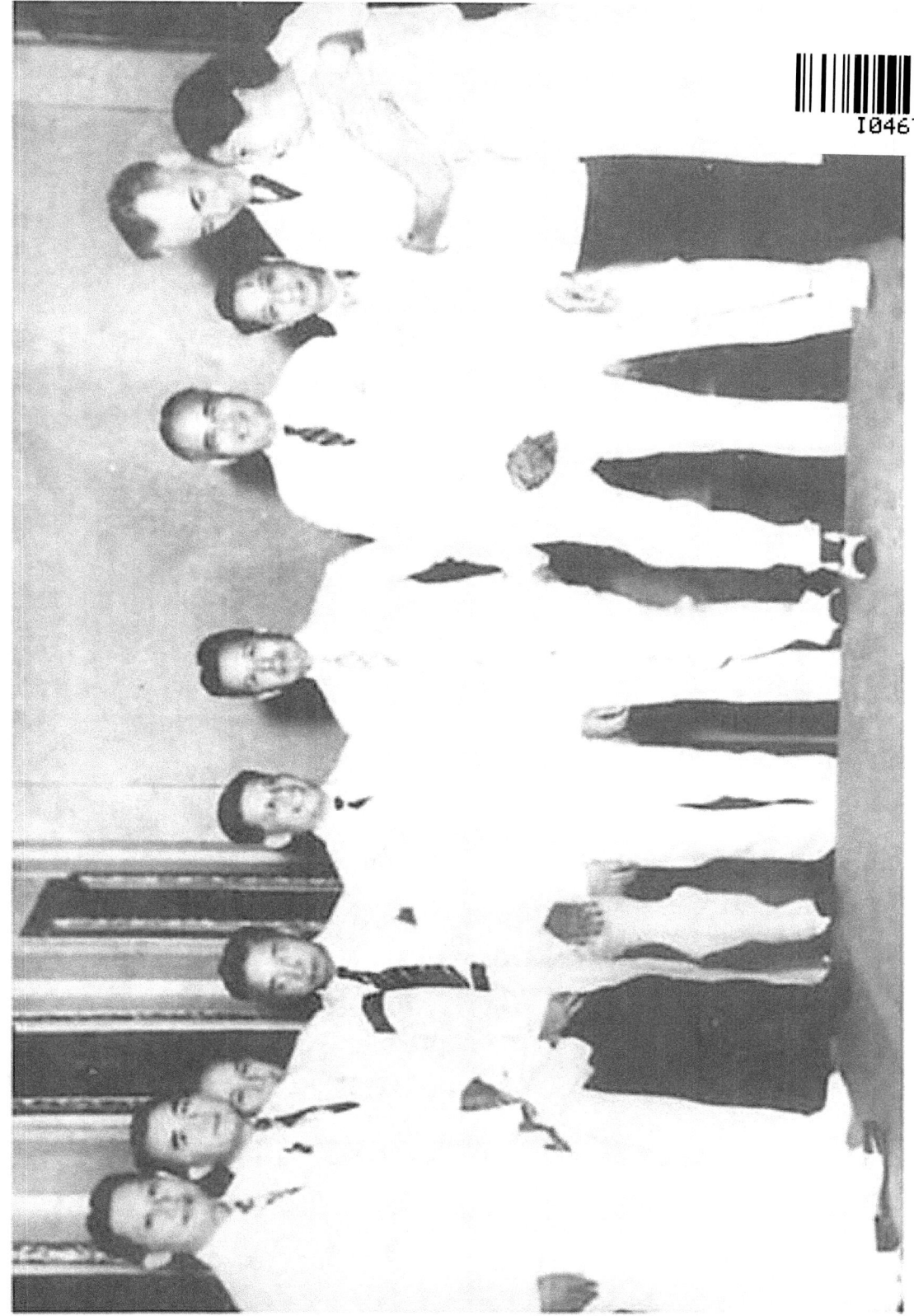

Cabinet of President Manuel L. Quezon. L-R: Benigno Aquino Sr., Jorge B. Vargas, Jesus Cuenco, Jorge Bocobo, Jose Avelino, Jose Abad Santos, Rafael Alunan, Manuel Roxas, President Quezon and First Lady Aurora Quezon. (Courtesy of Leslie Bocobo, facebook)

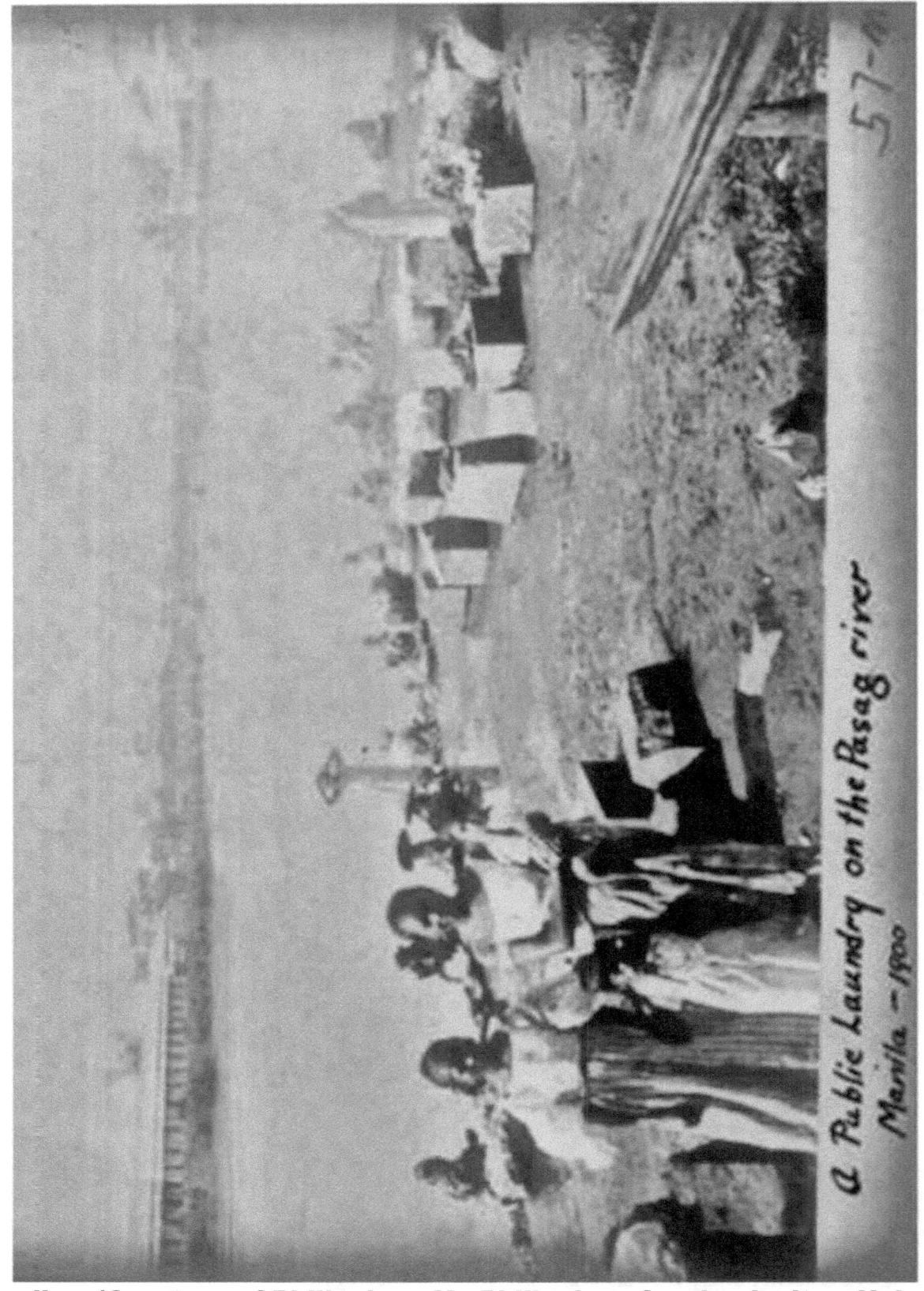

1900 Manila – (Courtesy of Philippines My Philippines facebook site – University of Michigan Library – Crist Ibarra)

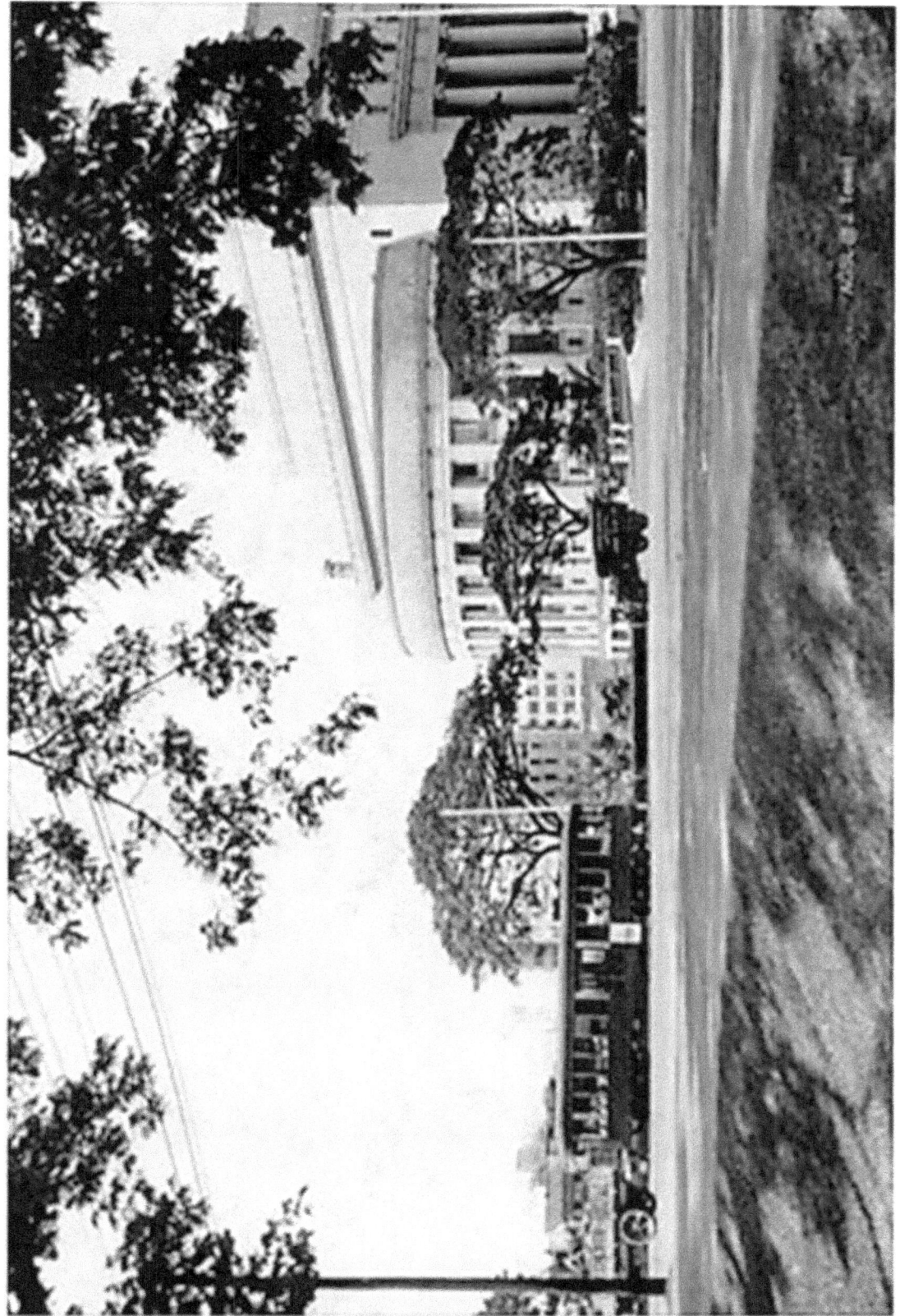

**1930s Manila – (courtesy of Philippines My Philippines facebook site –
John Tewell Collection – Crist Ibarra) – Editor's Note: I rode in that Tranvia
at age 7-8 with my mom in 1941-42, as residents of nearby Intramuros.**

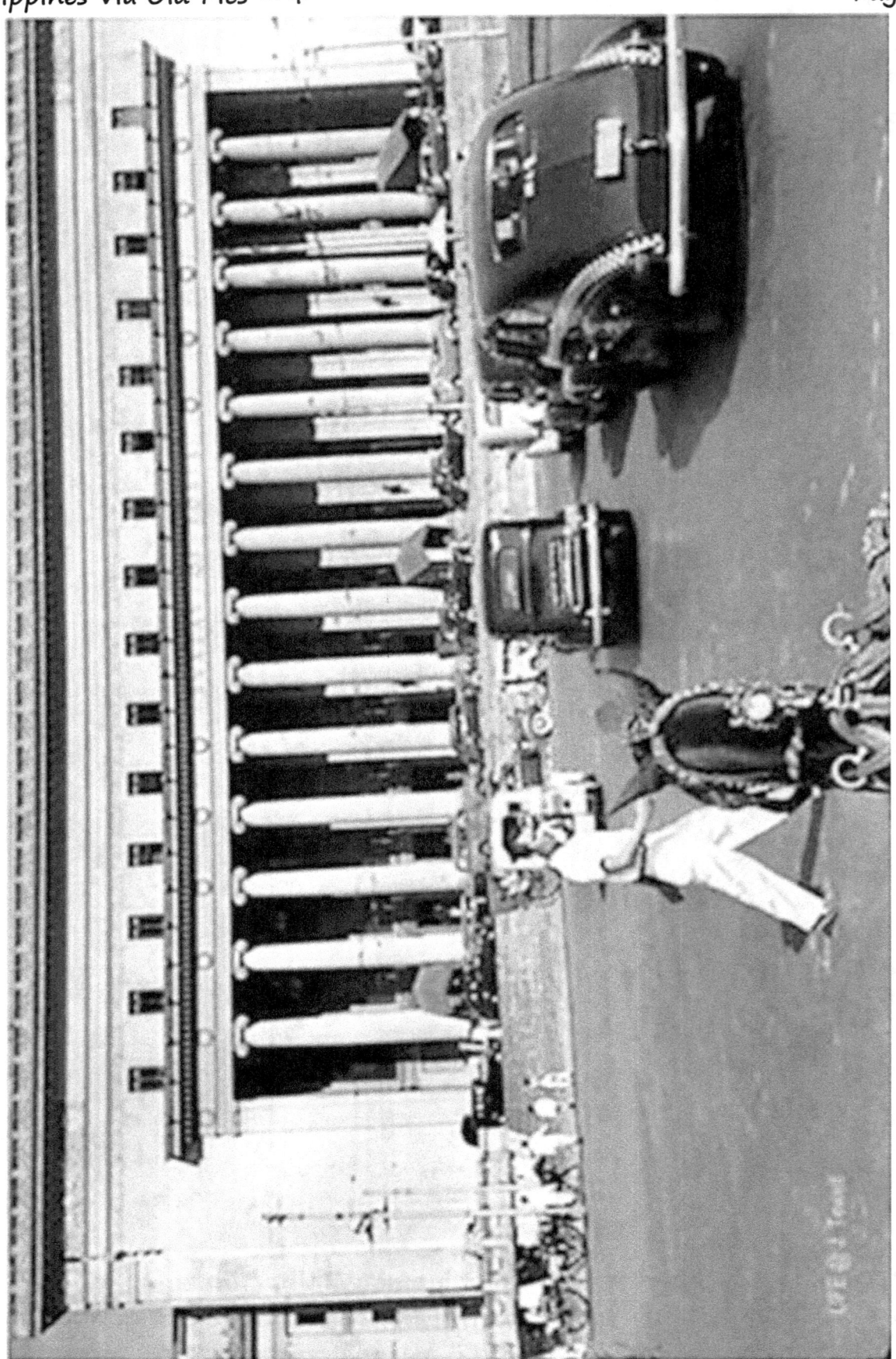

1941 Manila (courtesy of Philippines My Philippines facebook site – John Tewell collection – Crist Ibarra)

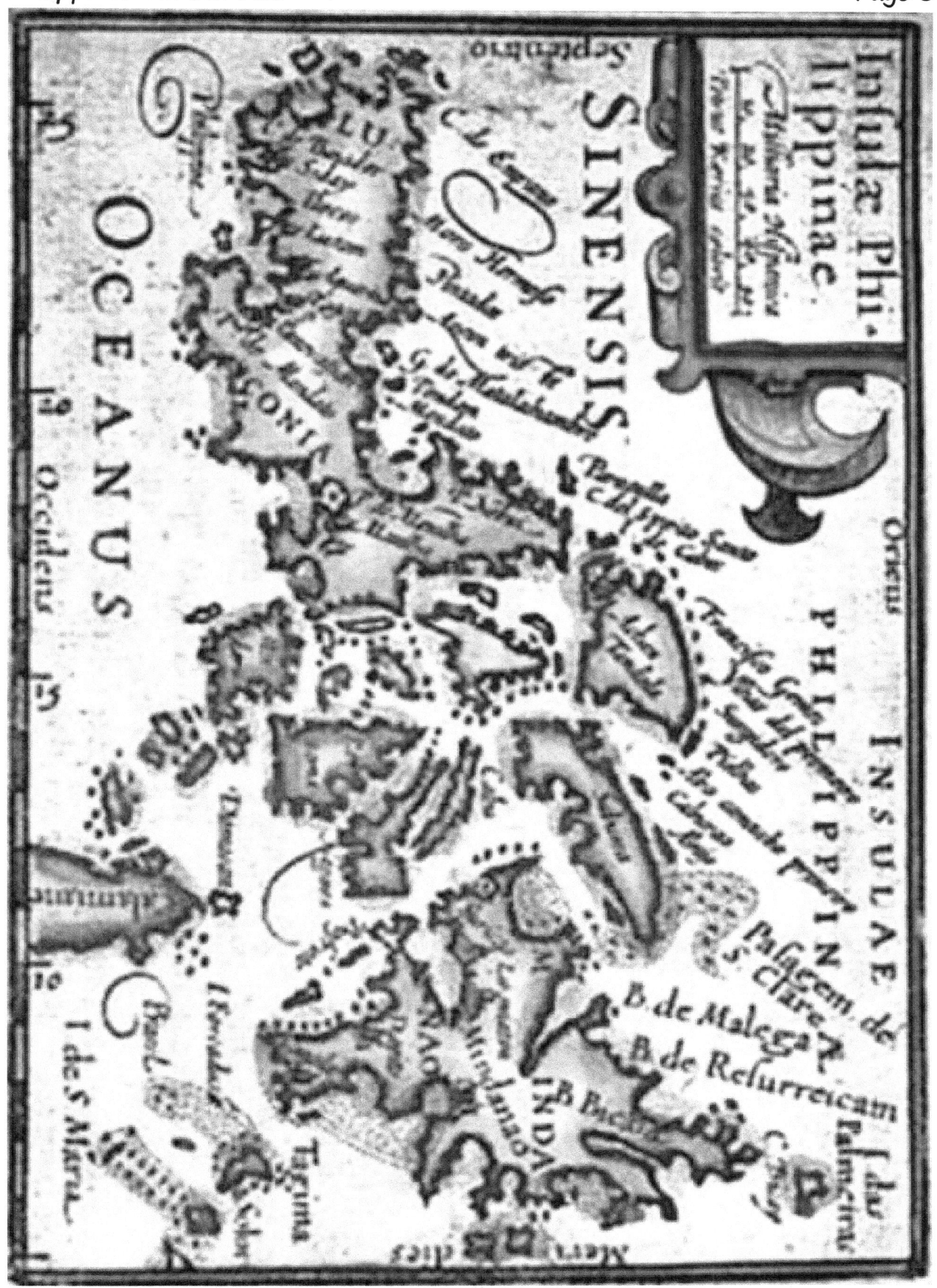

1599 Philippine Map (Courtesy Philippines My Philippines facebook Site)

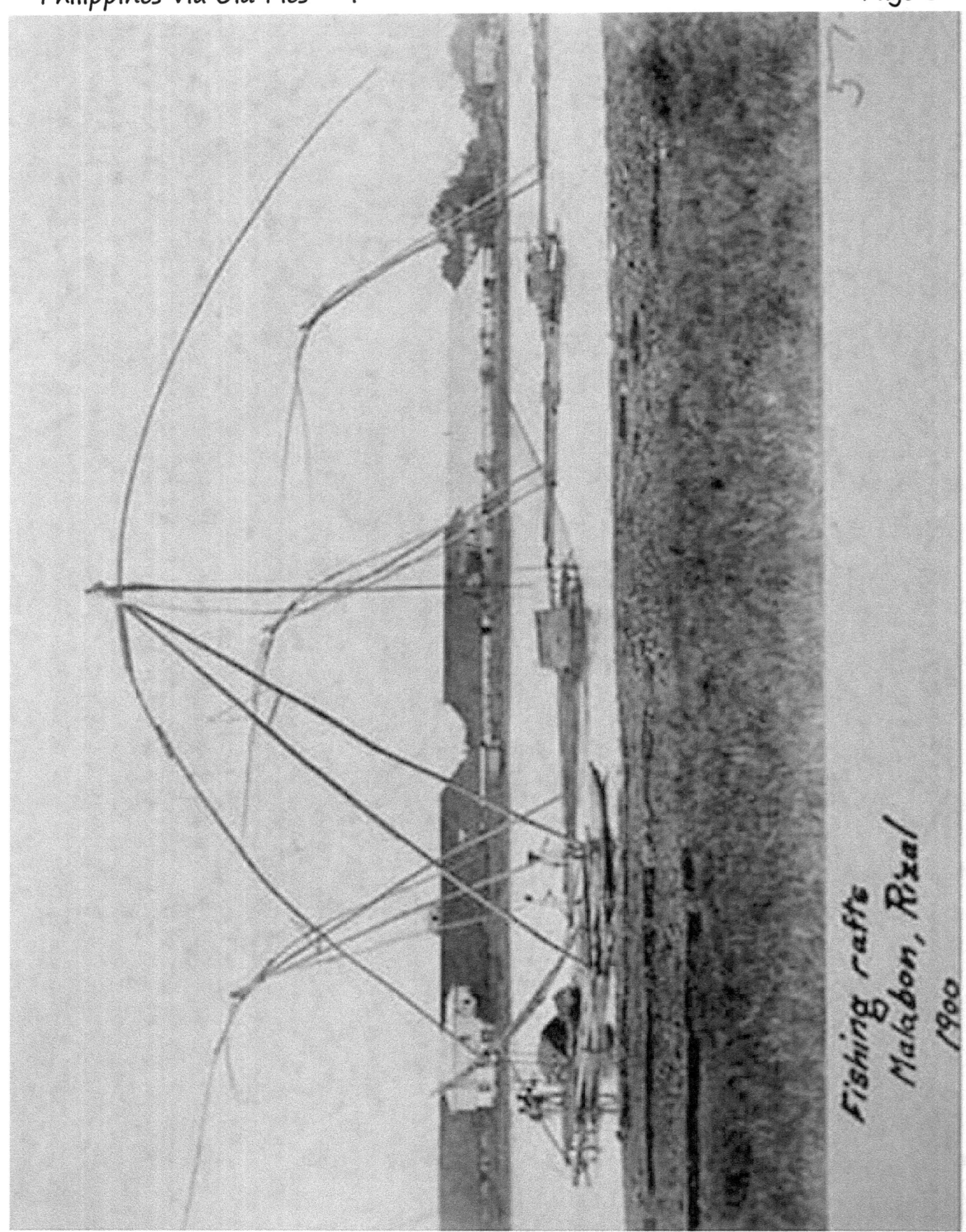

**1900 Malabon (courtesy of Philippines My Philippines facebook site –
University of Michigan Library – Crist Ibarra)**

Pag-ibig Sa Tinubuang Lupa

Ni Andres Bonifacio

Aling pag-ibig pa ang hihigit kaya
sa pagka-dalisay at pagka-dakila
gaya ng pag-ibig sa tinubuang lupa?
Alin pag-ibig pa? Wala na nga, wala.

Ulit-ulitin mang basahin ng isip
at isa-isahing talastasing pilit
ang salita't buhay na limbag at titik
ng isang katauhan ito'y namamasid.

Banal na pag-ibig pag ikaw ang nukal
sa tapat na puso ng sino't alinman,
imbit taong gubat, maralita't mangmang
nagiging dakila at iginagalang.

Pagpuring lubos ang nagiging hangad
sa bayan ng taong may dangal na ingat,
umawit, tumula, kumatha't sumulat,
kalakhan din nila'y isinisiwalat.

Walang mahalagang hindi inihandog
ng pusong mahal sa Bayang nagkupkop,
dugo, yaman, dunong, tiisa't pagod,
buhay ma'y abuting magkalagot-lagot.

Bakit? Ano itong sakdal nang laki
na hinahandugan ng buong pag kasi
na sa kalong mahal kapangyayari
at ginugugulan ng buhay na iwi.

Ay! Ito'y ang Inang Bayang tinubuan,
siya'y ina't tangi na kinamulatan
ng kawili-wiling liwanag ng araw
na nagbibigay init sa lunong katawan.

Sa kanya'y utang ang unang pagtanggol
ng simoy ng hanging nagbigay lunas,
sa inis na puso na sisinghap-singhap,
sa balong malalim ng siphayo't hirap.

Kalakip din nito'y pag-ibig sa Bayan
ang lahat ng lalong sa gunita'y mahal
mula sa masaya't gasong kasanggulan.
hanggang sa katawan ay mapasa-libingan.

Ang na nga kapanahon ng aliw,
ang inaasahang araw na darating
ng pagka-timawa ng mga alipin,
liban pa ba sa bayan tatanghalin?

At ang balang kahoy at ang balang sanga
na parang niya't gubat na kaaya-aya
sukat ang makita't sasa-ala-ala
ang ina't ang giliw lampas sa saya.

Tubig niyang malinaw sa anak'y bulog
bukal sa batisang nagkalat sa bundok
malambot na huni ng matuling agos
na nakaa-aliw sa pusong may lungkot.

Sa kaba ng abang mawalay sa Bayan!
gunita ma'y laging sakbibi ng limbay
walang ala-ala't inaasam-asam
kundi ang makita'ng lupang tinubuan.

Pati na'ng magdusa't sampung kamatayan
waring masarap kung dahil sa Bayan
at lalong maghirap, O! himalang bagay,
lalong pag-irog pa ang sa kanya'y alay.

Kung ang bayang ito'y nasa panganib
at siya ay dapat na ipagtangkilik
ang anak, asawa, magulang, kapatid
isang tawag niya'y tatalikdang pilit.

Datapwa kung bayan ng ka-Tagalogan
ay nilalapastangan at niyuyurakan
katwiran, puri niya't kamahalan
ng sama ng lilong ibang bayan.

Di gaano kaya ang paghinagpis
ng pusong Tagalog sa puring nakit
at aling kaluoban na lalong tahimik
ang di pupukawin sa paghihimagsik?

Saan magbubuhat ang paghihinay
sa paghihiganti't gumugol ng buhay
kung wala ring ibang kasasadlakan
kundi ang lugami sa ka-alipinan?

Kung ang pagka-baon niya't pagka-busabos
sa lusak ng daya't tunay na pag-ayop
supil ng pang-hampas tanikalang gapos
at luha na lamang ang pinaa-agos

Sa kanyang anyo'y sino ang tutunghay
na di-aakayin sa gawang magdamdam
pusong naglilipak sa pagka-sukaban
na hindi gumagalang dugo at buhay.

Mangyari kayang ito'y masulyap
ng mga Tagalog at hindi lumingap
sa naghihingalong Inang nasa yapak
ng kasuklam-suklam na Castilang hamak.

Nasaan ang dangal ng mga Tagalog,
nasaan ang dugong dapat na ibuhos?
bayan ay inaapi, bakit di kumikilos?
at natitilihang ito'y mapanuod.

Hayo na nga kayo, kayong ngang buhay
sa pag-asang lubos na kaginhawahan
at walang tinamo kundi kapaitan,
kaya nga't ibigin ang naaabang bayan.

Kayong antayan na sa kapapasakit
ng dakilang hangad sa batis ng dibdib
muling pabalungit tunay na pag-ibig
kusang ibulalas sa bayang piniit.

Kayong nalagasan ng bunga't bulaklak
kahoy niyaring buhay na nilant sukat
ng bala-balakit makapal na hirap
muling manariwa't sa baya'y lumiyag.

Kayong mga pusong kusang (pugal)
ng dagat at bagsik ng ganid na asal,
ngayon magbangon't baya'y itanghal
agawin sa kuko ng mga sukaban.

Kayong mga dukhang walang tanging (lasap)
kundi ang mabuhay sa dalita't hirap,
ampunin ang bayan kung nasa ay lunas
sapagkat ang ginhawa niya ay sa lahat.

Ipaghandog-handog ang buong pag-ibig
hanggang sa mga dugo'y ubusang itigis
kung sa pagtatanggol, buhay ay (mailit)
ito'y kapalaran at tunay na langit.

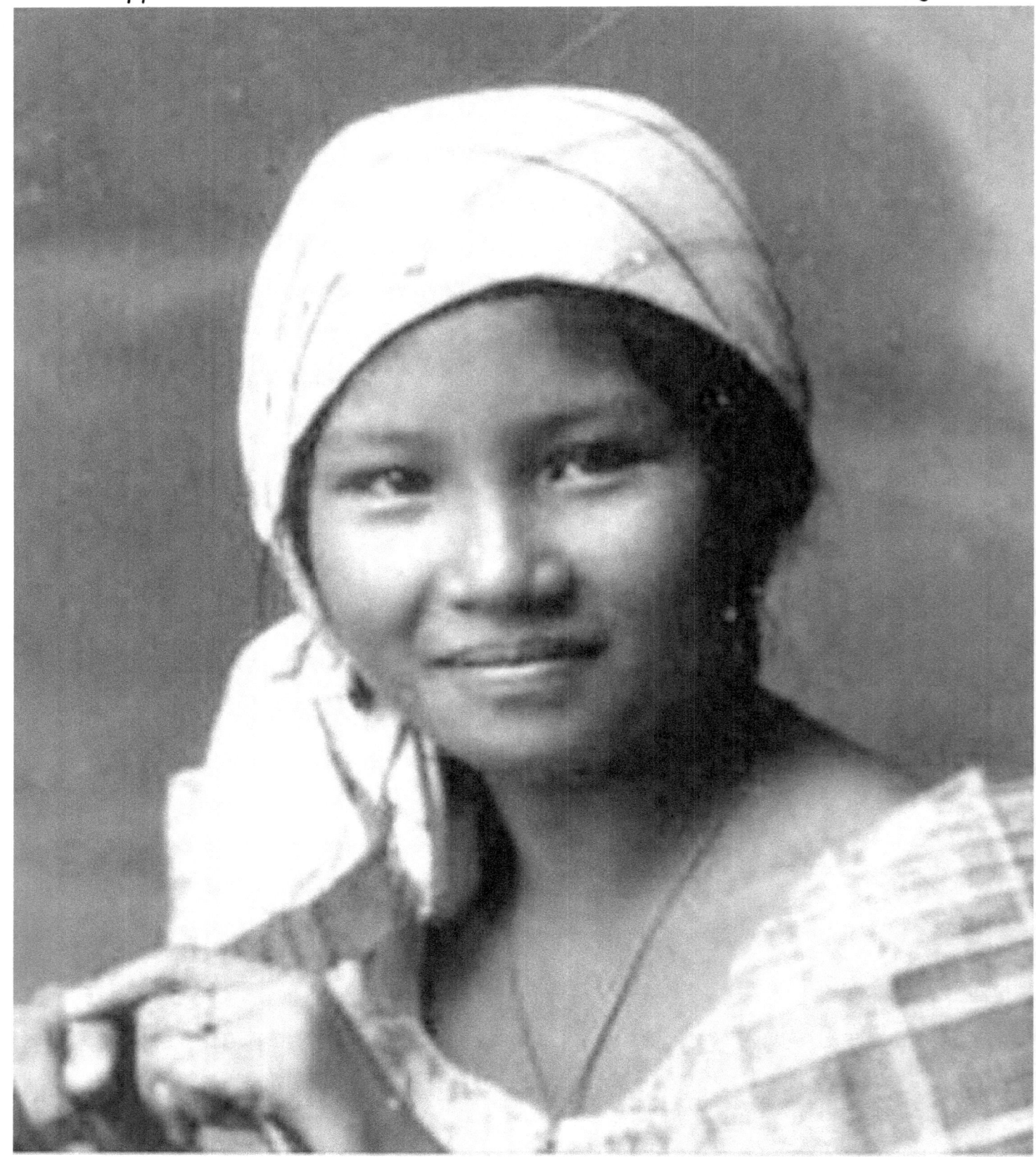

Early 1900s – Typical Filipina Beauty (courtesy of Philippines My Philippines facebook site)

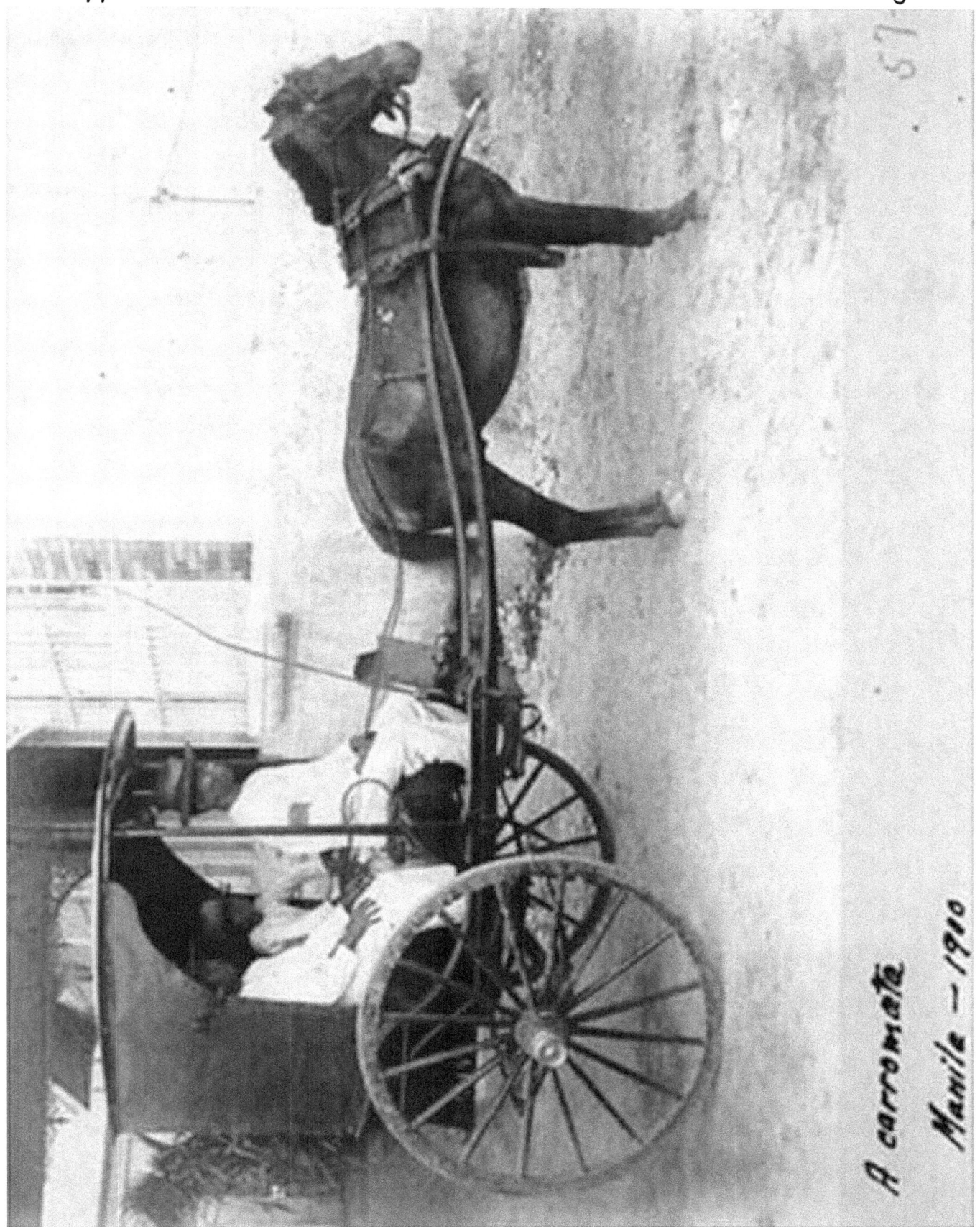

1900 Manila – Carromata (courtesy of Philippines My Philippines Facebook site)

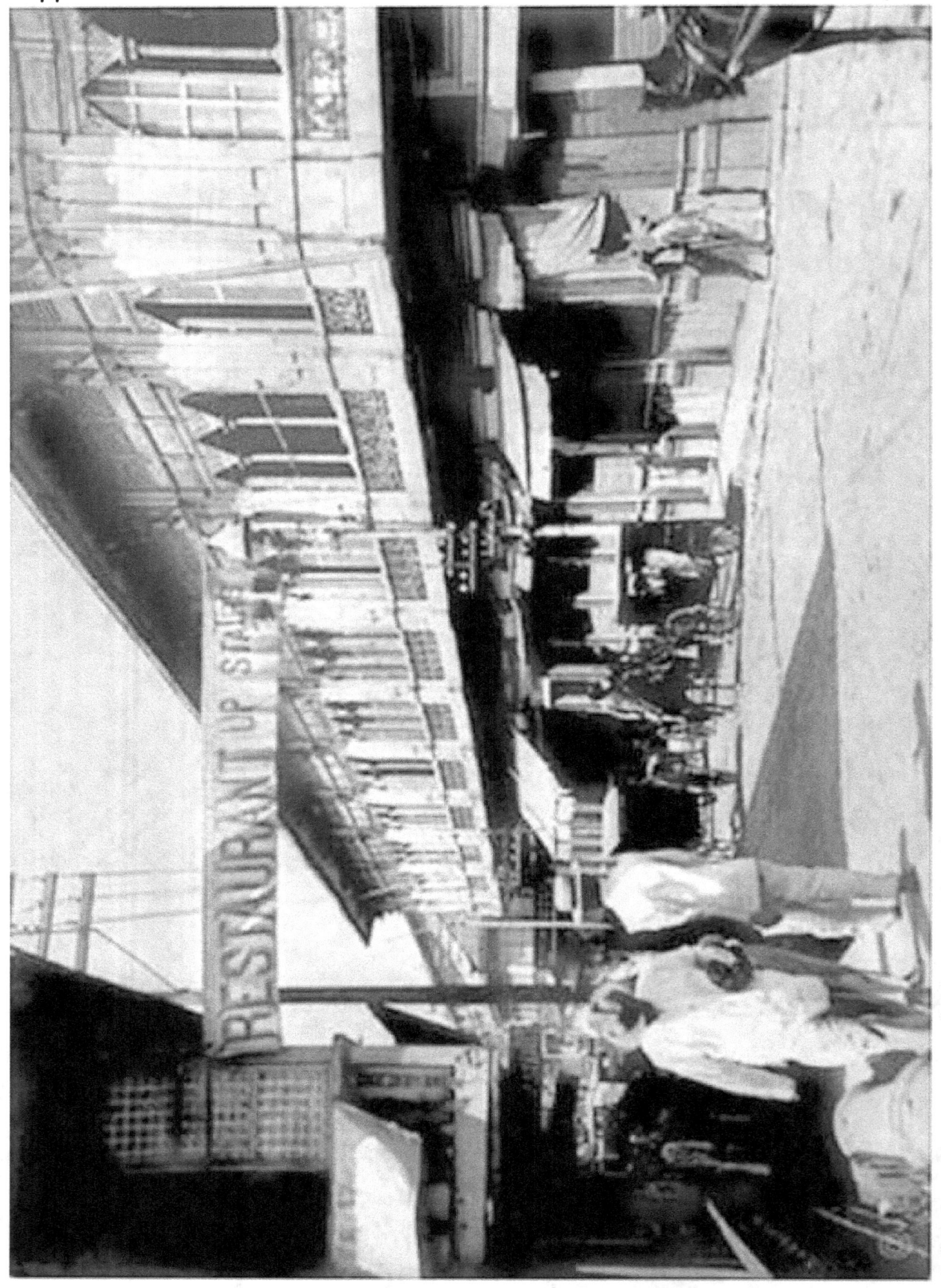

1902 Manila – Escolta – (courtesy of Philippines My Philippines Facebook site – John Tewell Collection – Crist Ibarra)

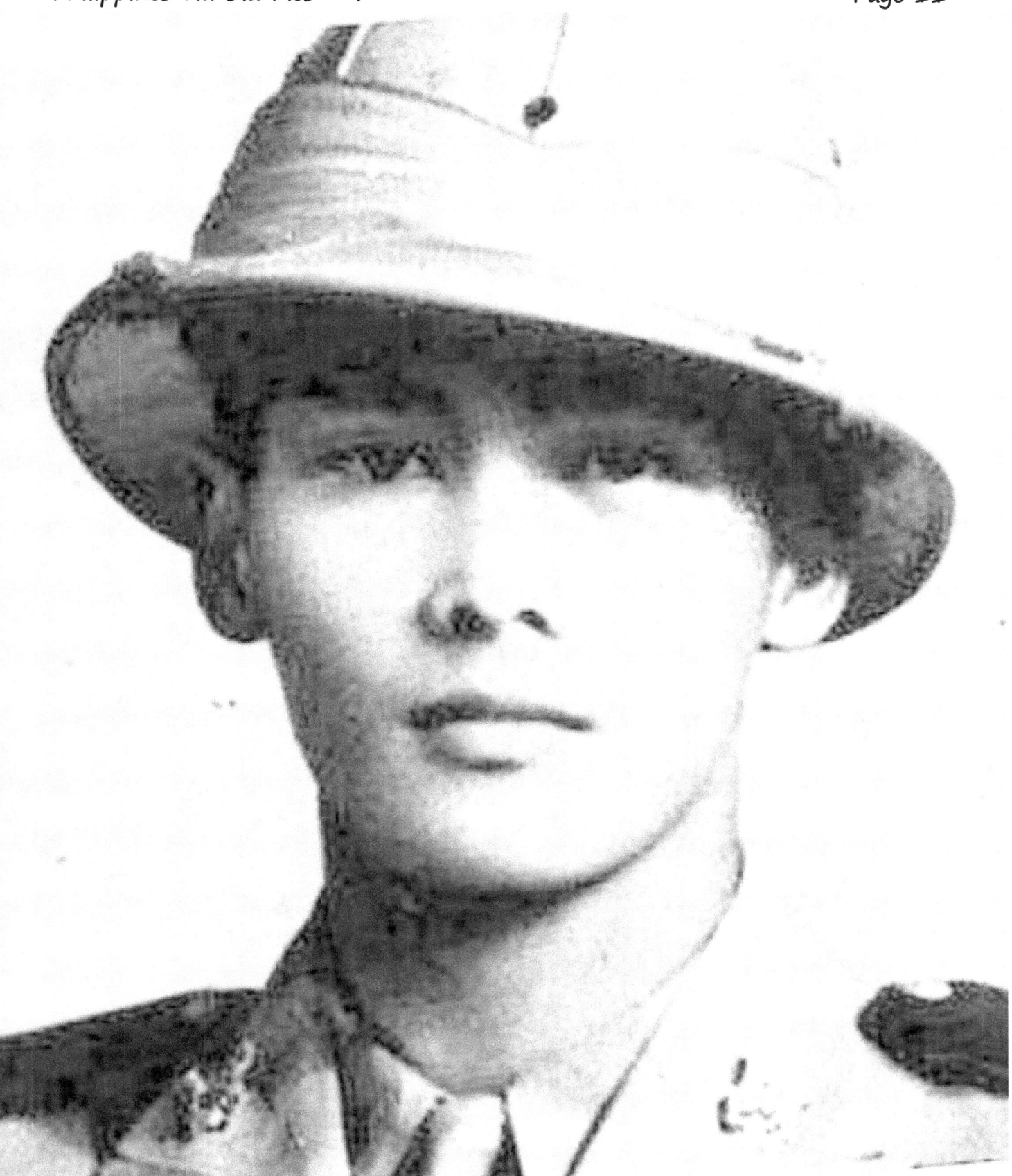

Lt. Cesar Fernando Basa, in whose memory Basa Airfield was named. (courtesy of Philippines My Philippines facebook site)

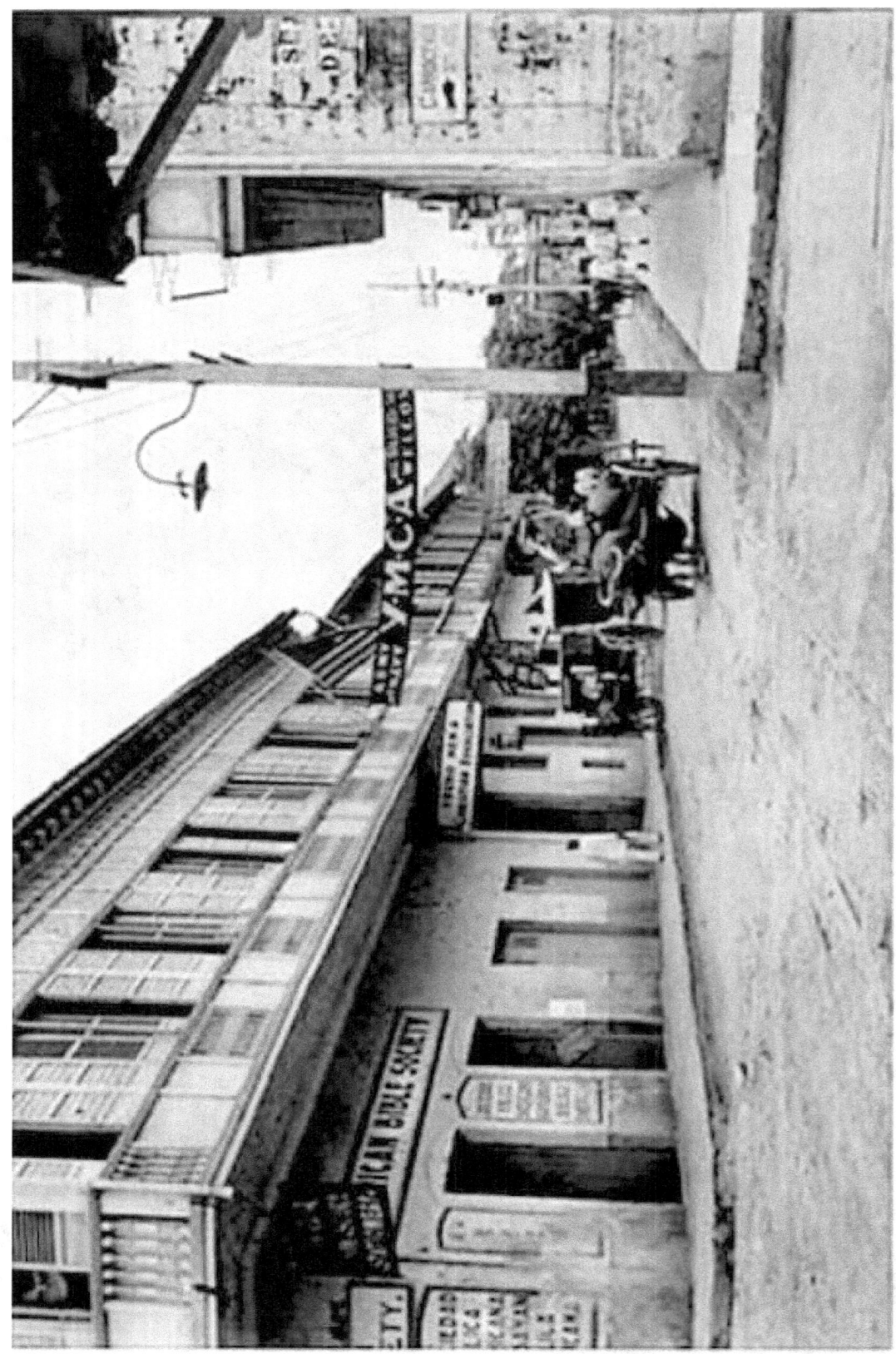

1902 Intramuros Manila – Calle Real corner Calle de Lagazpi. San Juan De Dios Hospital is on the right. Gate Parian is at end. (courtesy of Philippines My Philippines facebook site – John Tewell collection – Crist Ibarra) – Editor's note: I was born in that hospital in 1934.

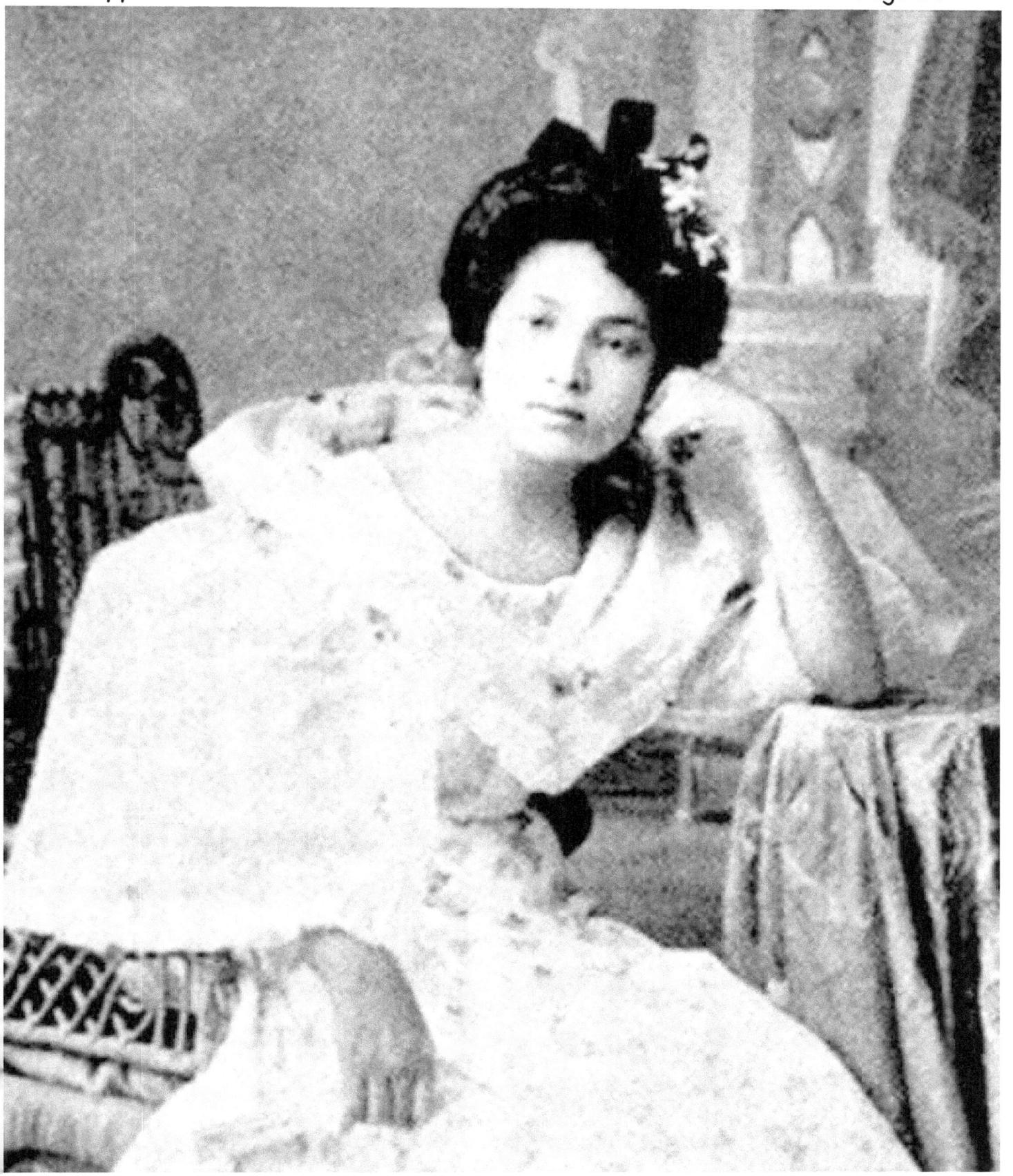

**1912 Filipina Beauty (courtesy of Philippines My Philippines facebook
Site – Cornell Univ. Library – Crist Ibarra)**

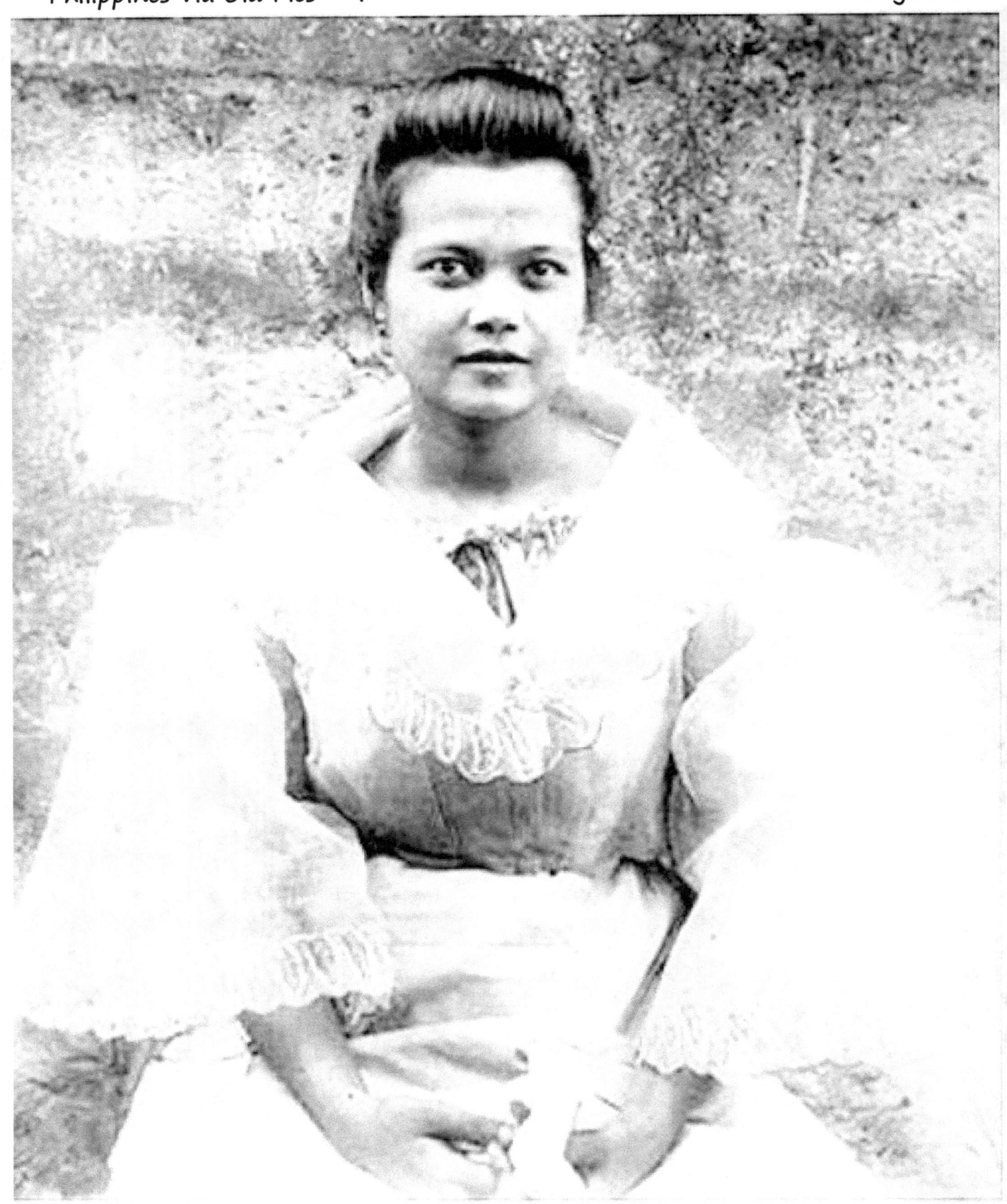

**1901 Filipina Beauty (courtesy of Philippines My Philippines facebook
Site – Univ. of Michigan Library – Crist Ibarra)**

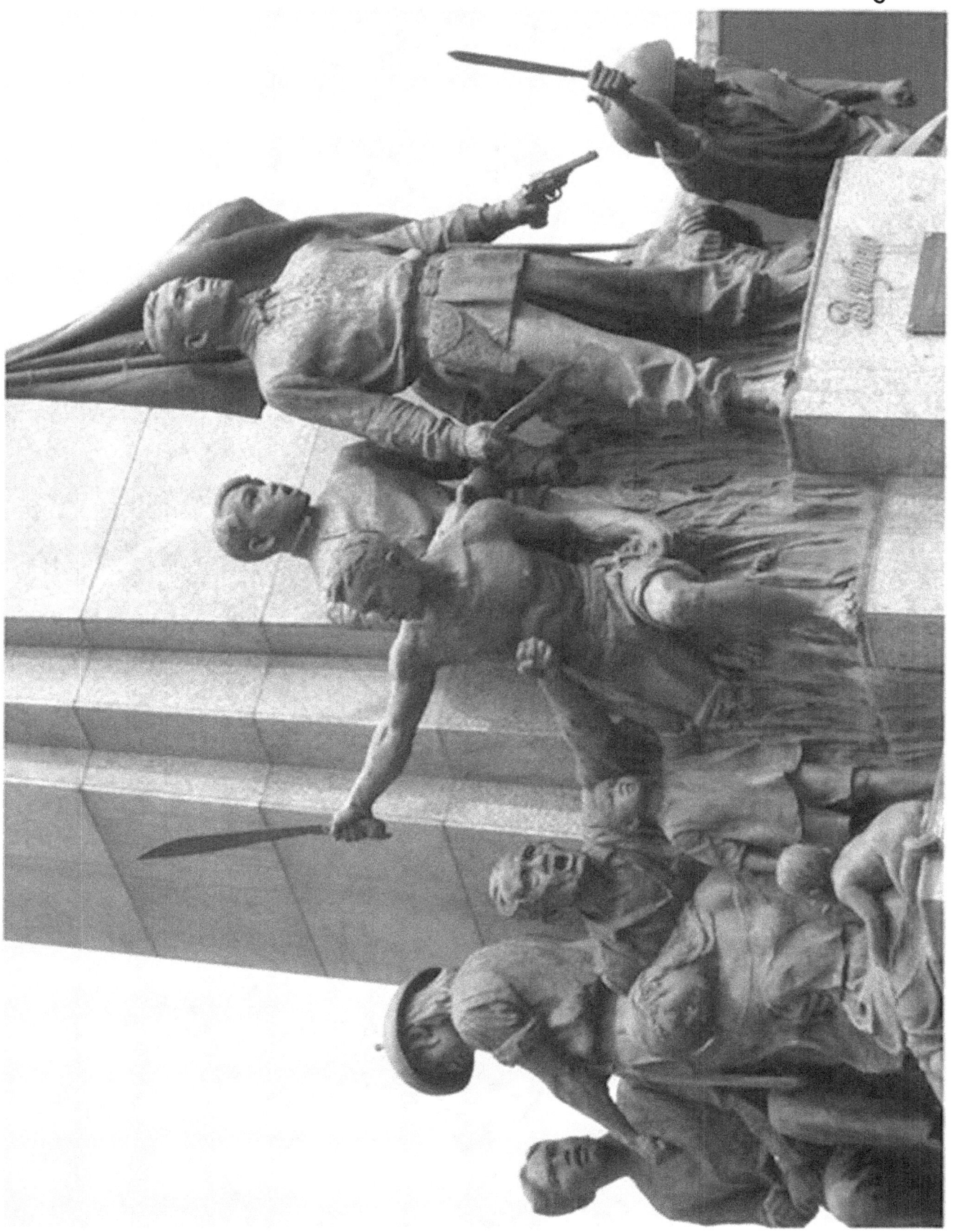

Bonifacio Monument (Courtesy of Philippines My Philippines facebook site - Salvador Rada)

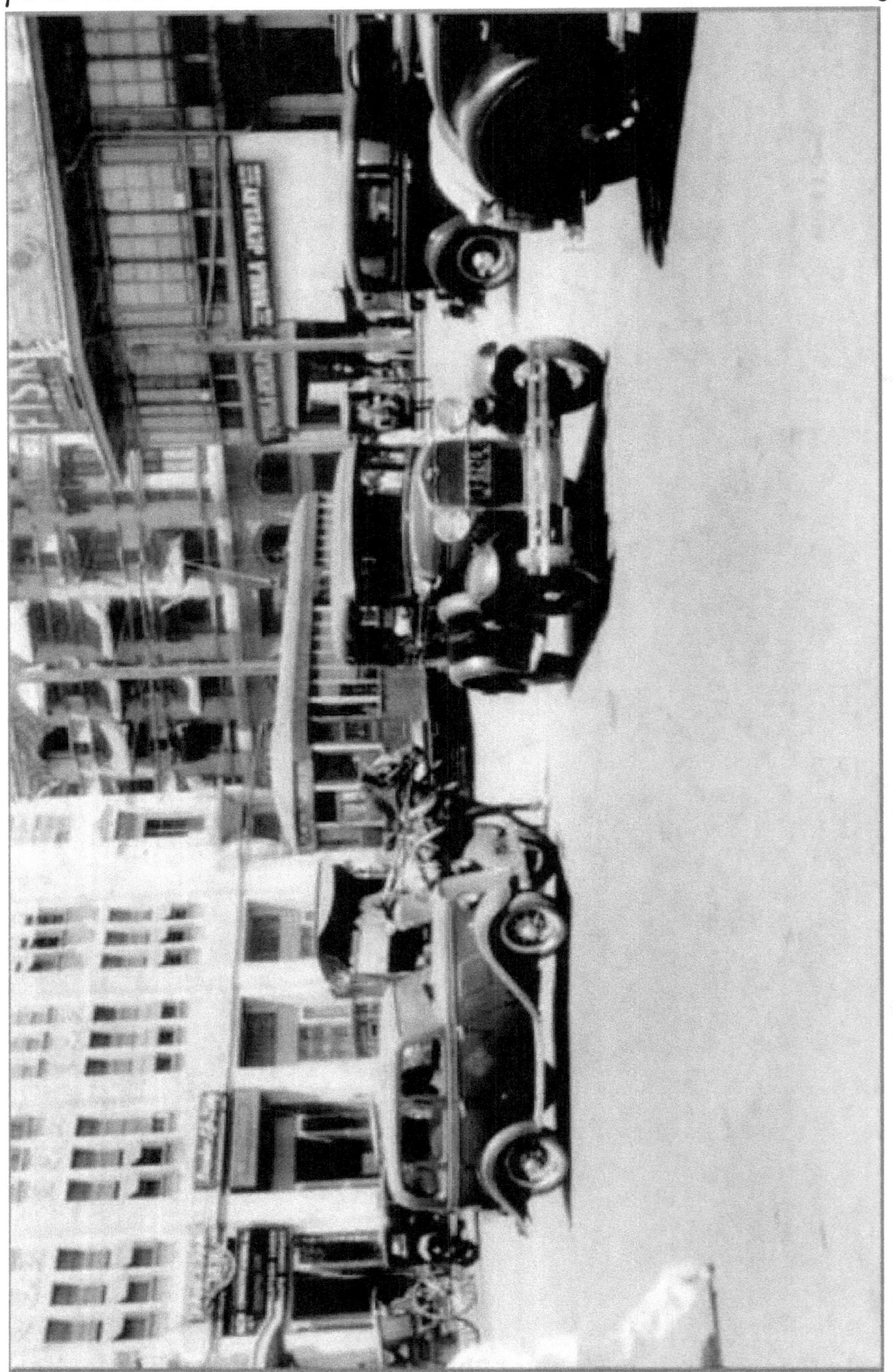

1930s Downtown Manila – Plaza Morga near Escolta – (courtesy of Philippines My Philippines facebook site)

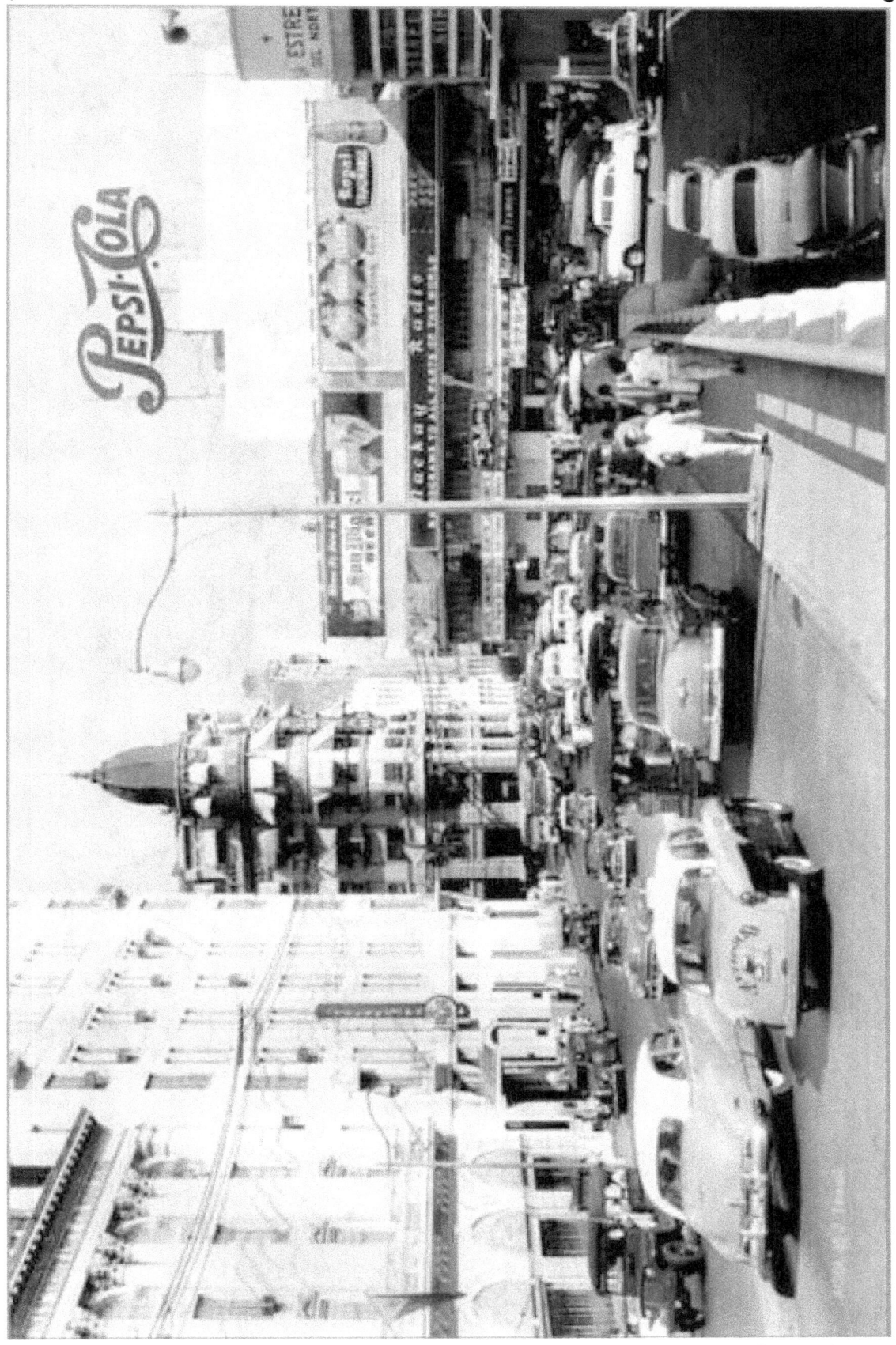

1950s Downtown Manila, near Jones Bridge & Escolta – (courtesy of Philippines My Philippines facebook site)

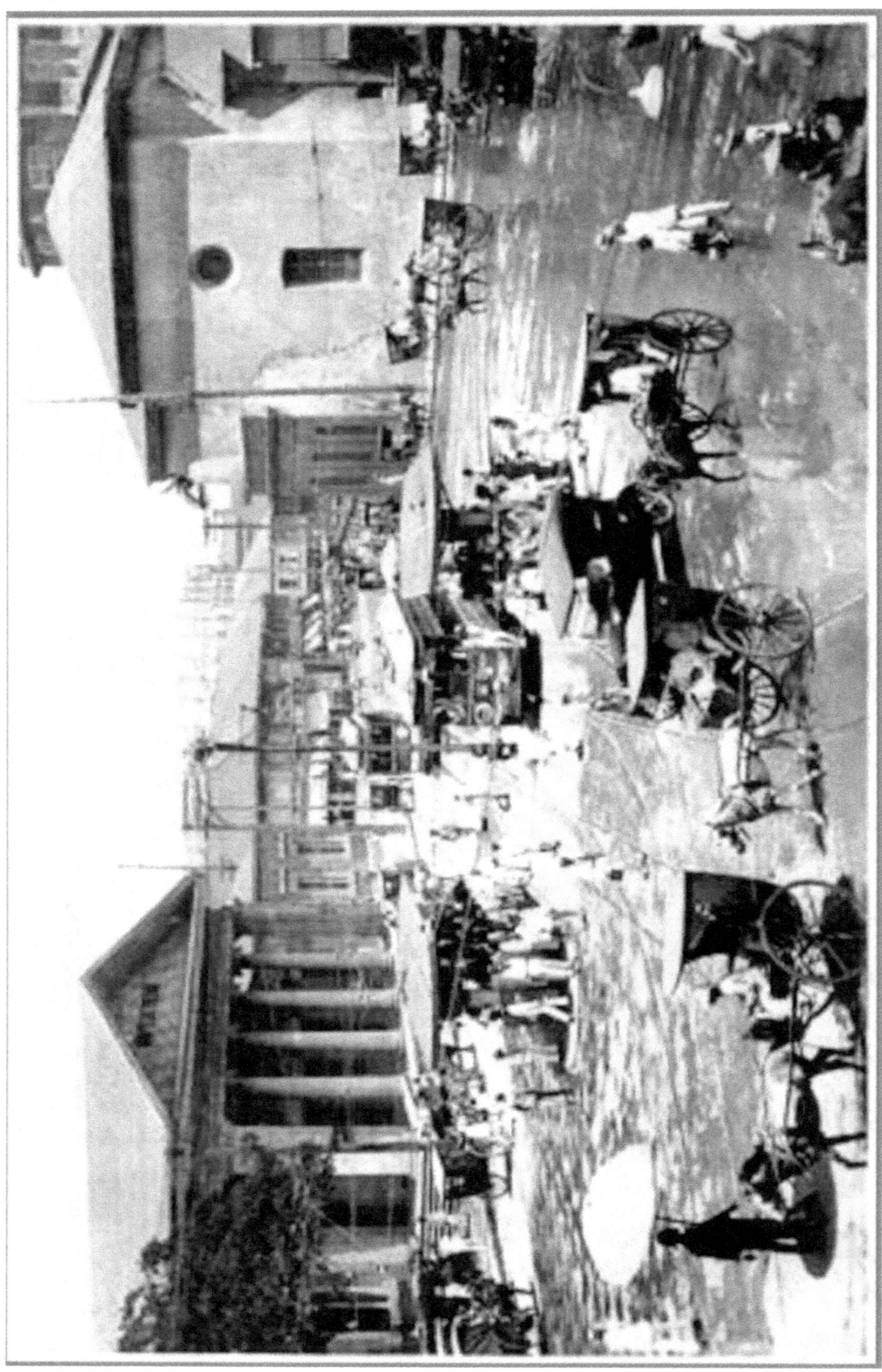

Plaza Goiti, Manila, 1920-1940 - horse-drawn carriages and trollies as well as people Monte de Piedad bank building on the left. (Courtesy of Philippines My Philippines Facebook - USC Digital Library Intl. Mission Photography Archive (IMPA)

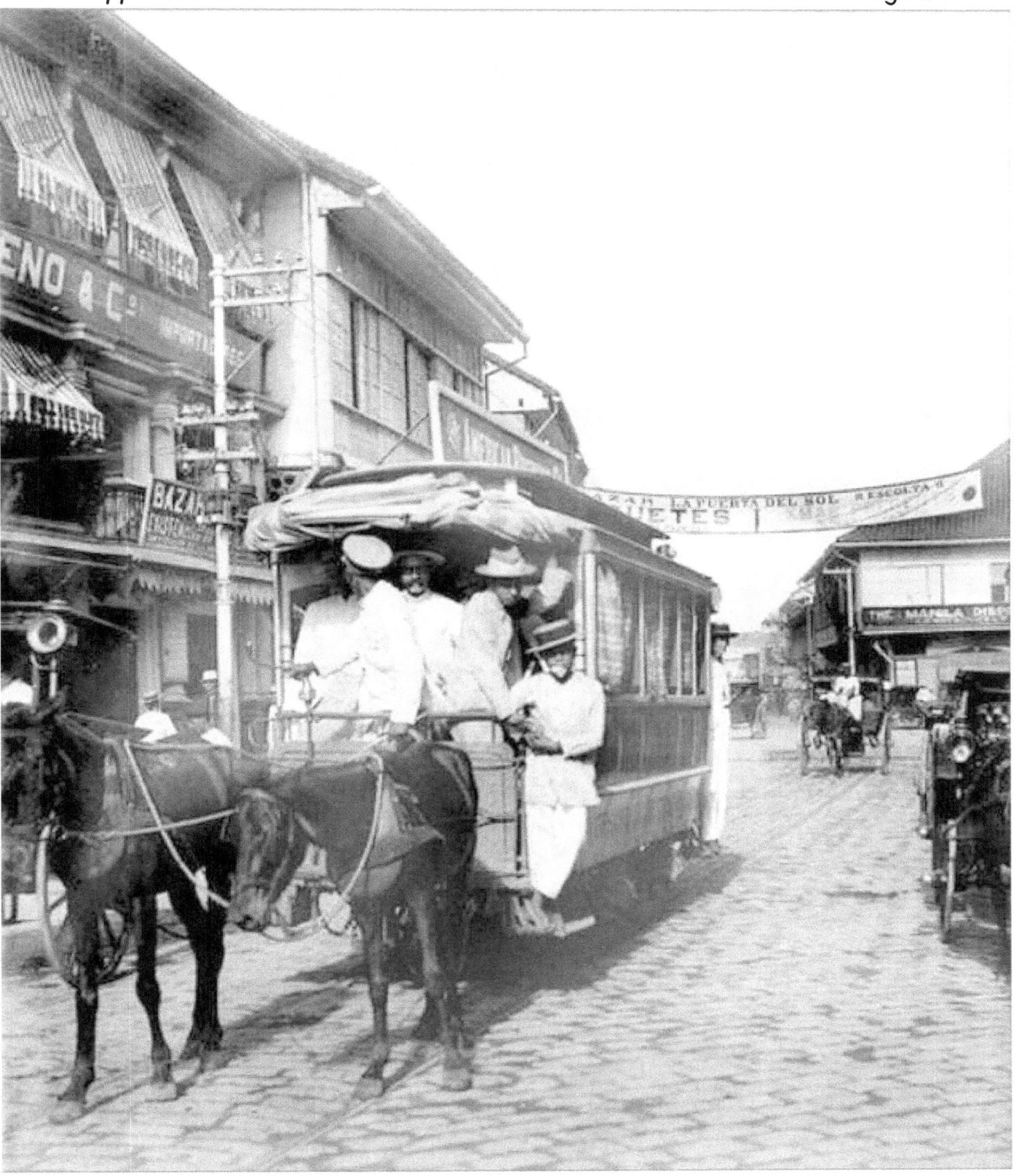

**1910 Horse-drawn Tranvia (courtesy of Philippines My Philippines facebook
site – Lou Gopal – Nostalgia Manila)**

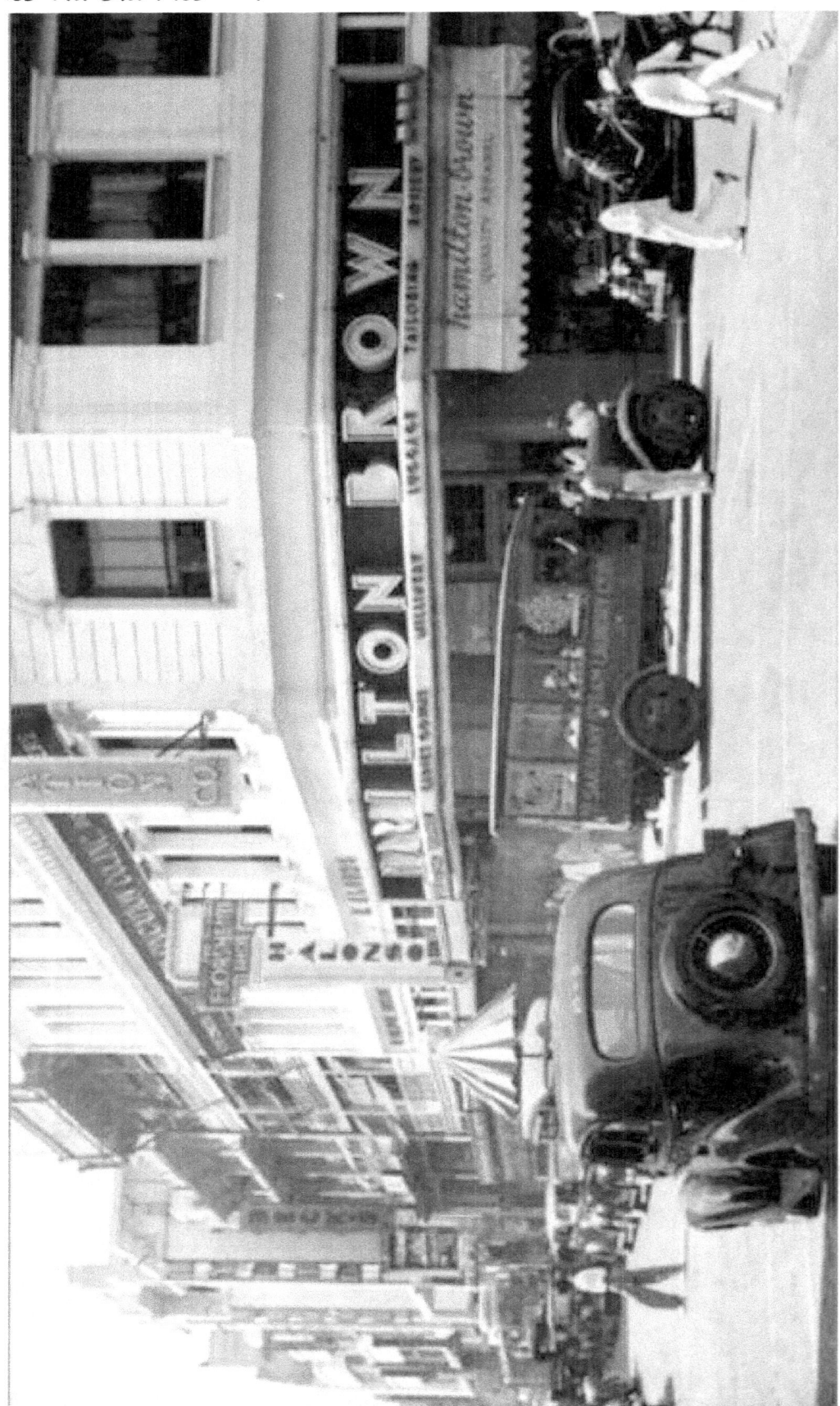

1920s Escolta St cor. Tomas Pinpin, Manila. Natividad Building with Hamilton Brown Store (courtesy of Philippines My Philippines facebook – Mnl. Nostalgia)

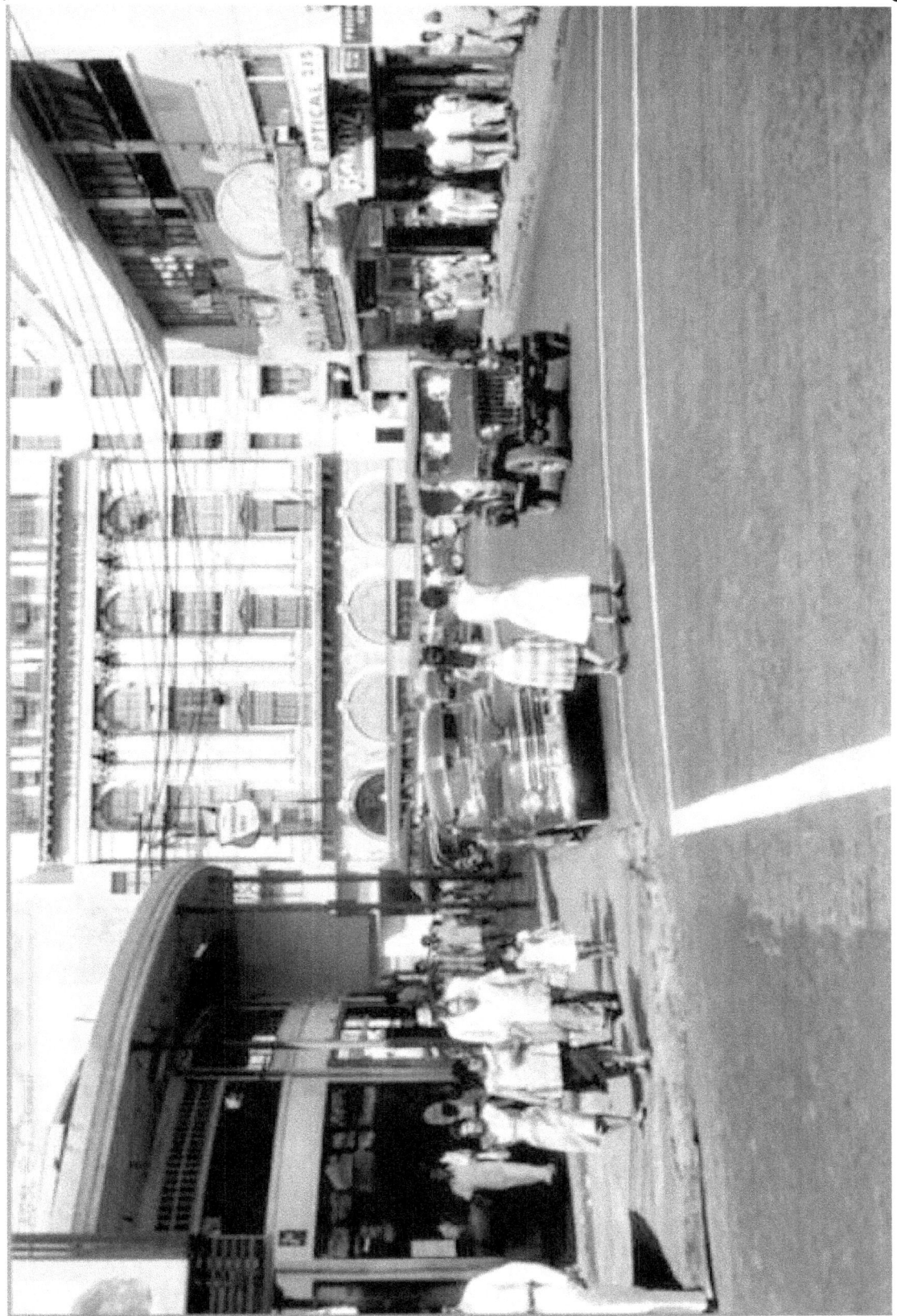

1950s - Escolta Street +Plaza/Calle Moraga - "Filipinas Insurance Co Building" has La Estrella Del Norte Jewelry Store became Savory Chicken Restaurant; the side street leads to Binondo. The other road turning left leads to Jones Bridge – (courtesy of Philippines My Philippines facebook - image AGSL - J. Tewell)

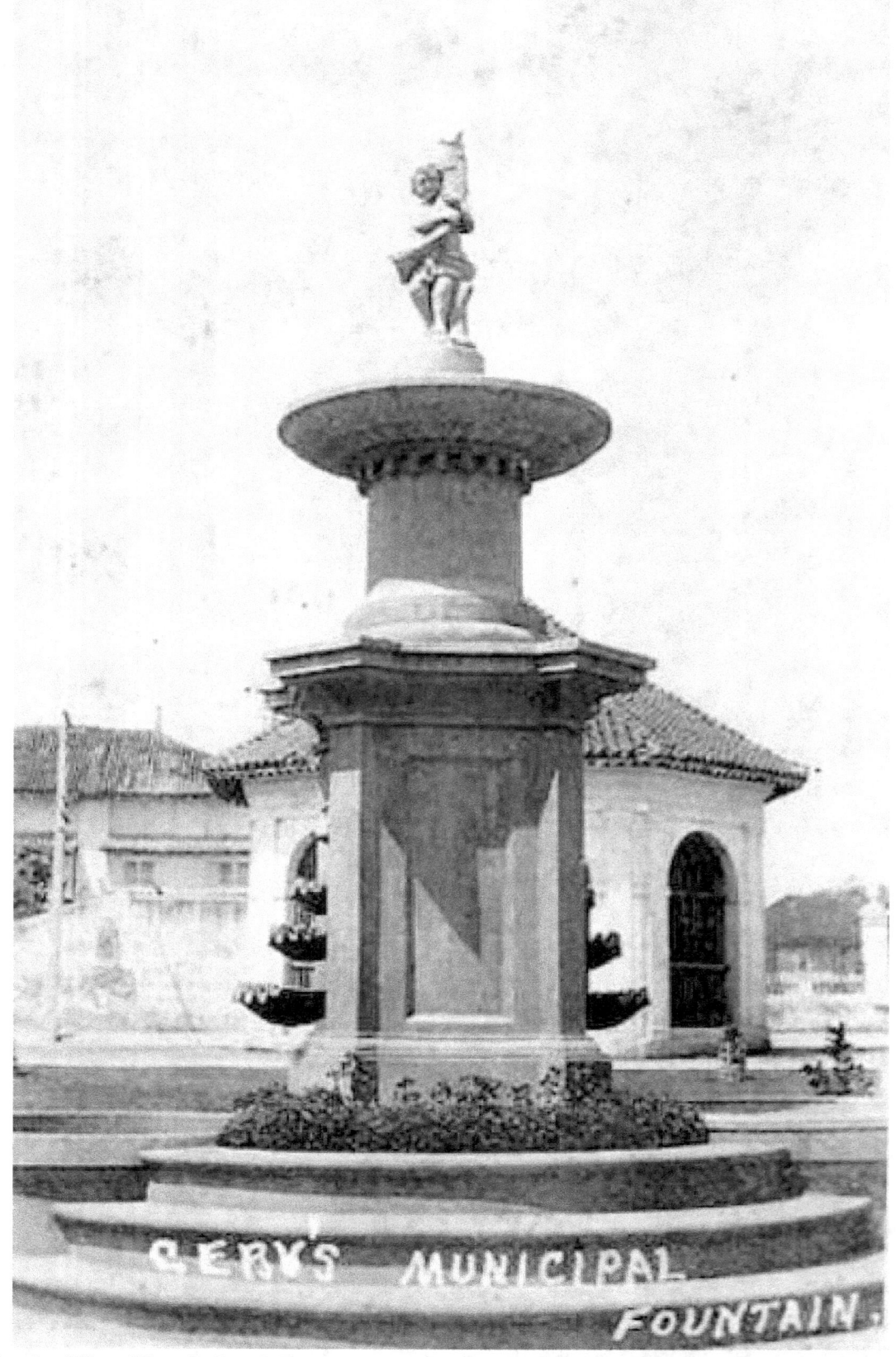

Undated - The Municipal Fountain, Plaza Rizal, Cebu City. Kiosk at back is Magellan Cross and Fort San Pedro – (courtesy of Philippines My Philippines Facebook - simoun - image Filipinas Retrato Collection)

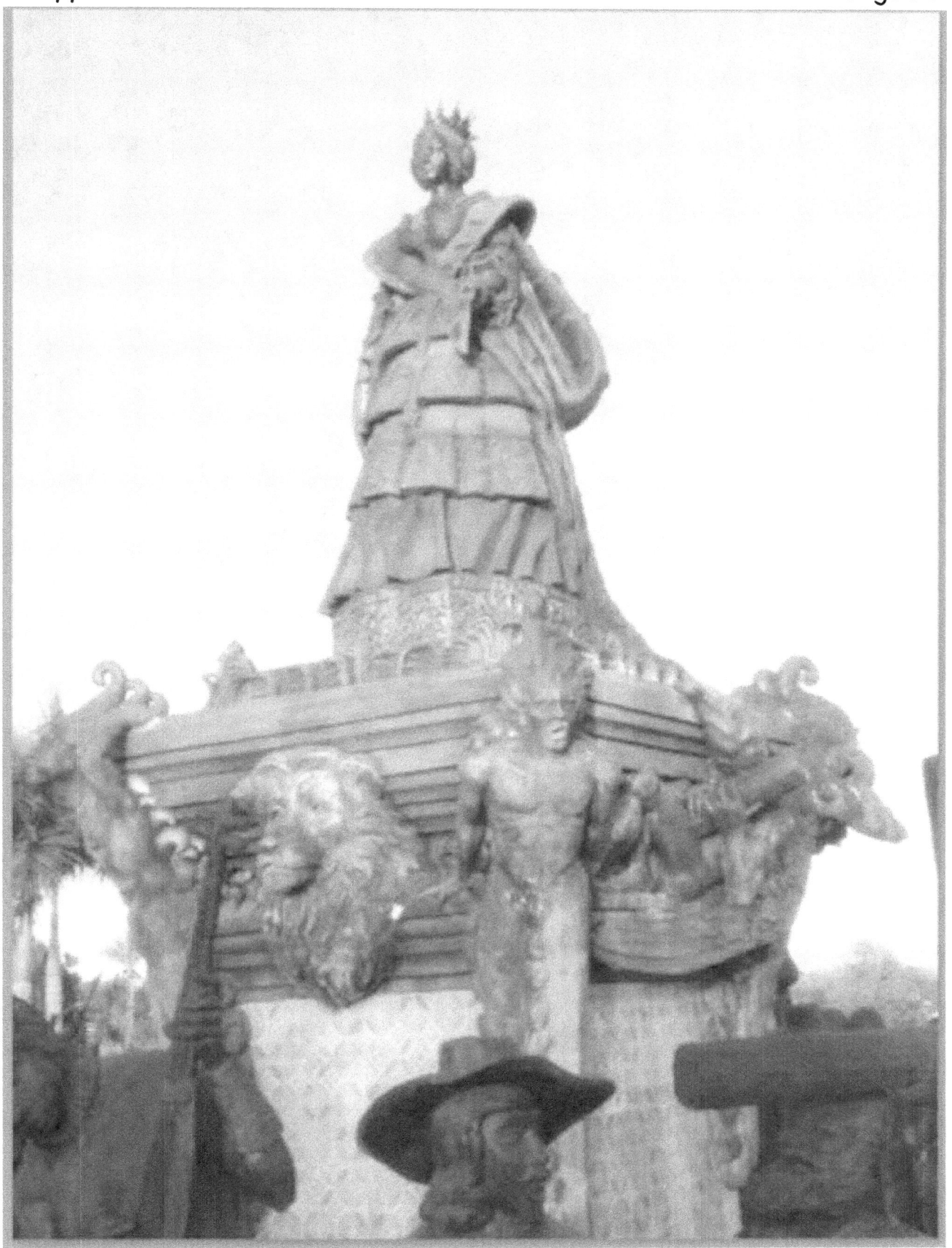

The "other" Isabella Statue, Isabela Province – (courtesy of Philippines My Philippines facebook site)

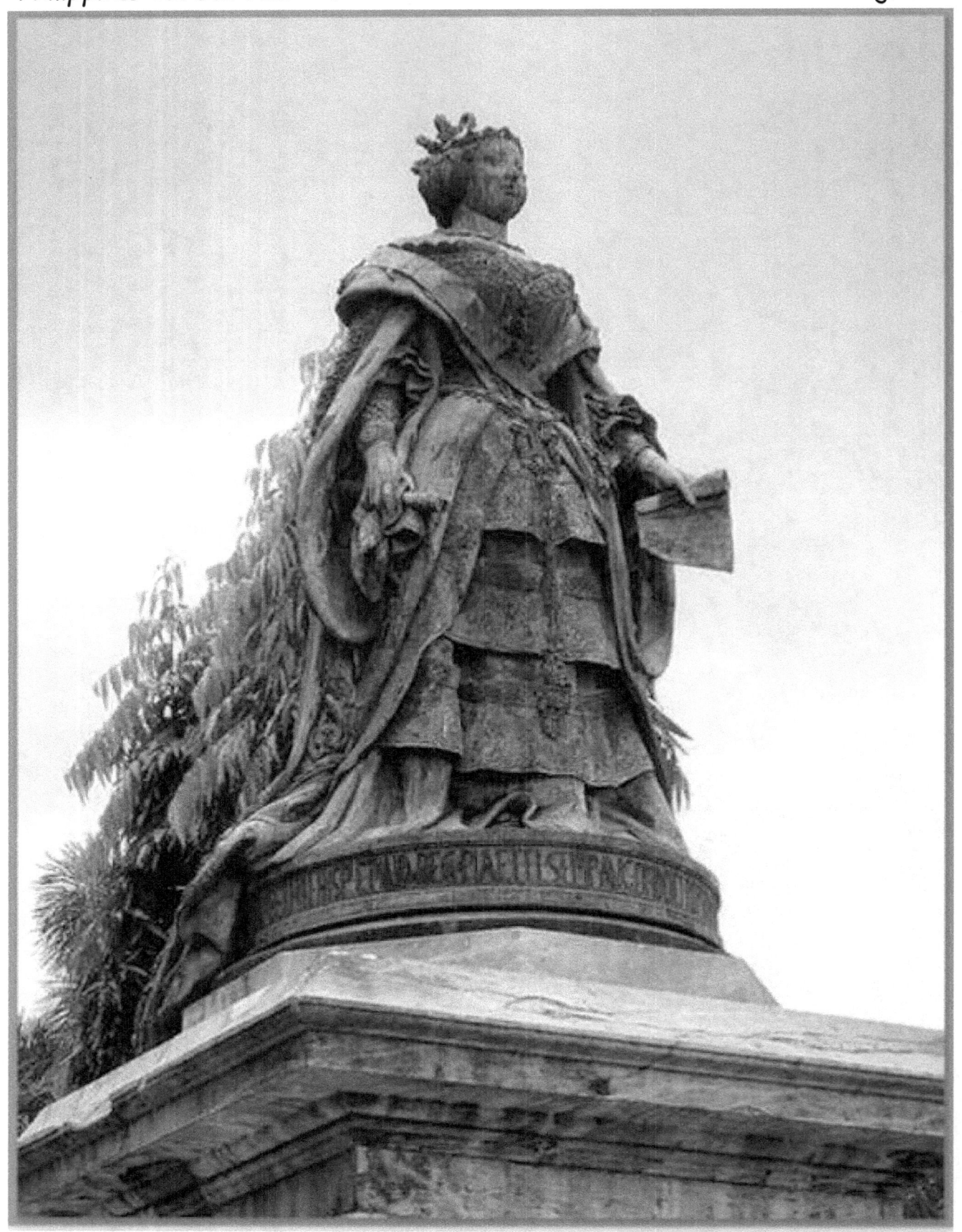

Queen Isabella Statue, Intramuros Manila (courtesy of Philippines My Philippines facebook site)

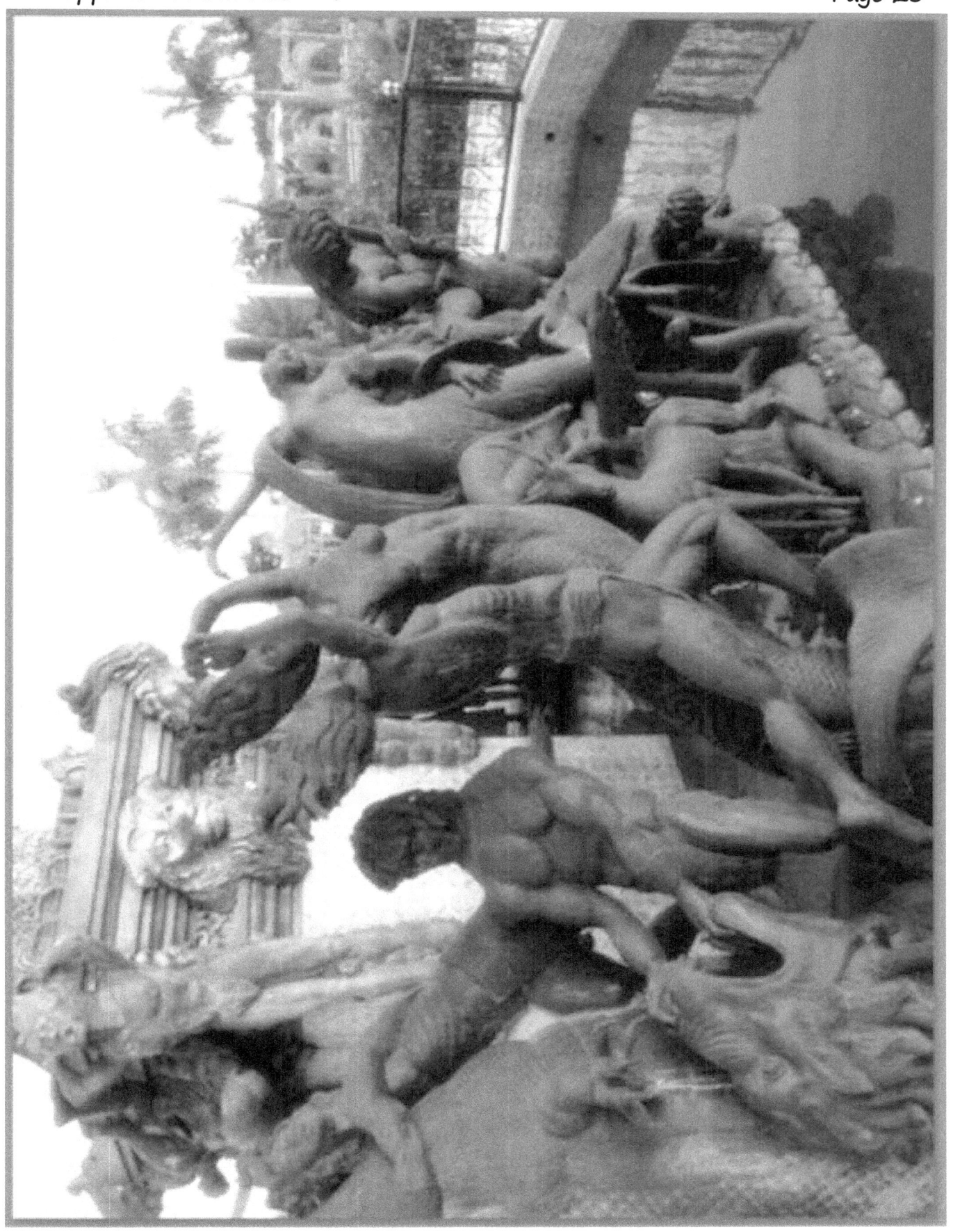

Elaborate sculpture at foot of Queen Isabella Statue

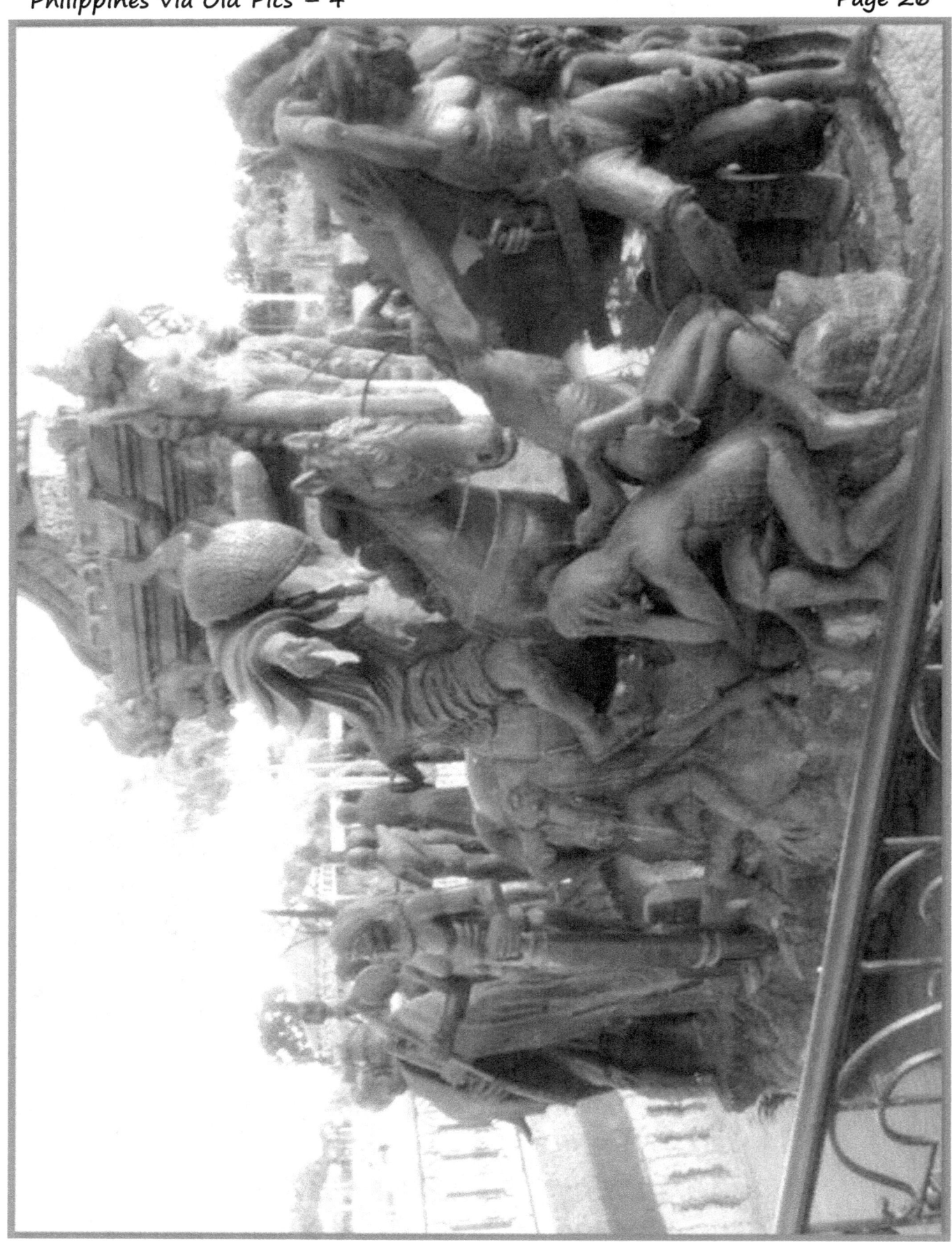

Elaborate sculpture at foot of Queen Isabella Statue

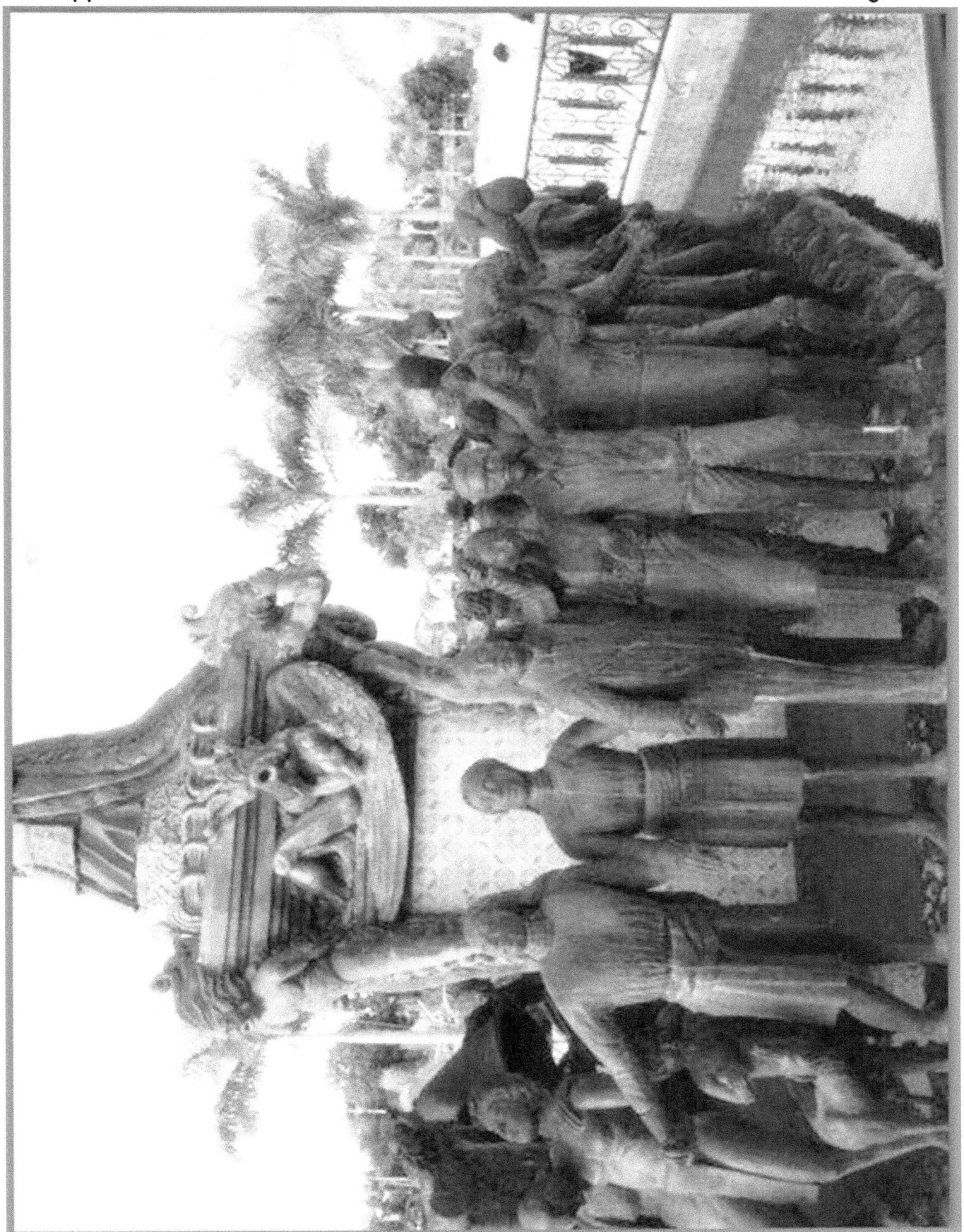

Elaborate sculpture at foot of Queen Isabella Statue

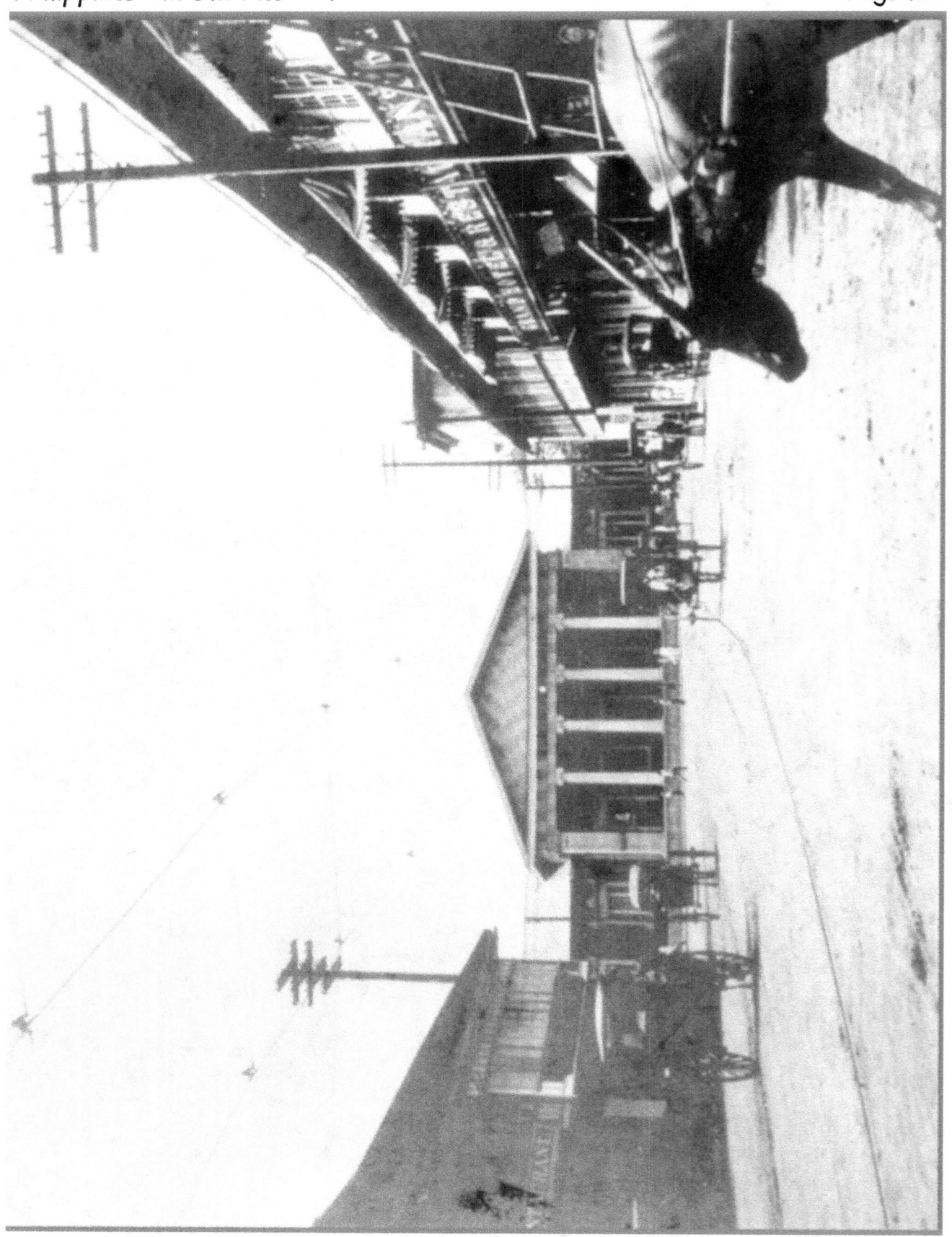

1900s before World War II, Binondo District, Manila. Destroyed by war. – (courtesy of Philippines My Philippines facebook site)

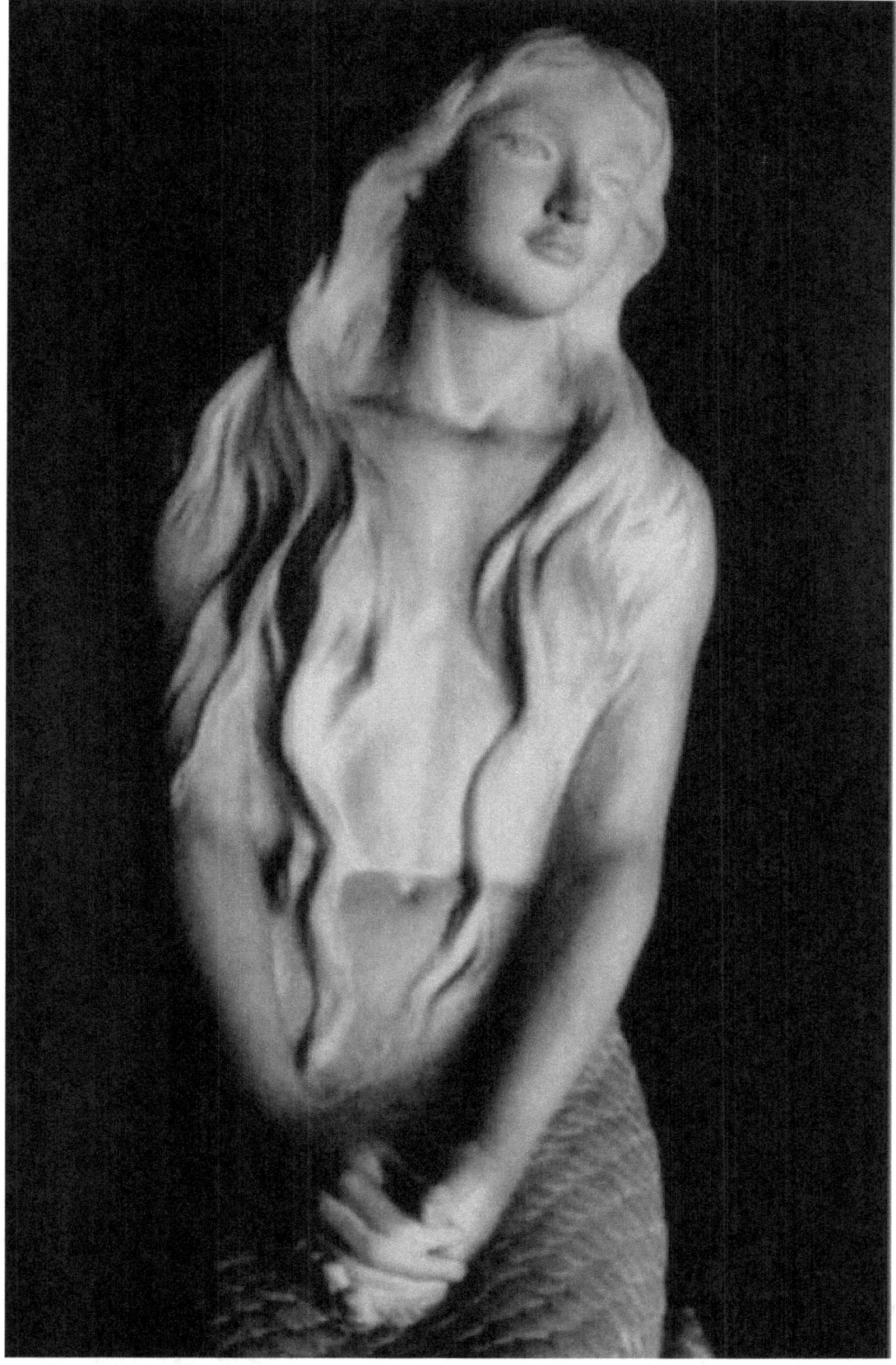

Symbolic Filipina Statue of the famous Song, Mutya Ng Pasig by Nicanor Abelardo, lyrics by A.S.delRosario (courtesy of Philippines My Philippines facebook site)

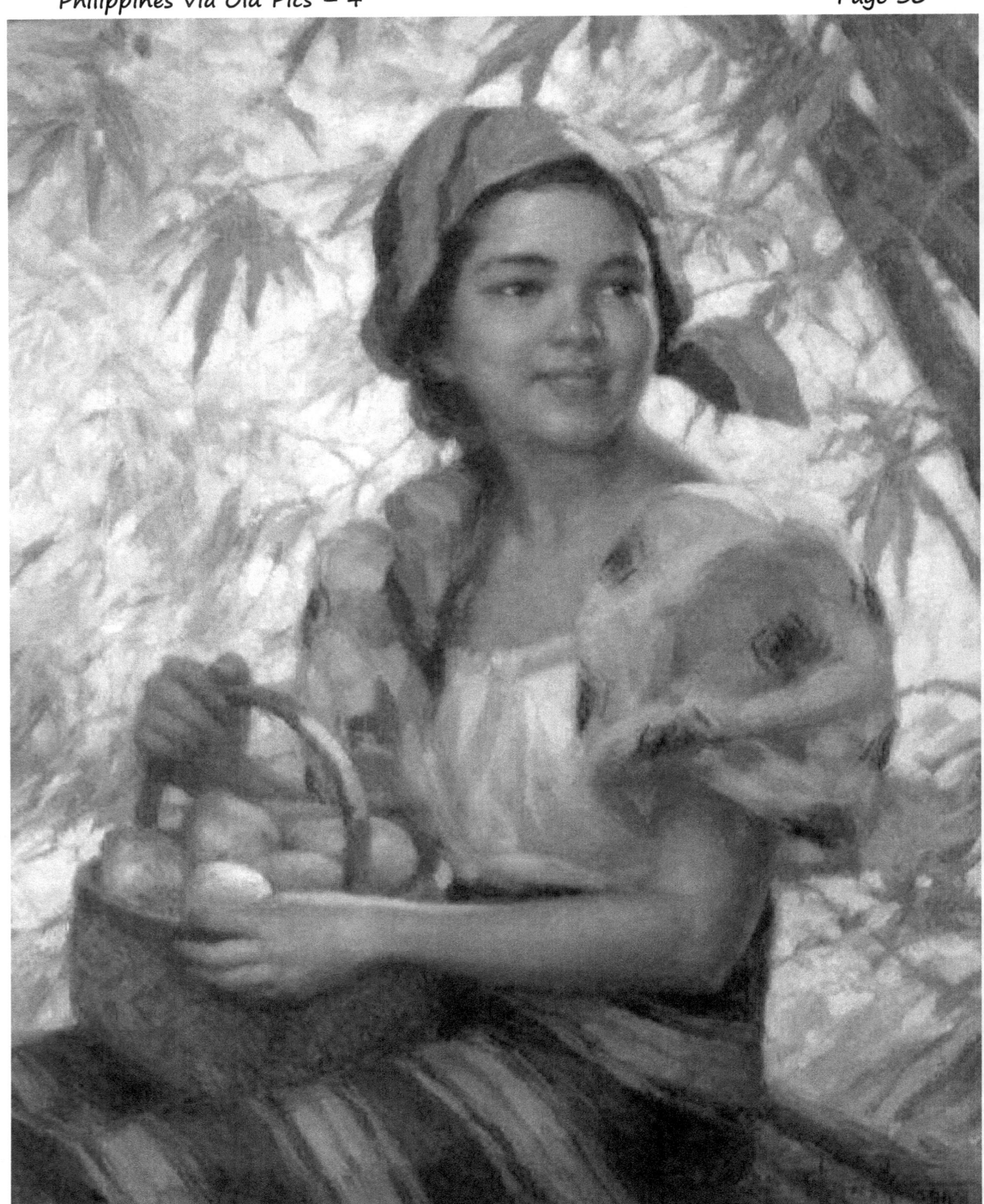

An Amorsolo Painting (courtesy of Philippines My Philippines FB)

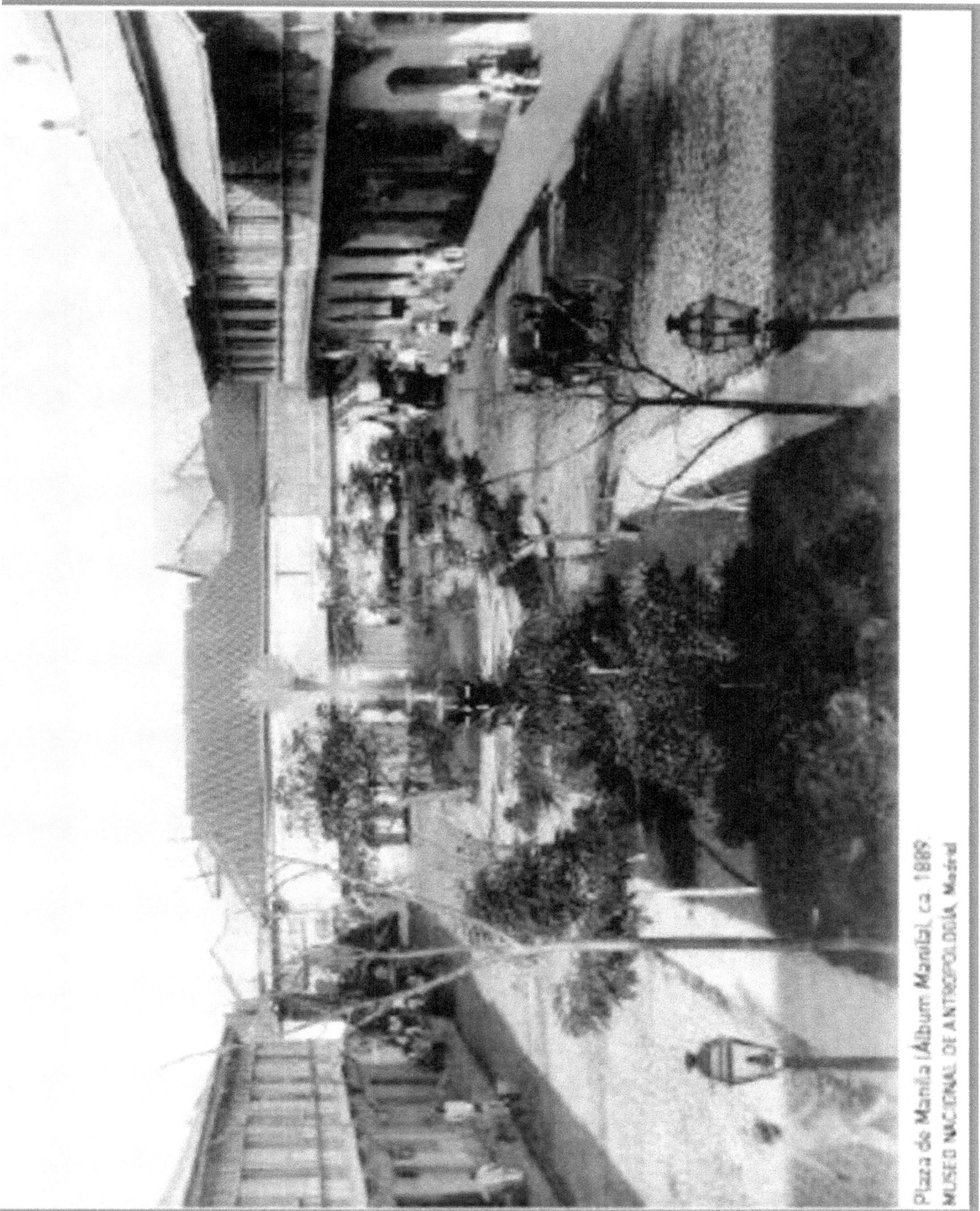

Plaza de Manila (Álbum Manila), ca. 1889.
MUSEO NACIONAL DE ANTROPOLOGÍA, Madrid

1889 Madrid Spain, Plaza de Manila (Philippines My Philippines facebook)

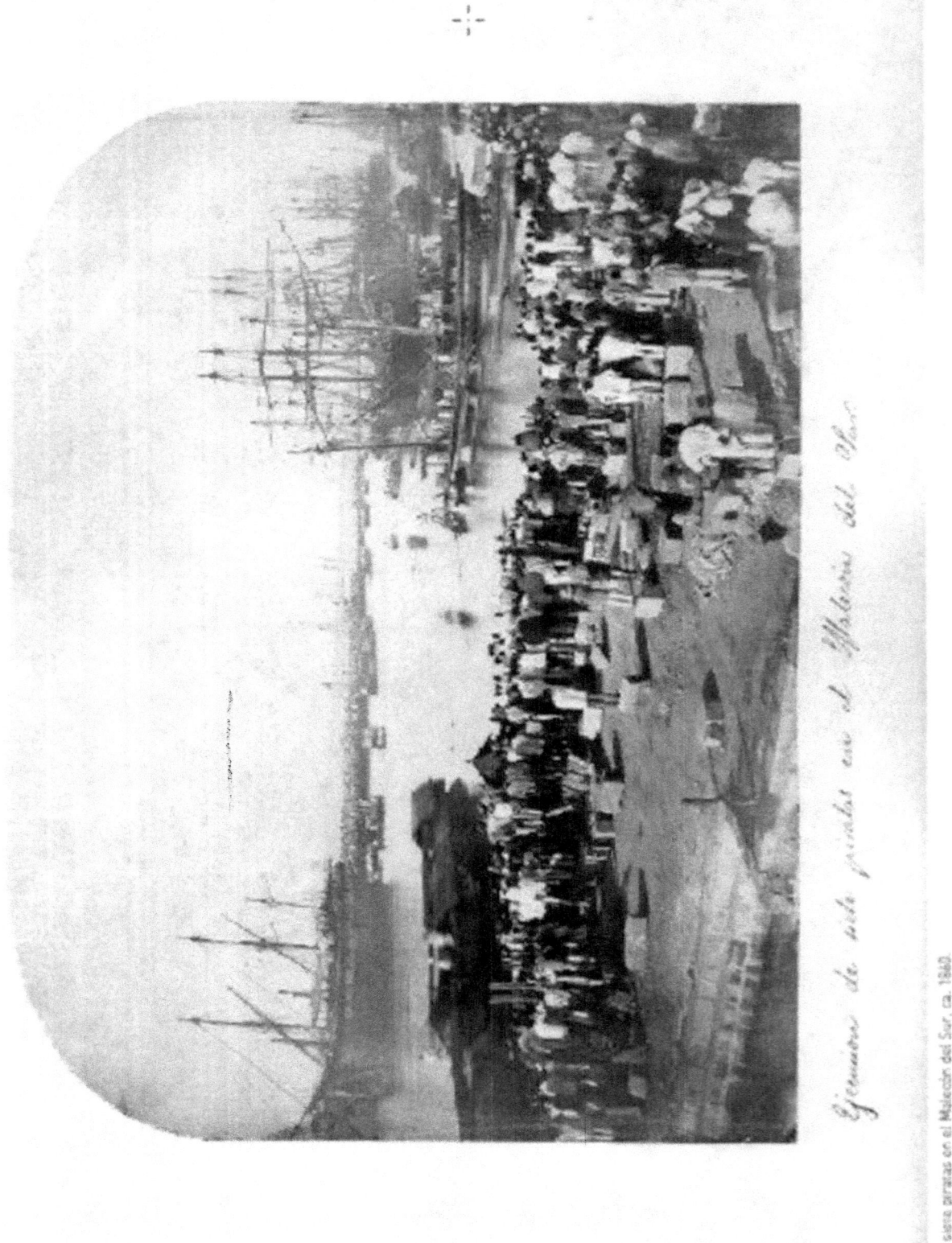

**1862, very old picture of Philippines in Spanish era, showing execution
Of pirates (courtesy of Philippines My Philippines FB site – Maria Llandelar)**

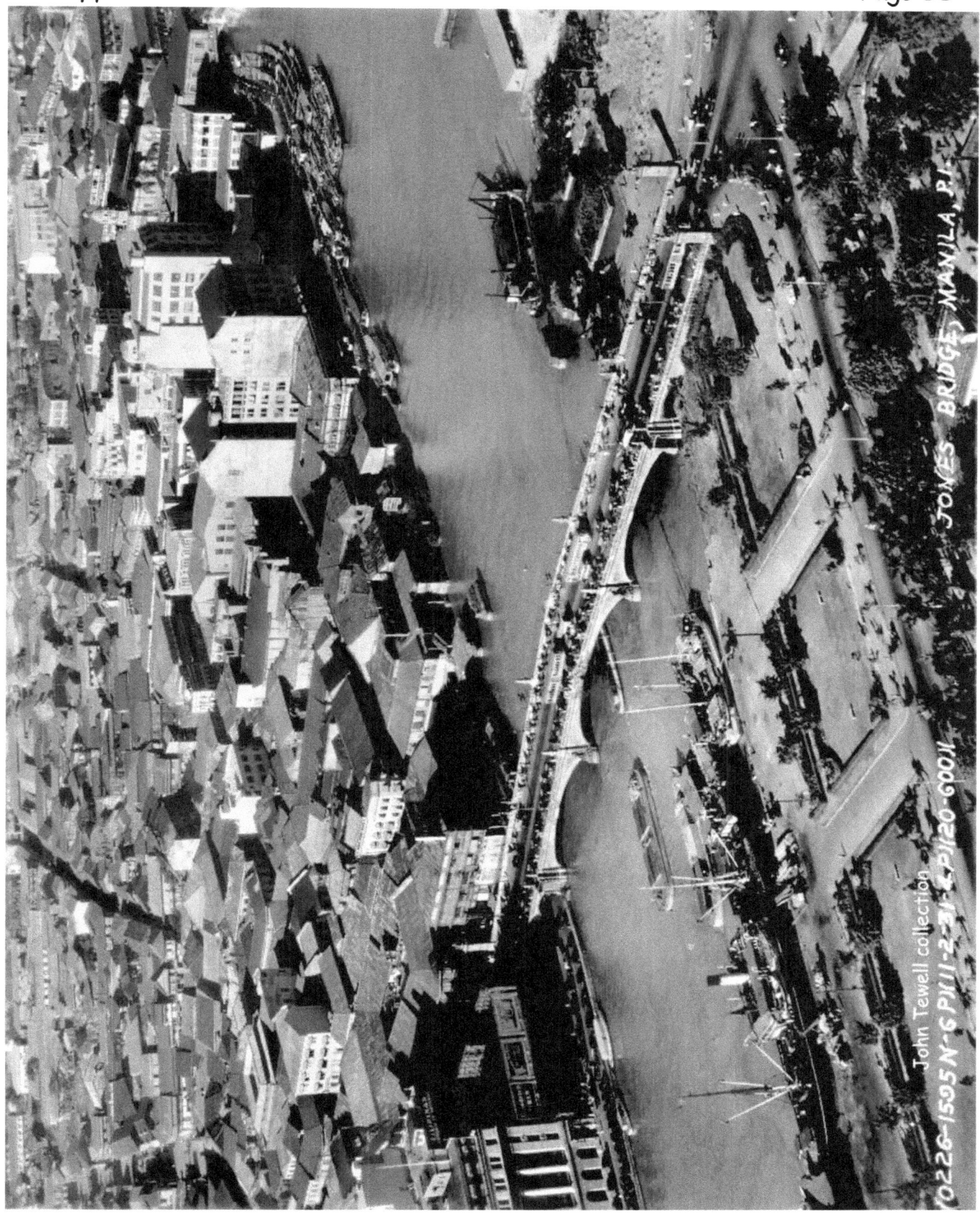

The Jones Bridge. Manila, Philippines, 1931. Designed as work of art. Sadly destroyed by the Japanese during WWII. (Courtesy of Philippines My Philippines – John Tewell Collection - https://www.flickr.com/photos/johntewell/**)**

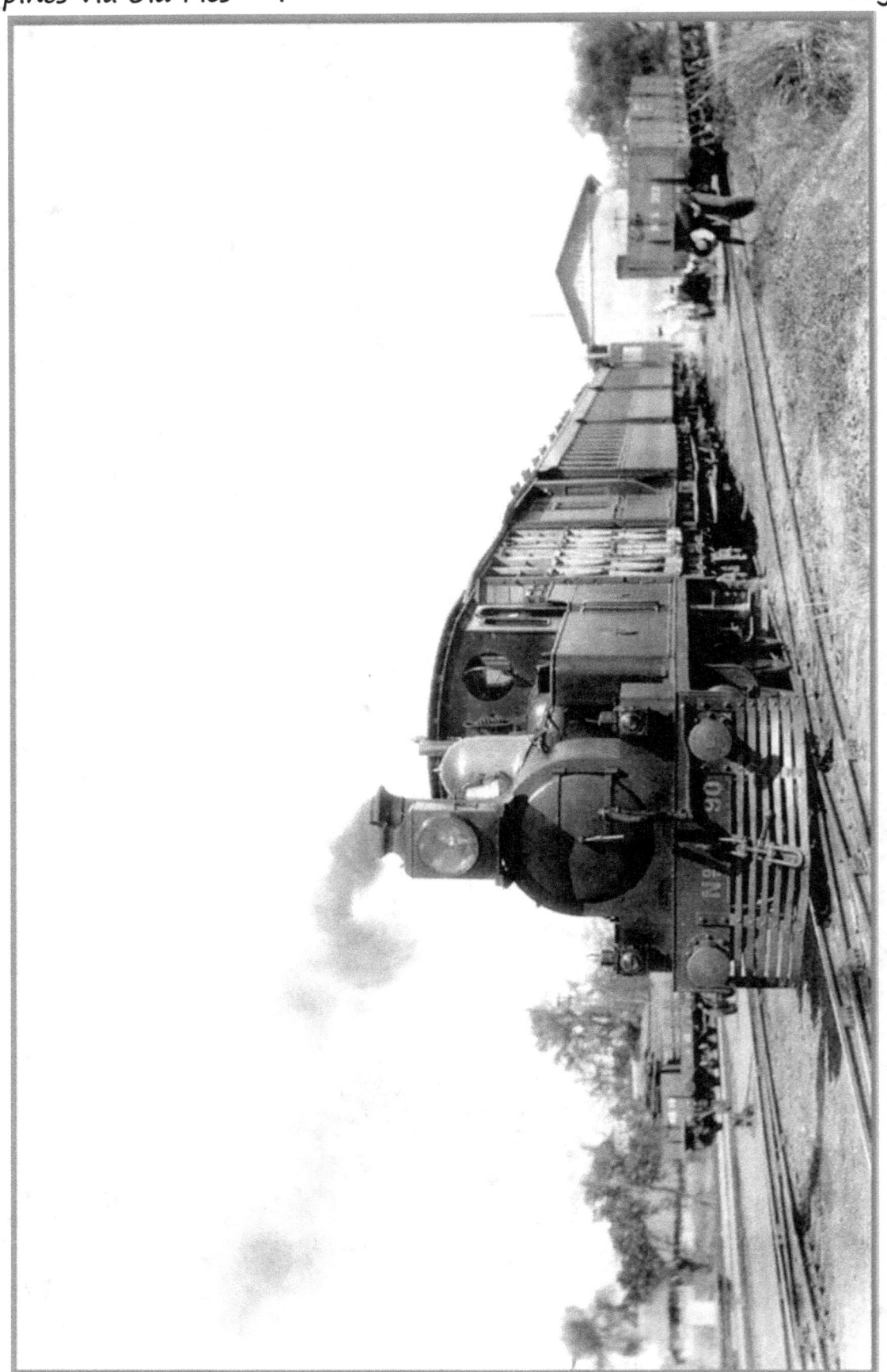

1915 Steam-powered Locomotive, Los Banos, Laguna – (courtesy of Philippines My Philippines facebook site – John Tewell Collection)

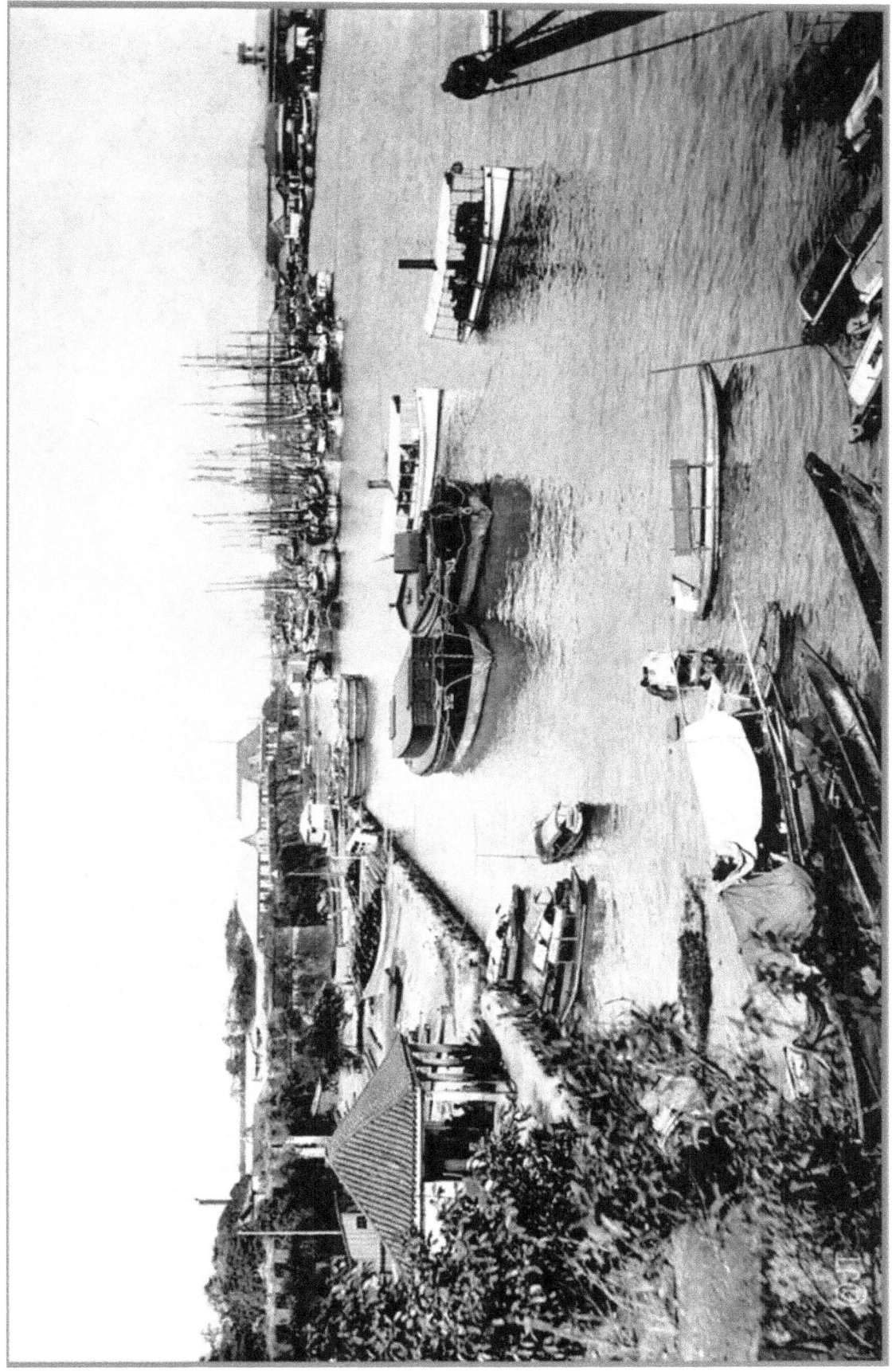

1902 Manila, Pasig River – (courtesy of Philippines My Philippines Facebook Site – John Tewel Collection)

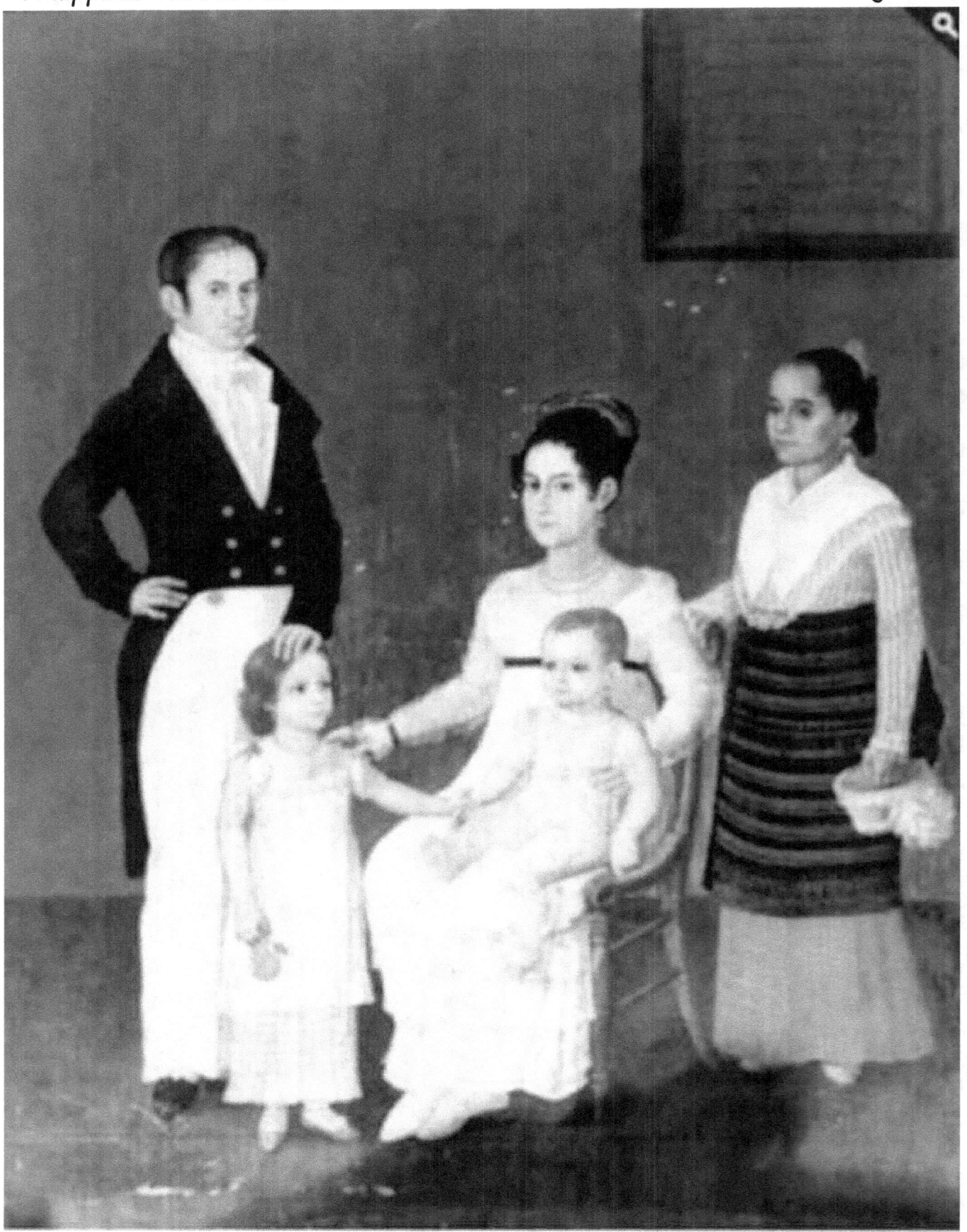

**19th Century Portrait of Spanish Family + Filipina Nanny in elegant dress –
(courtesy of Philippines My Philippines FB site – Nacpil Collection)**

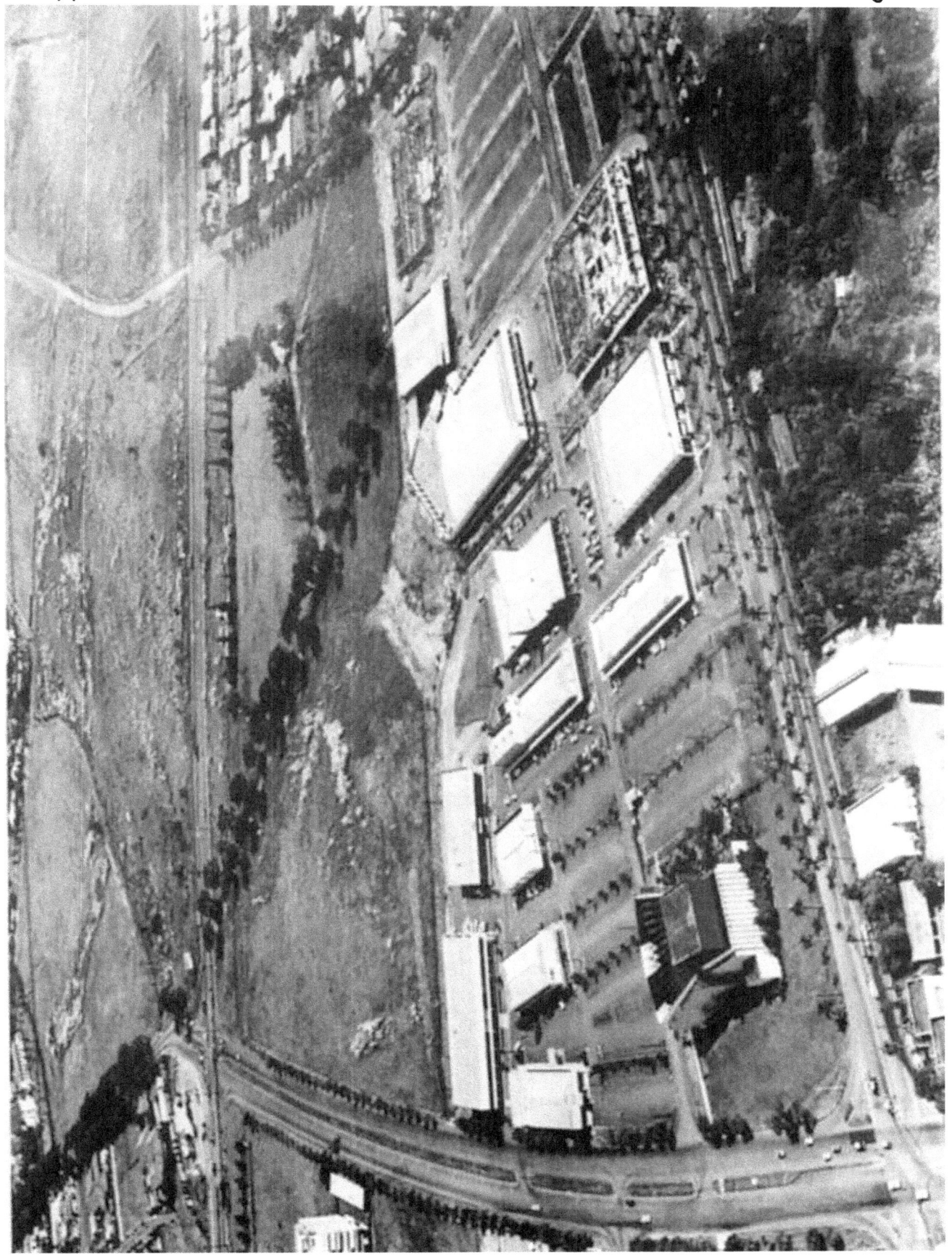

1960s Makati Development Taking Shape – (courtesy of Philippines My Philippines facebook site)

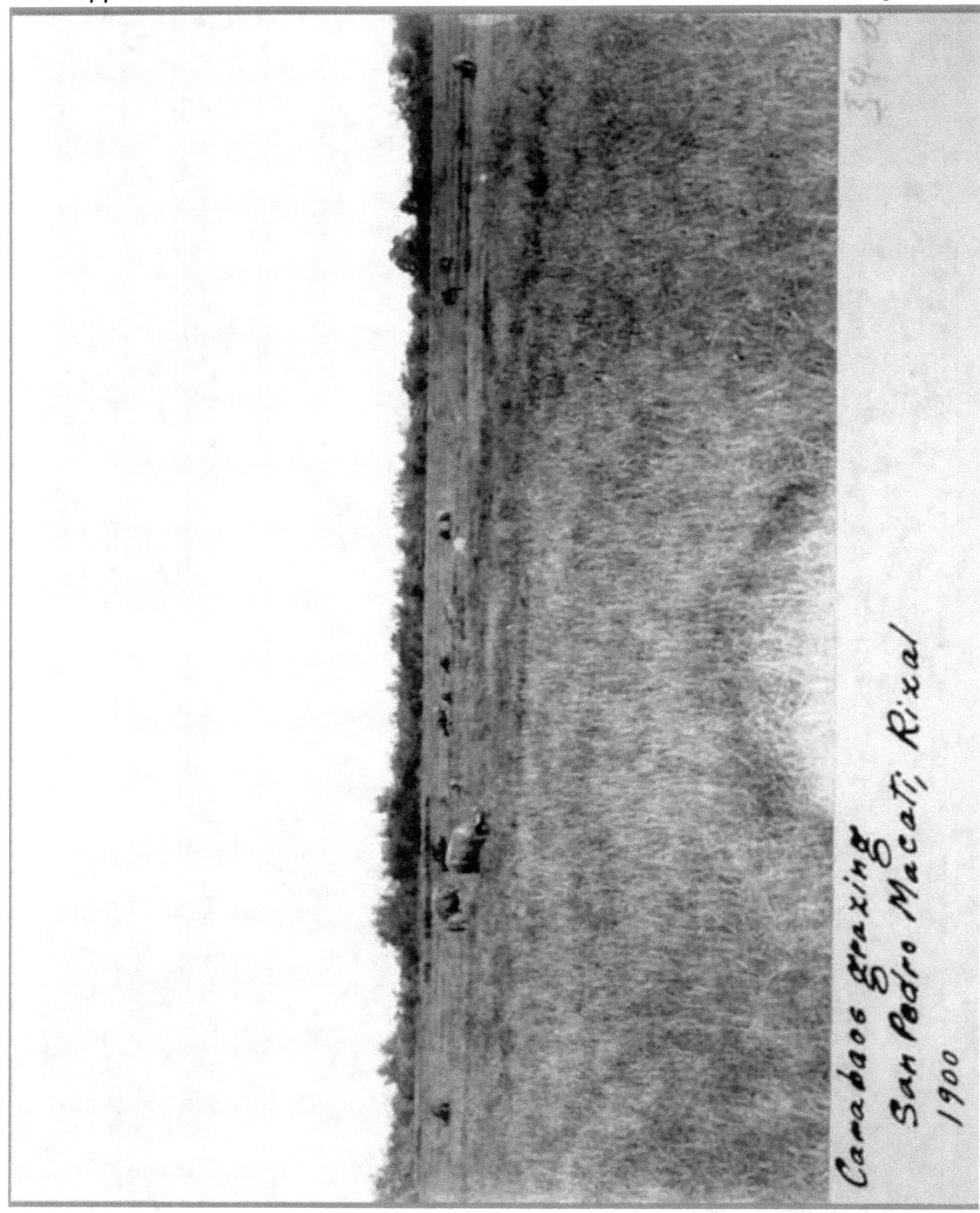

Carabaos grazing
San Pedro Macati, Rizal
1900

1900 Showing Original Makati as open grazing field, called then as San Pedro de Macati – (courtesy of Philippines My Philippines FB site)

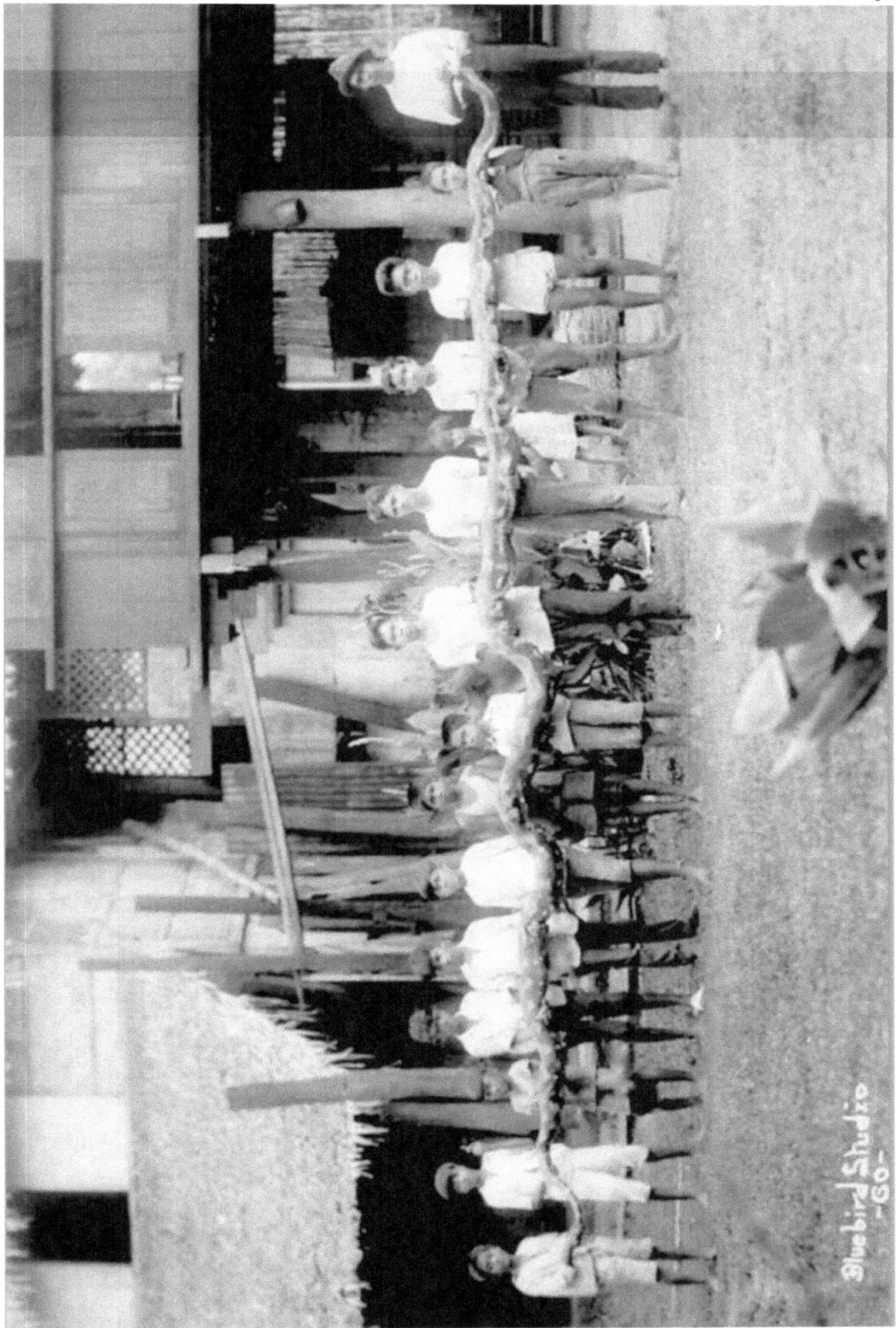

Early 1900s - A Massive Python caught in Palawan. (courtesy of Philippines My Philippines FB site - simoun - image Matthew Westfall FB page)

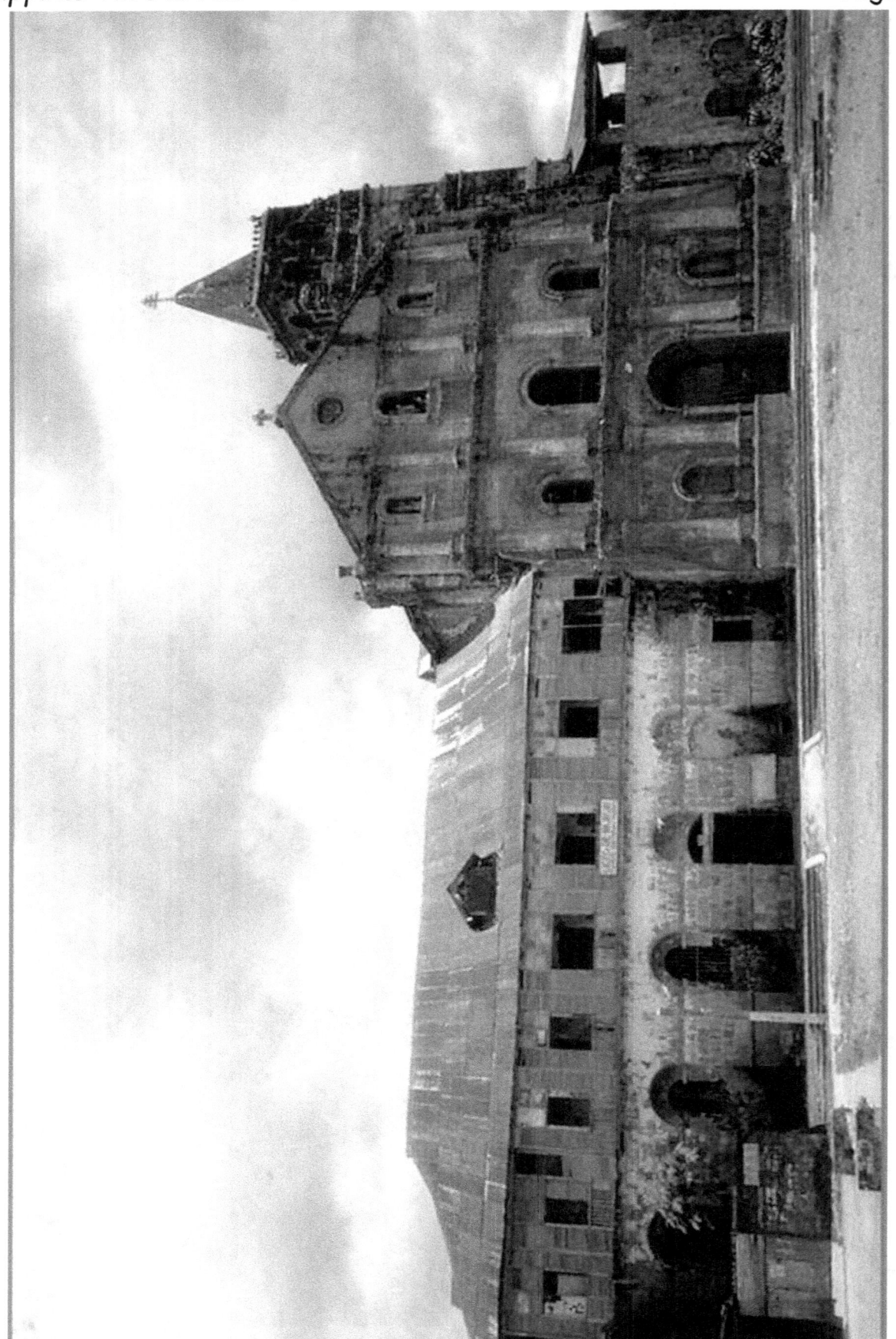

18th century-built San Gregorio Magno Church in Majayjay, Laguna, renoved several times – (courtesy of Philippines My Philippines FB site)

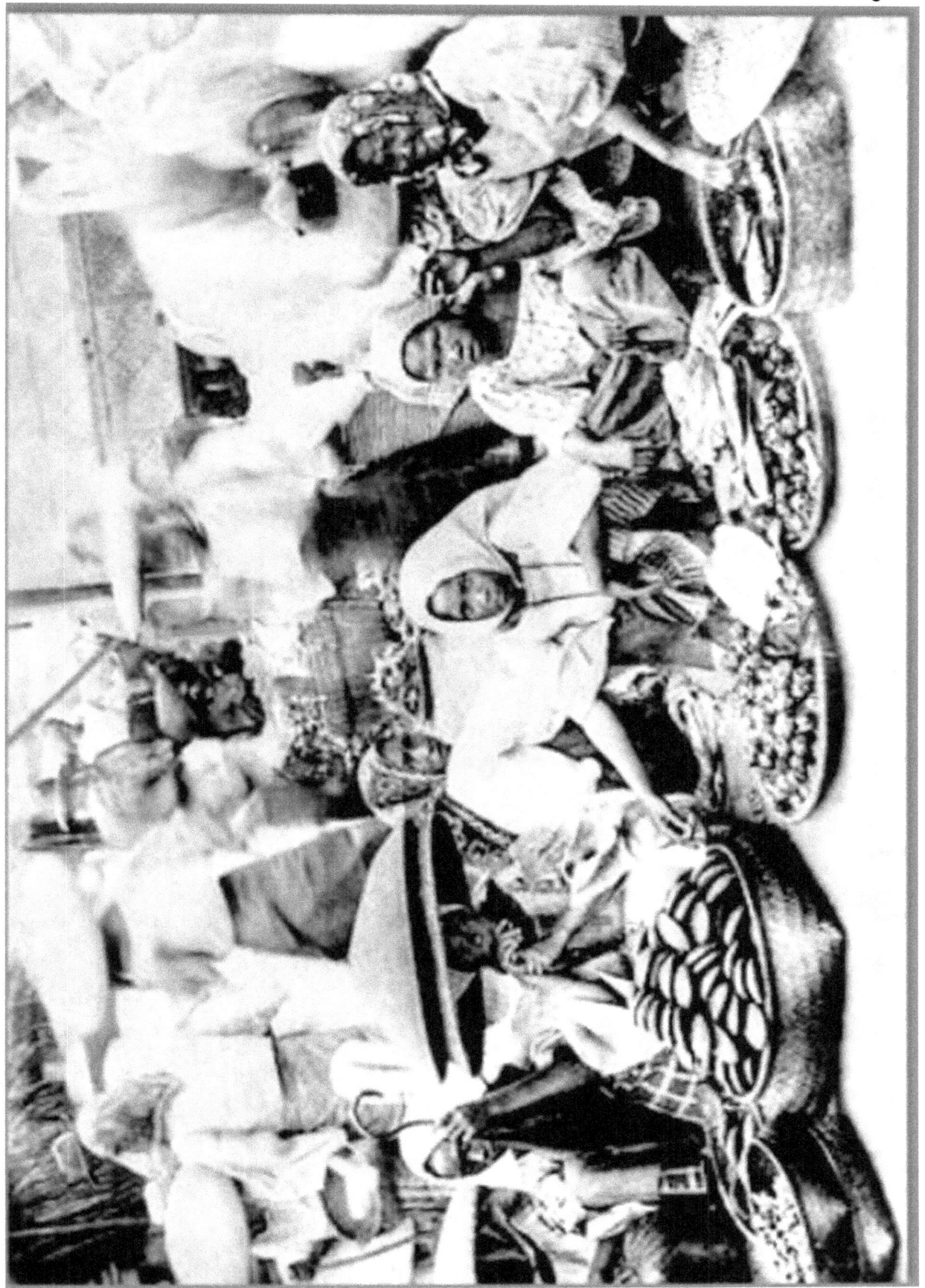

1900s Market Vendors – (courtesy of Philippines My Philippines FB site – Eric Degala Deramos)

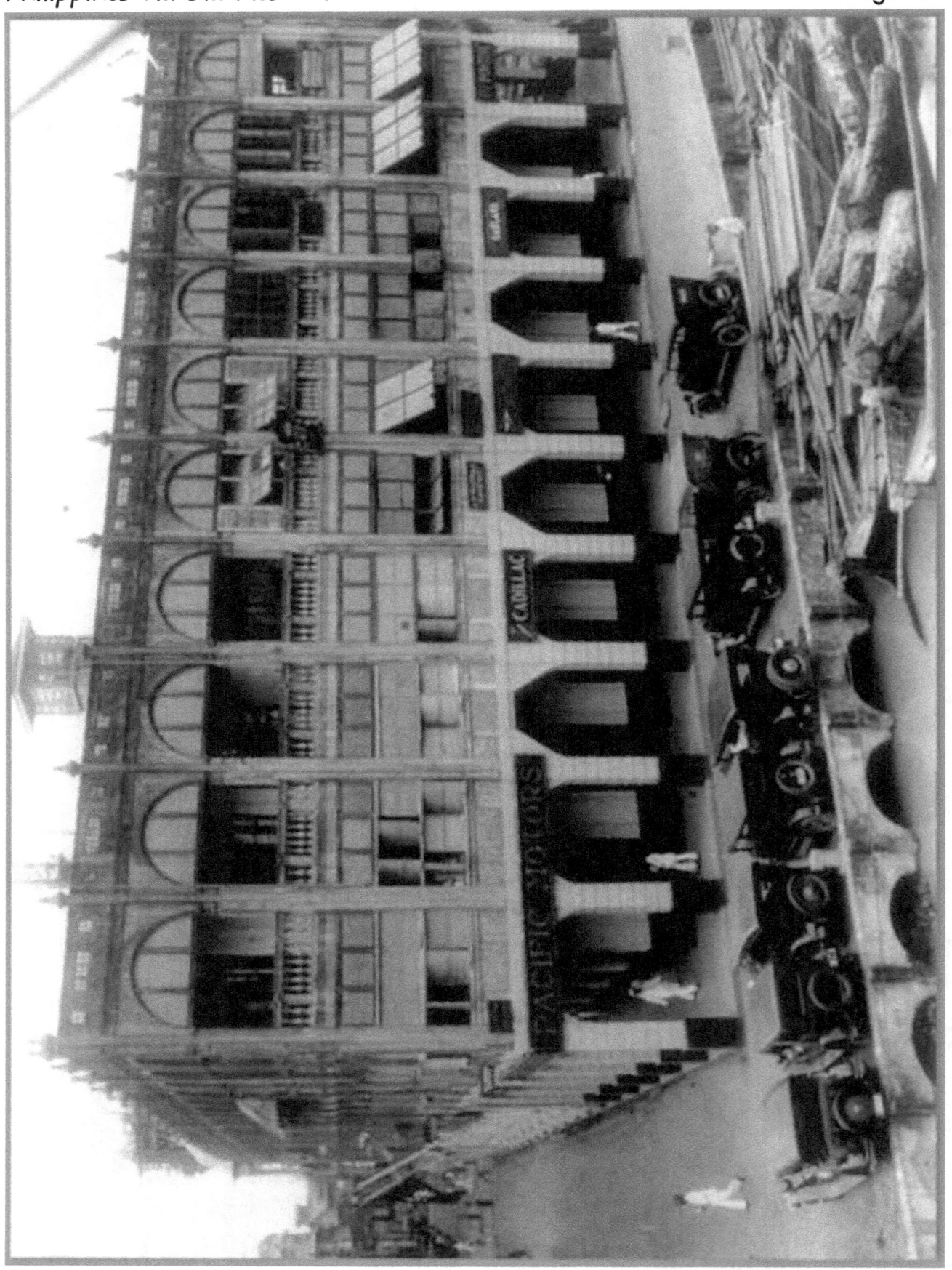

1928 Regina Bldg. Escolta – Cadillac cars line-up – (courtesy of Philippines My Philippines FB site – Seludong Tandang Sora)

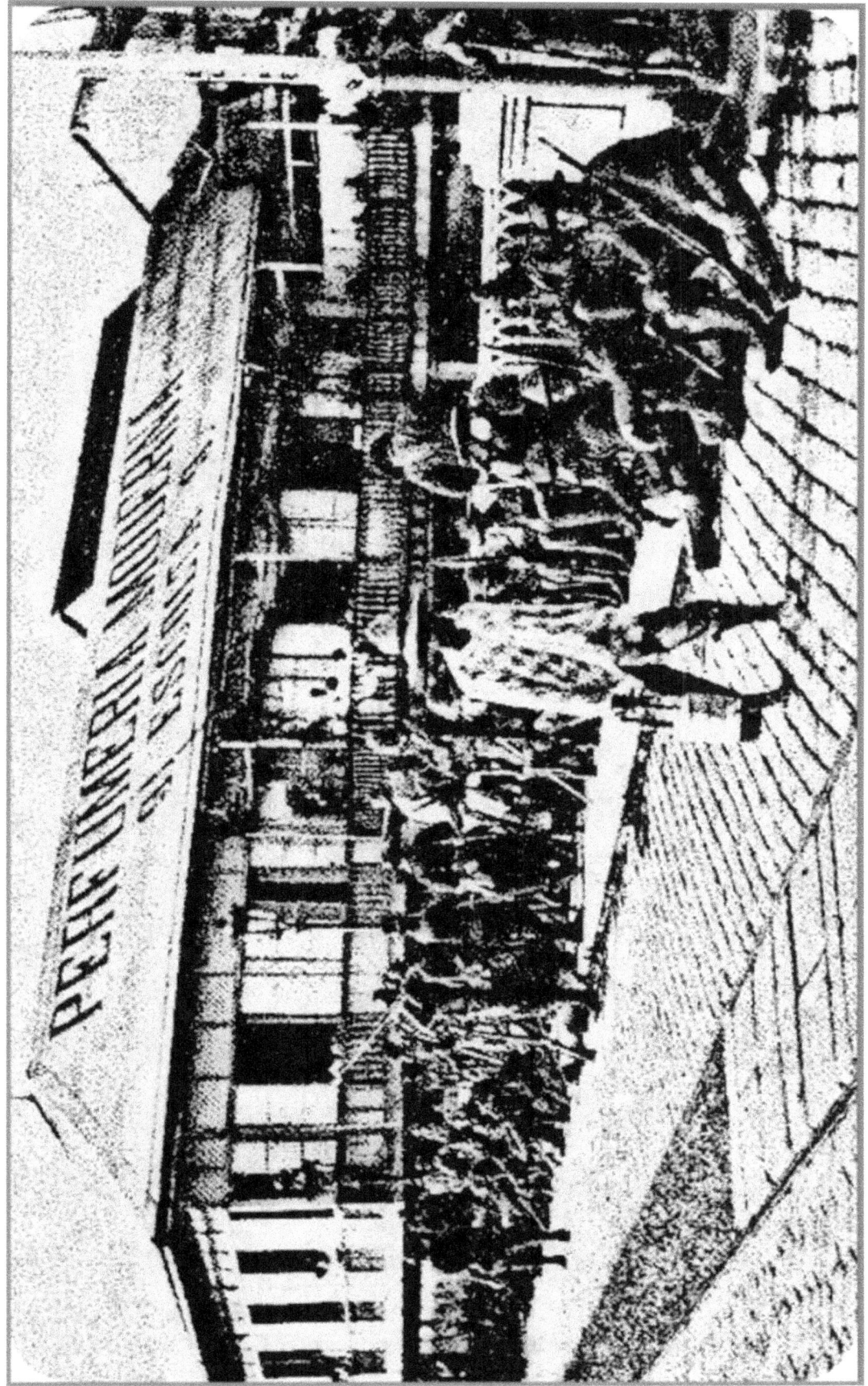

1898 – American Troop in Philpiine War – (courtesy of Philippines My Philippines FB site – Wikipedia – Inang Laya)

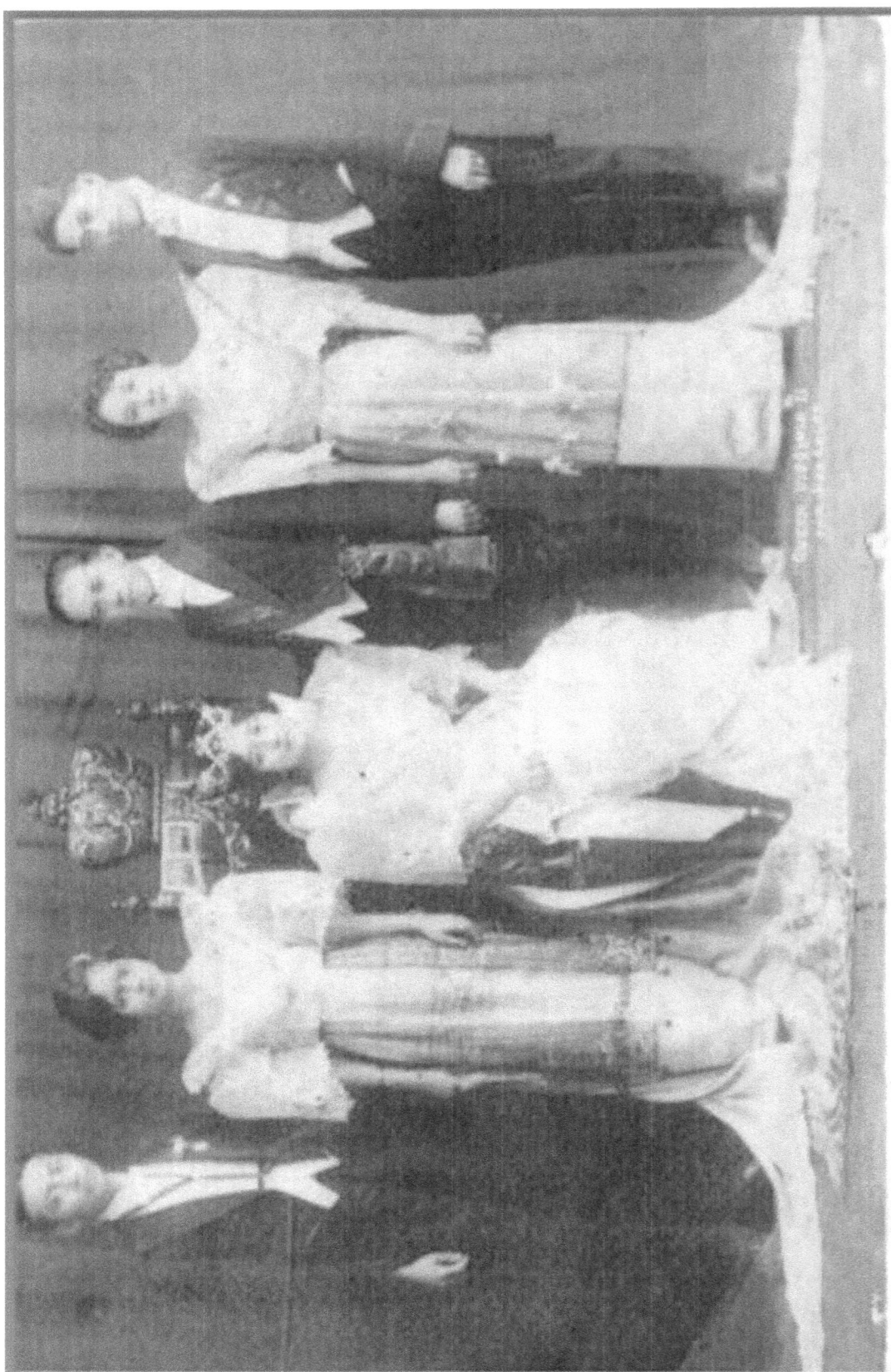

Miss Manila Carnival 1922 (MissPhilippines that time), Virginia Llamas of Pagsanjan, Laguna. Her prince consort was journalist Carlos P Romulo of Camiling, Tarlac, who she married later. Carlos P. Romulo was General Douglas McArthur aide-de-camp & UN Sec. General (Philippines My Philippines FB site)

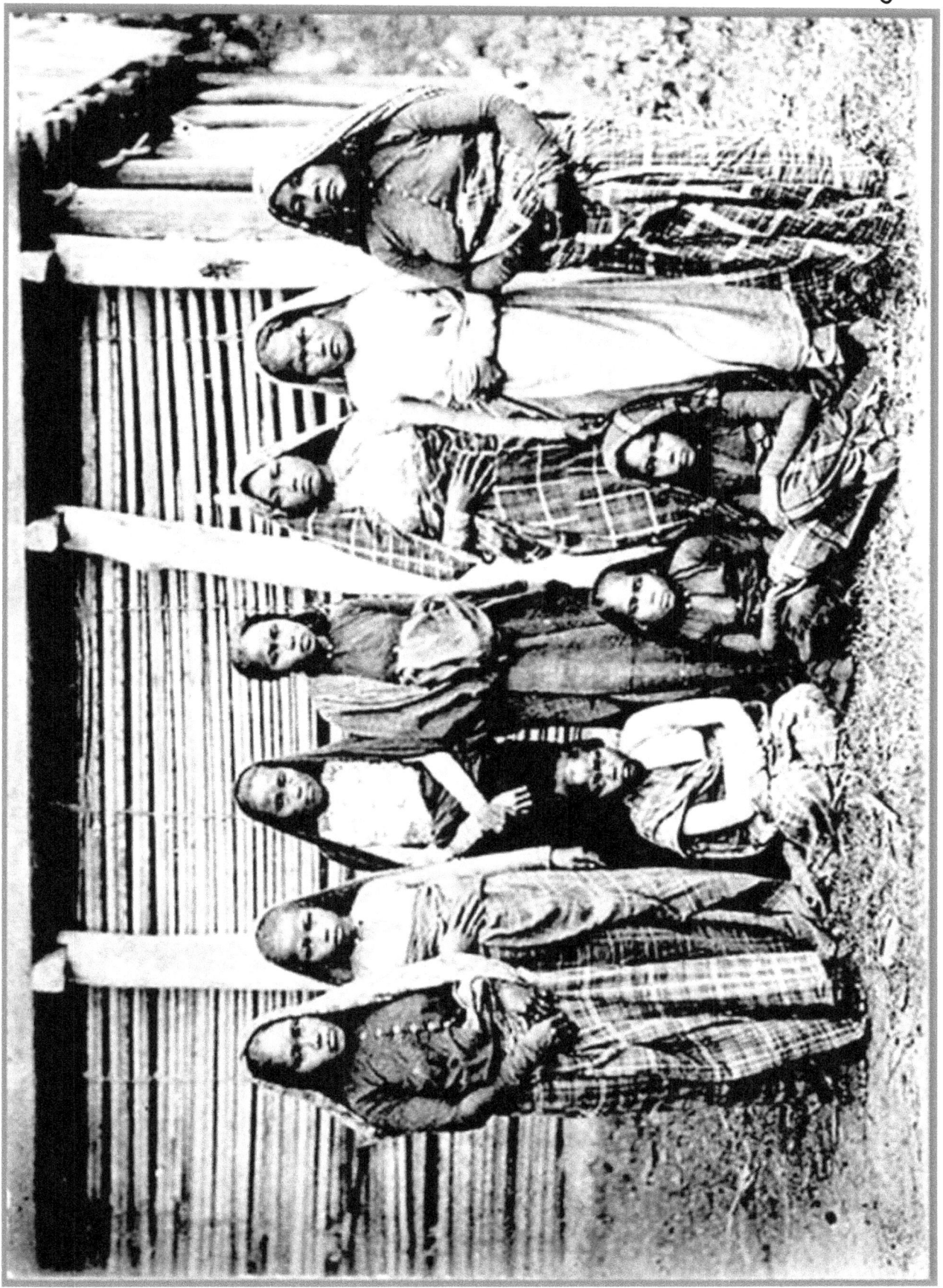

1900 Moro Women – (courtesy of Philippines My Philippines FB site – Maria Llanderal)

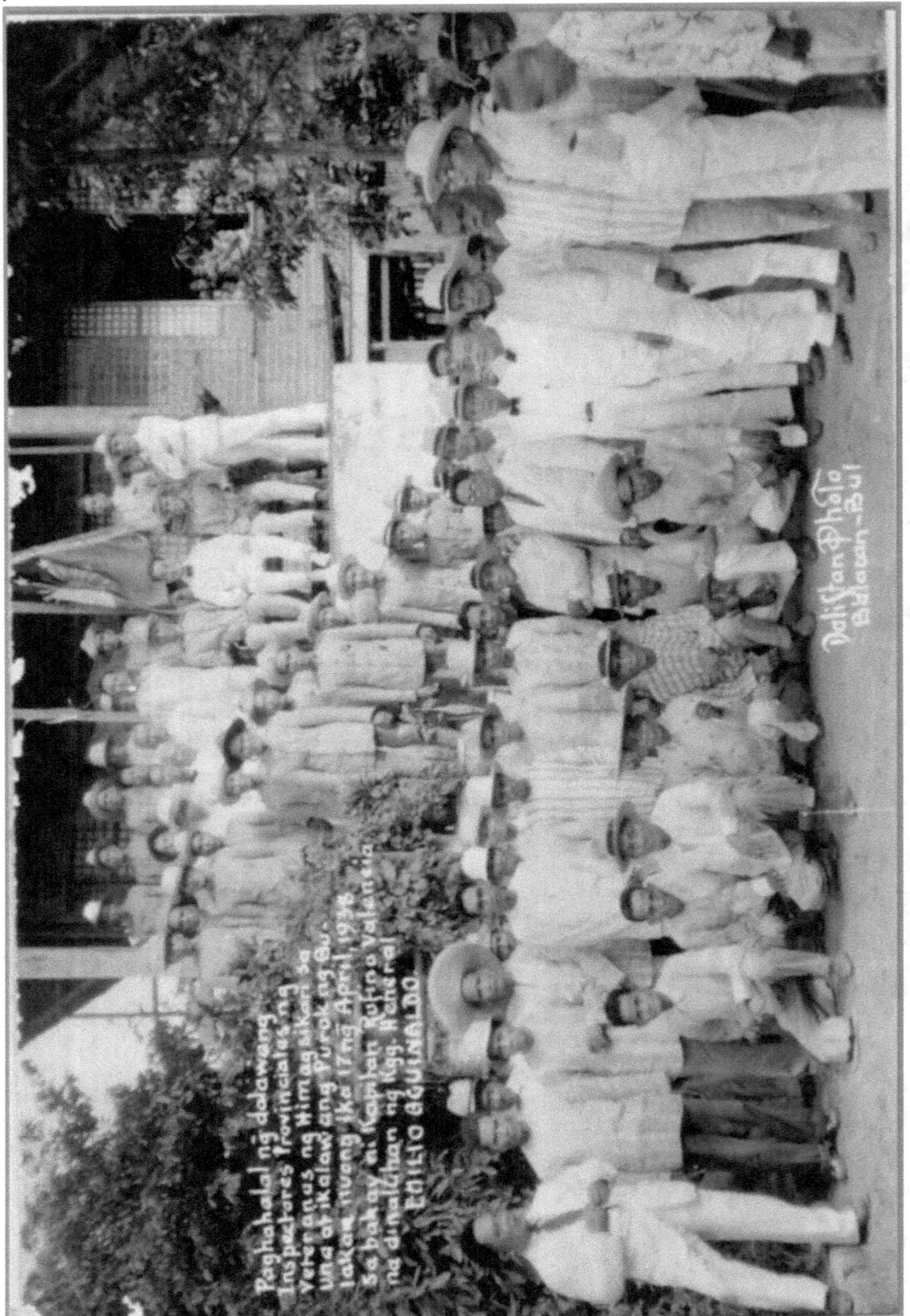

April 17, 1938 - Election of "Inspectores Provinciates" of "Veteranos ng Himagsikan" of Bulacan, Bulacan - Attended by Gen Emilio Aguinaldo and Jose SF Enriquez – (courtesy of Philippines, My Philippines FB site – A very well preserved photo - Beto Reyes & simoun)

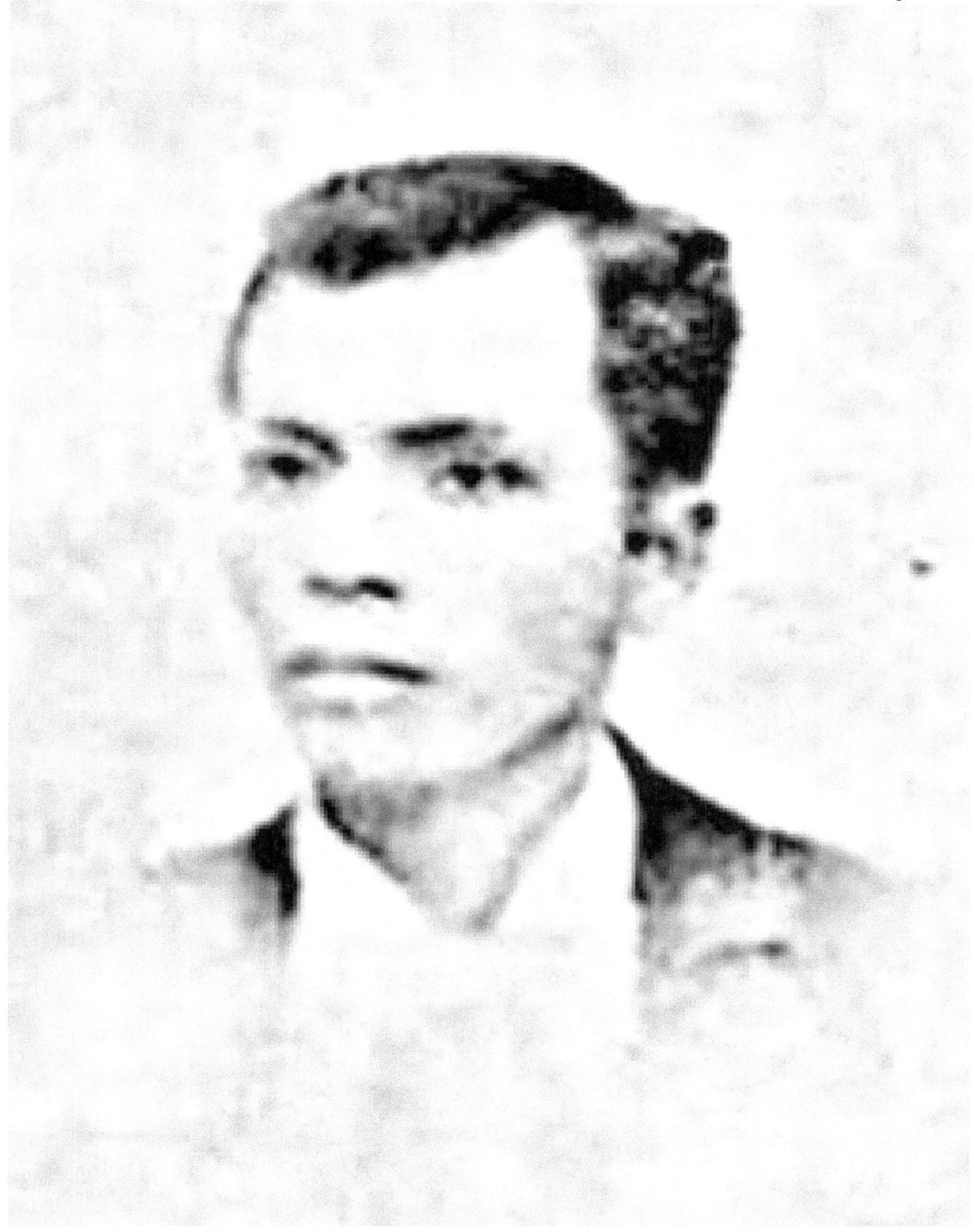

**Gat. Andres Bonifacio, The Great Plebean – Founder and Supremo
of the Katipunan Revolutionary Force at the turn of the 19th century –
(courtesy of Philippines My Philippines FB site)**

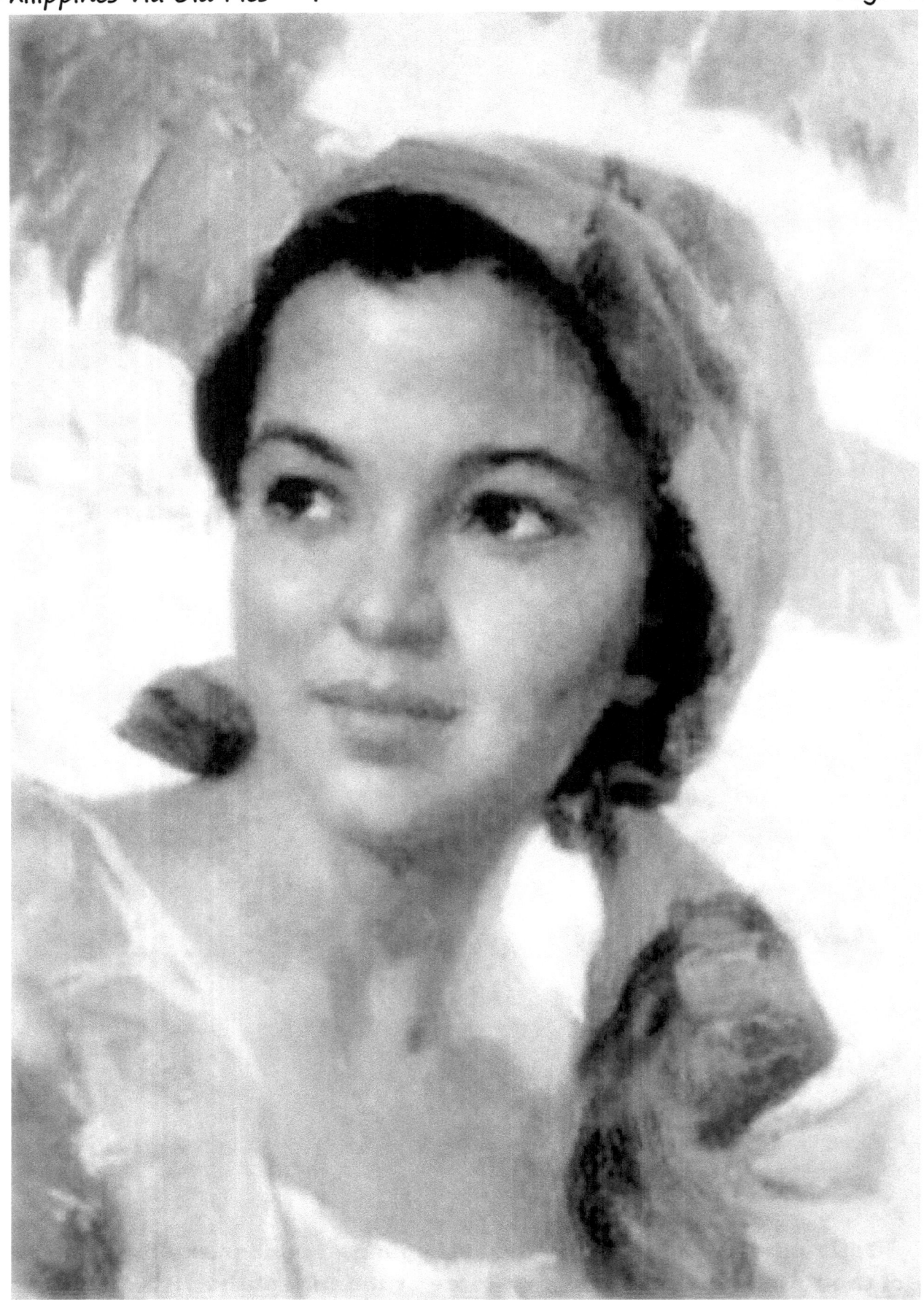

An Amorsolo Painting – (courtesy of Philippines My Philippines FB site)

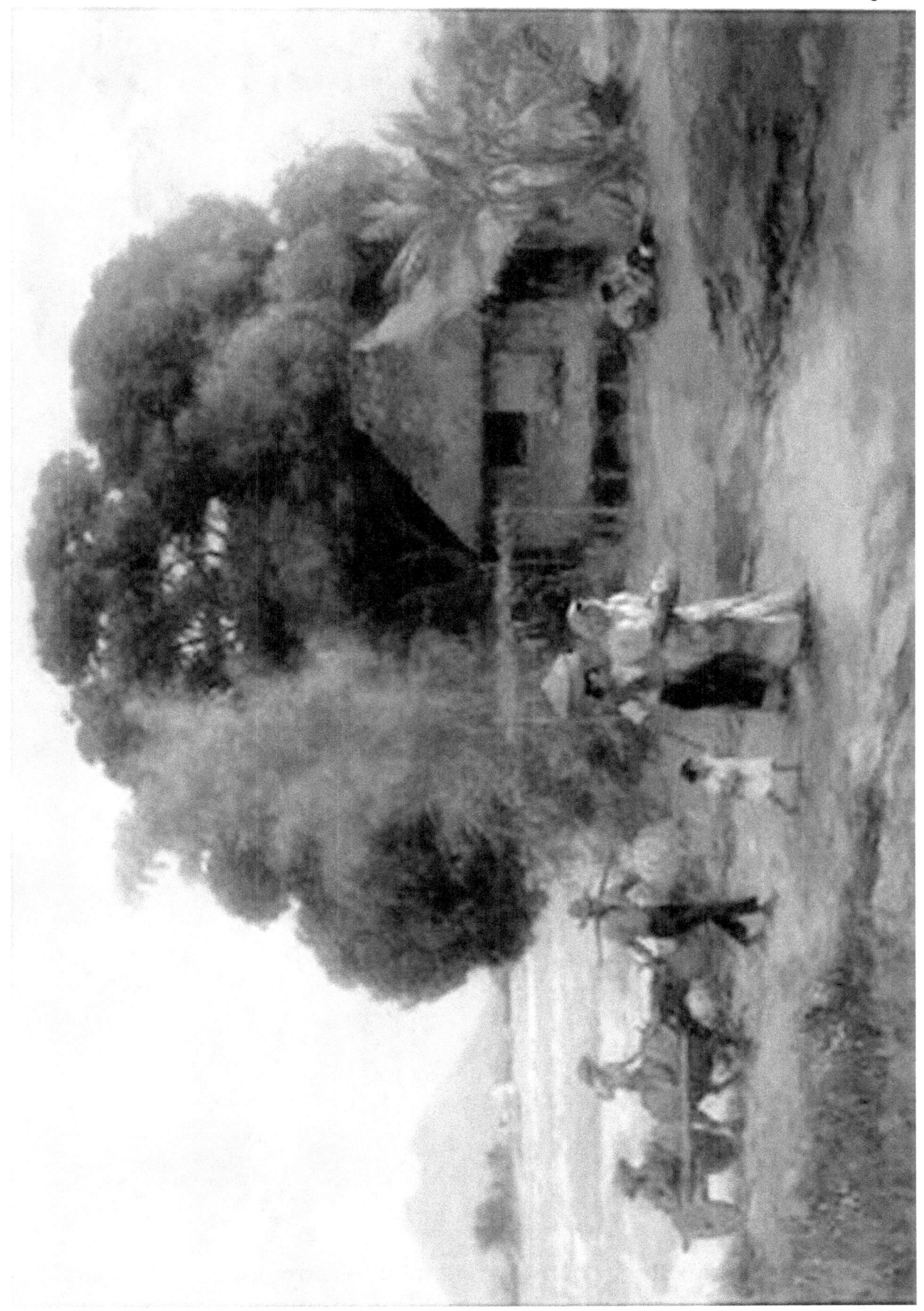

An Amorsolo Painting – (courtesy of Philippines My Philippines FB site)

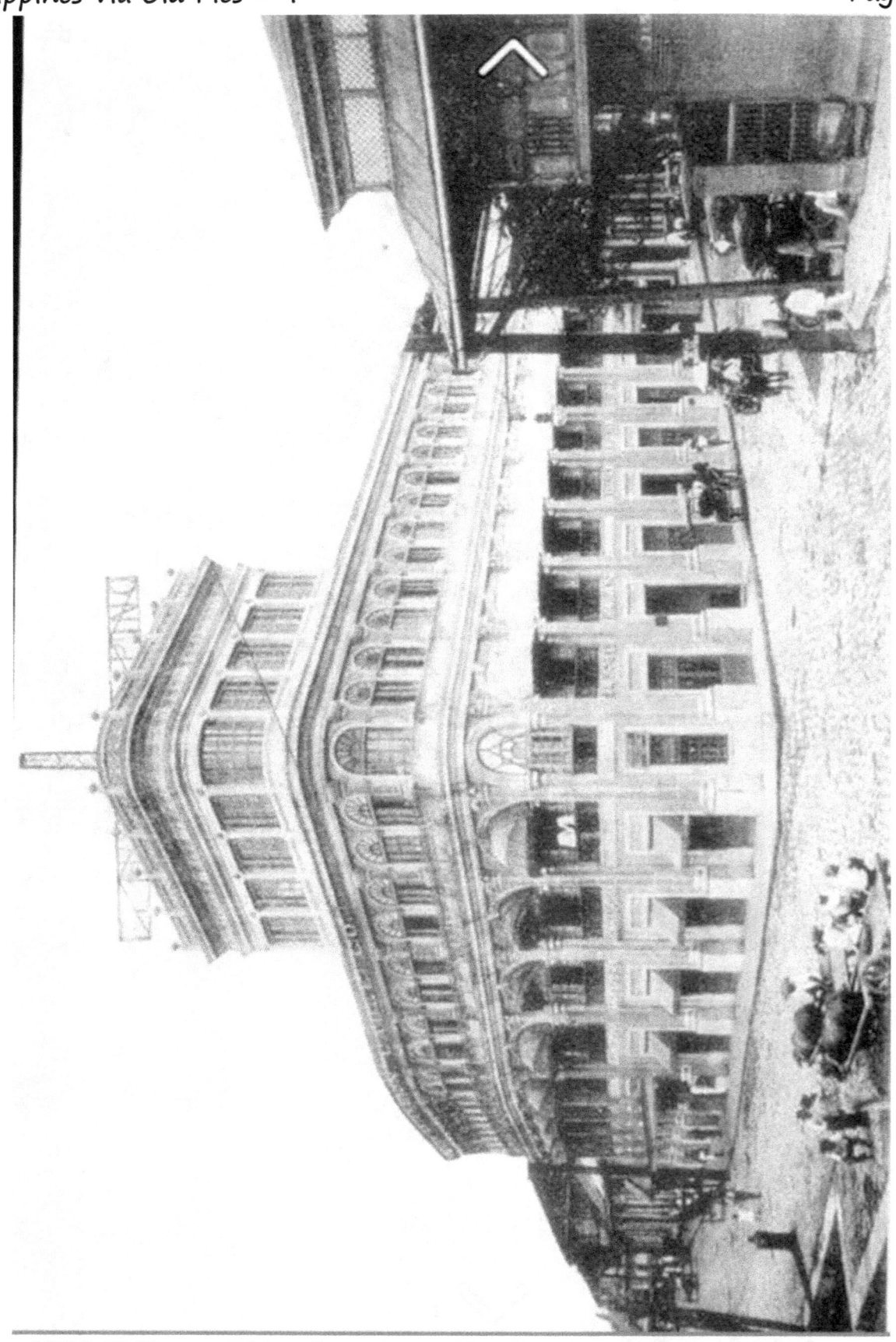

1900 El Hogar Bldg, downtown Manila, destroyed by WWII, but Dilapidated as of now, due for demolition – (courtesy of Philippines My Philippines FB site)

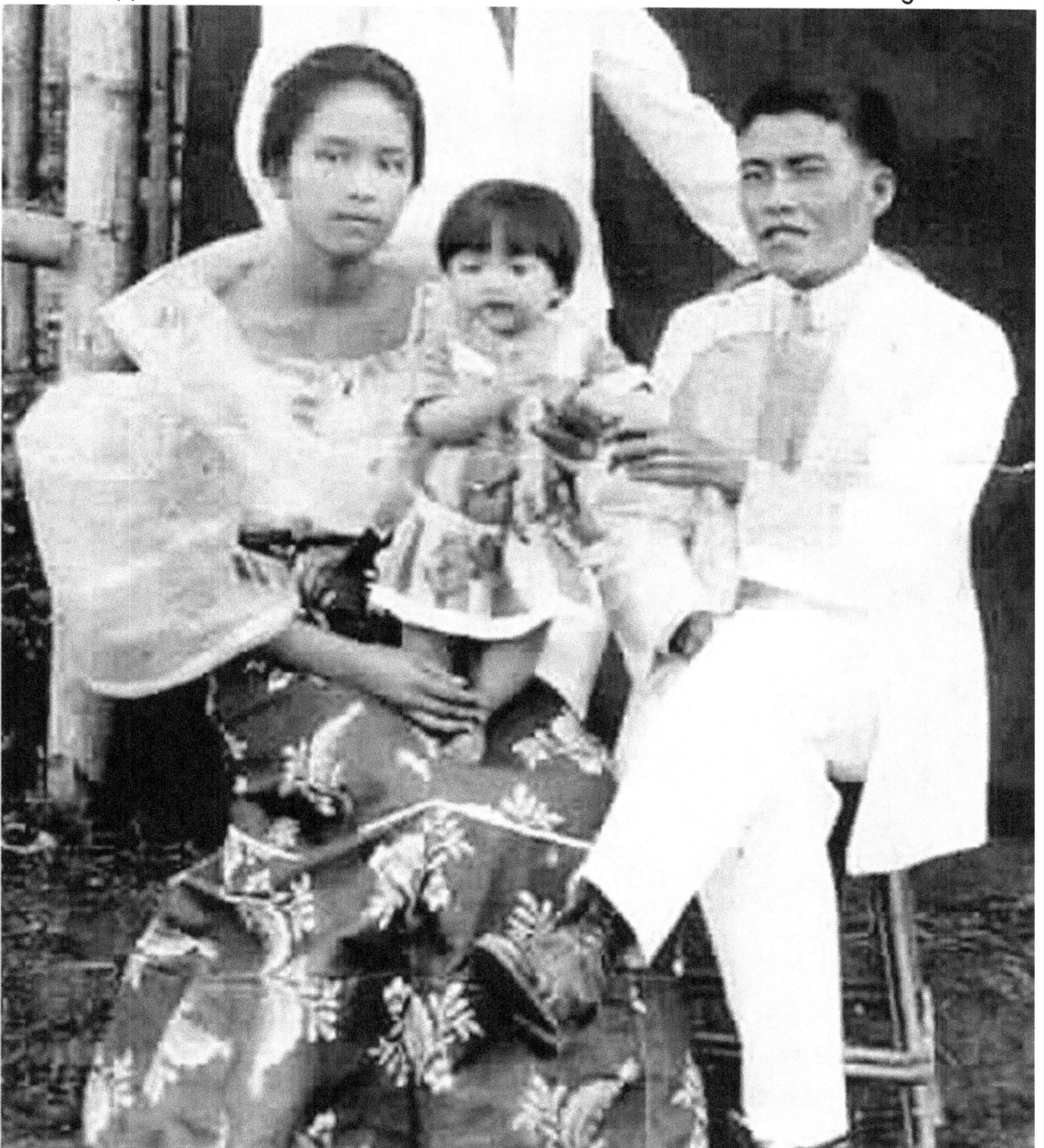

1914 Typical Young Filipino Couple with one child – Colorful attire

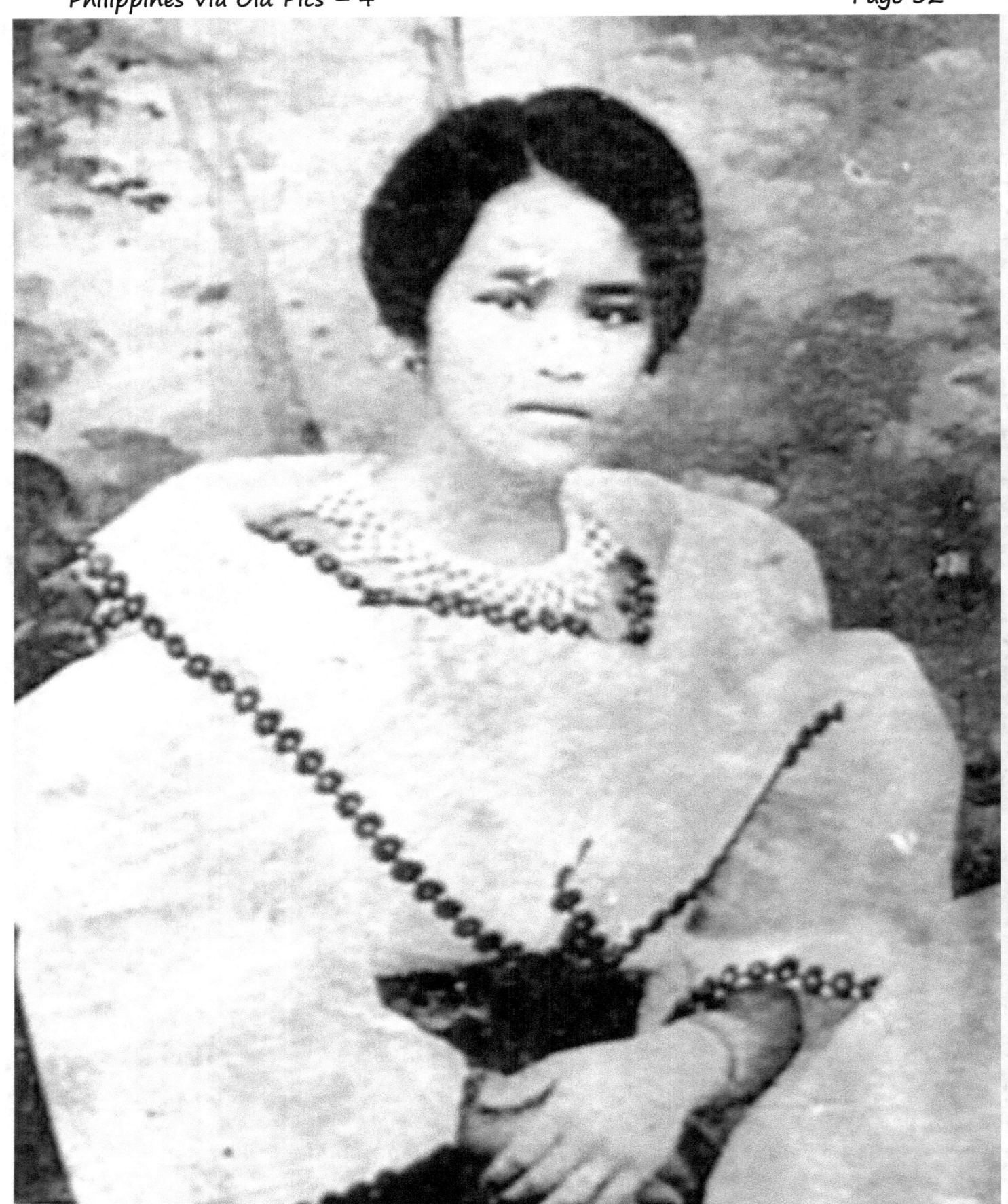

1913 Typical Young Lady in Pilipina Dress

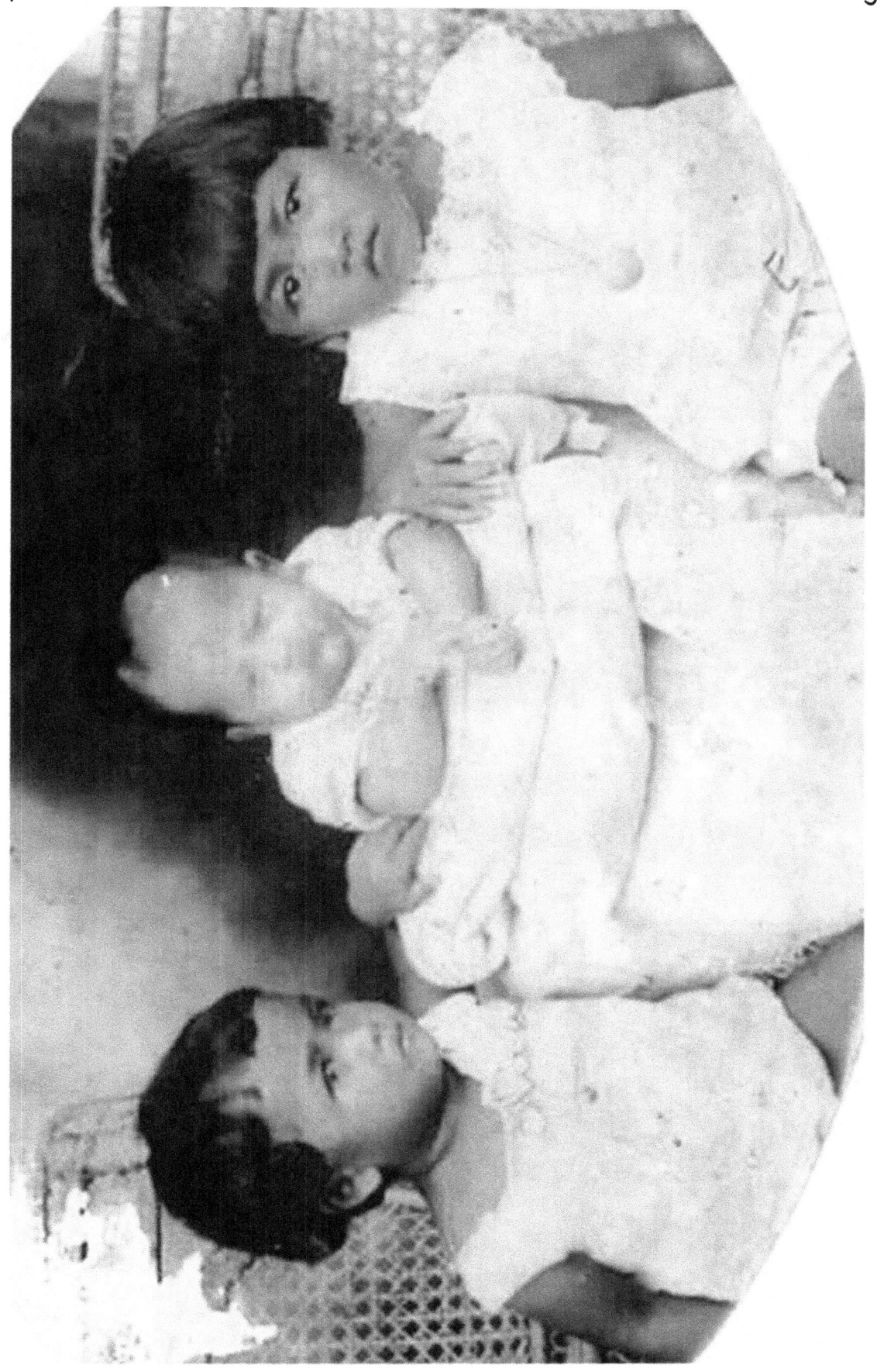

1918 Typical Filipino Children's photo

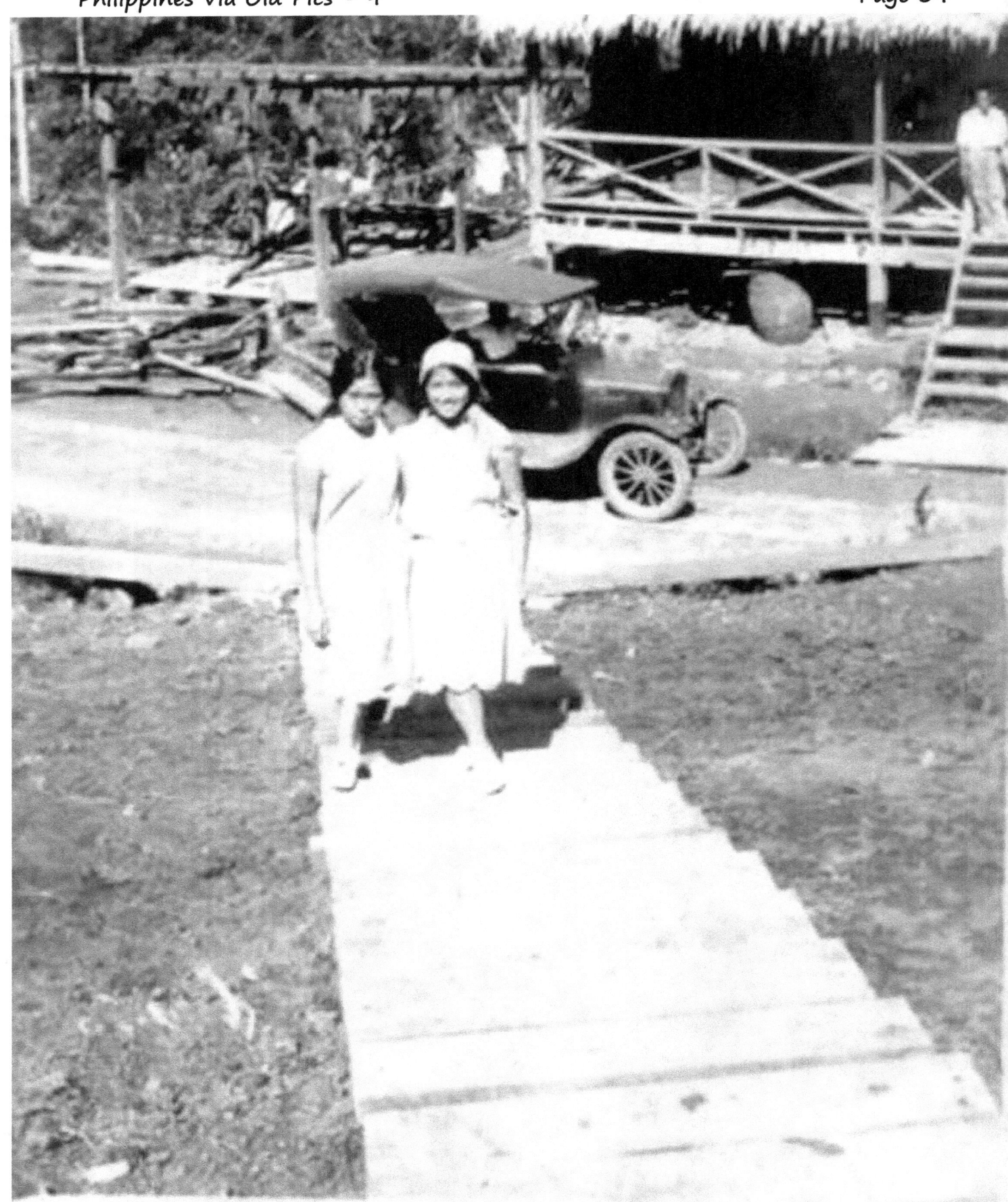

1920s Provincial Filipina girls with T-Ford car at background

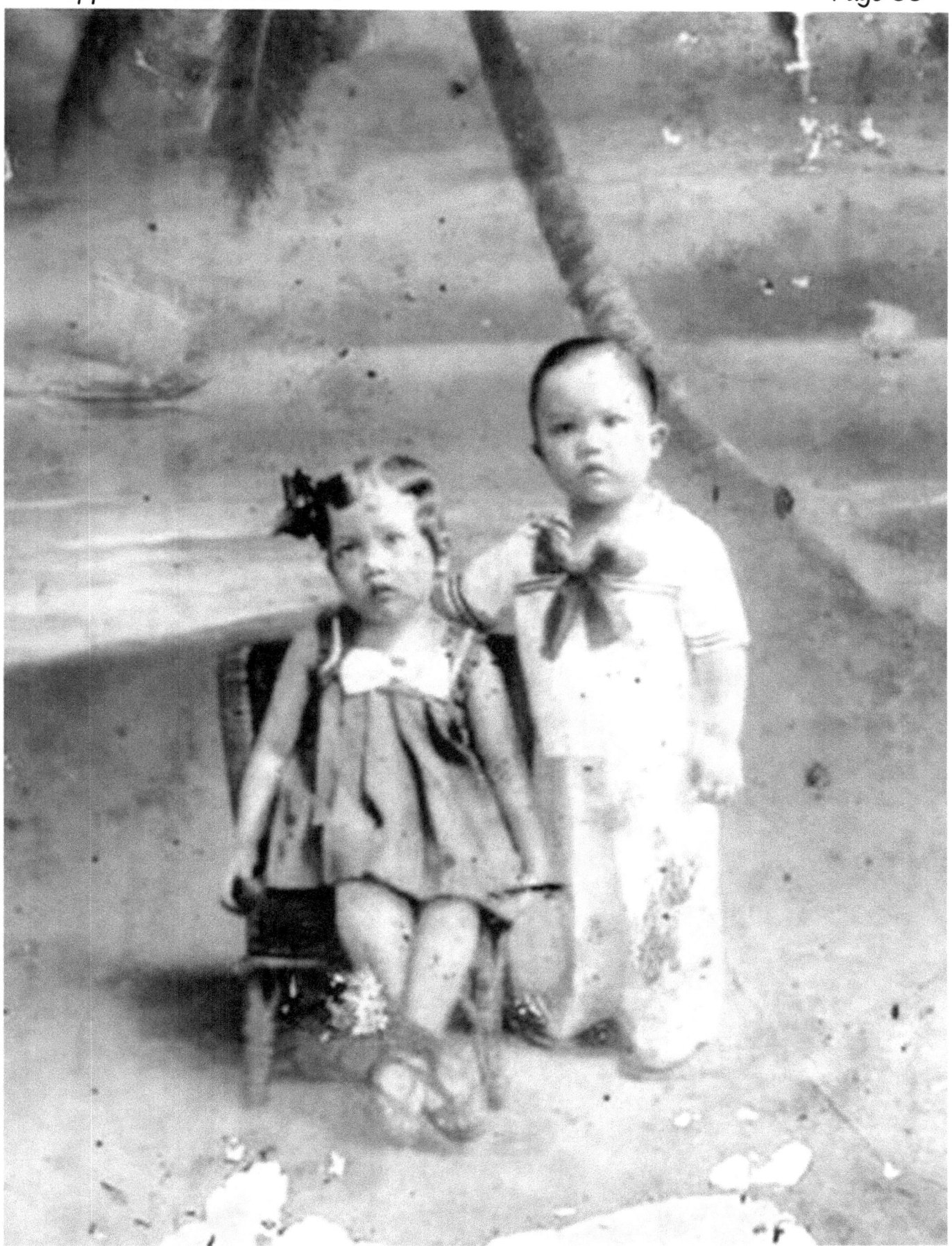

1930s Typical Filipino tots

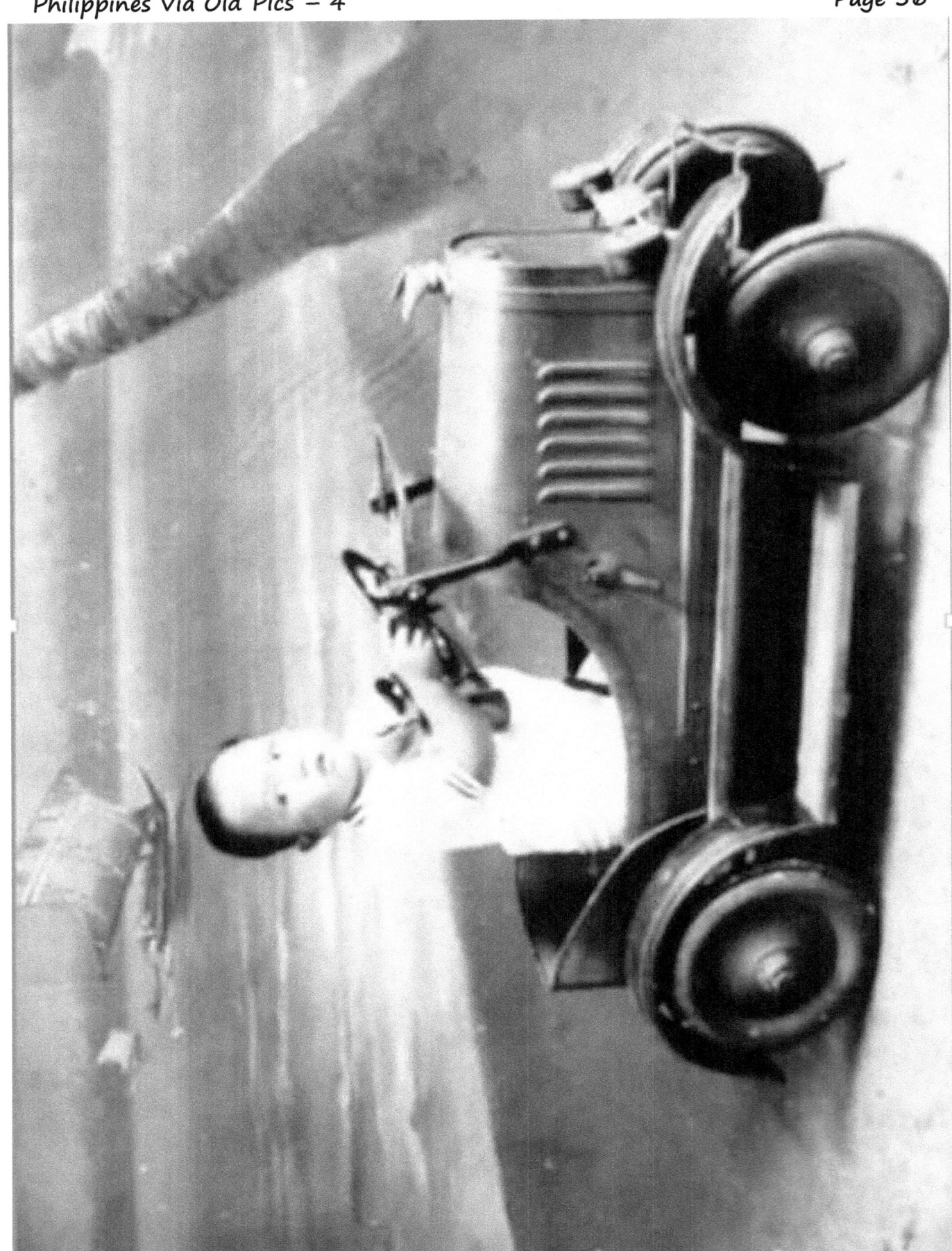

1930s Typical Filipino tot

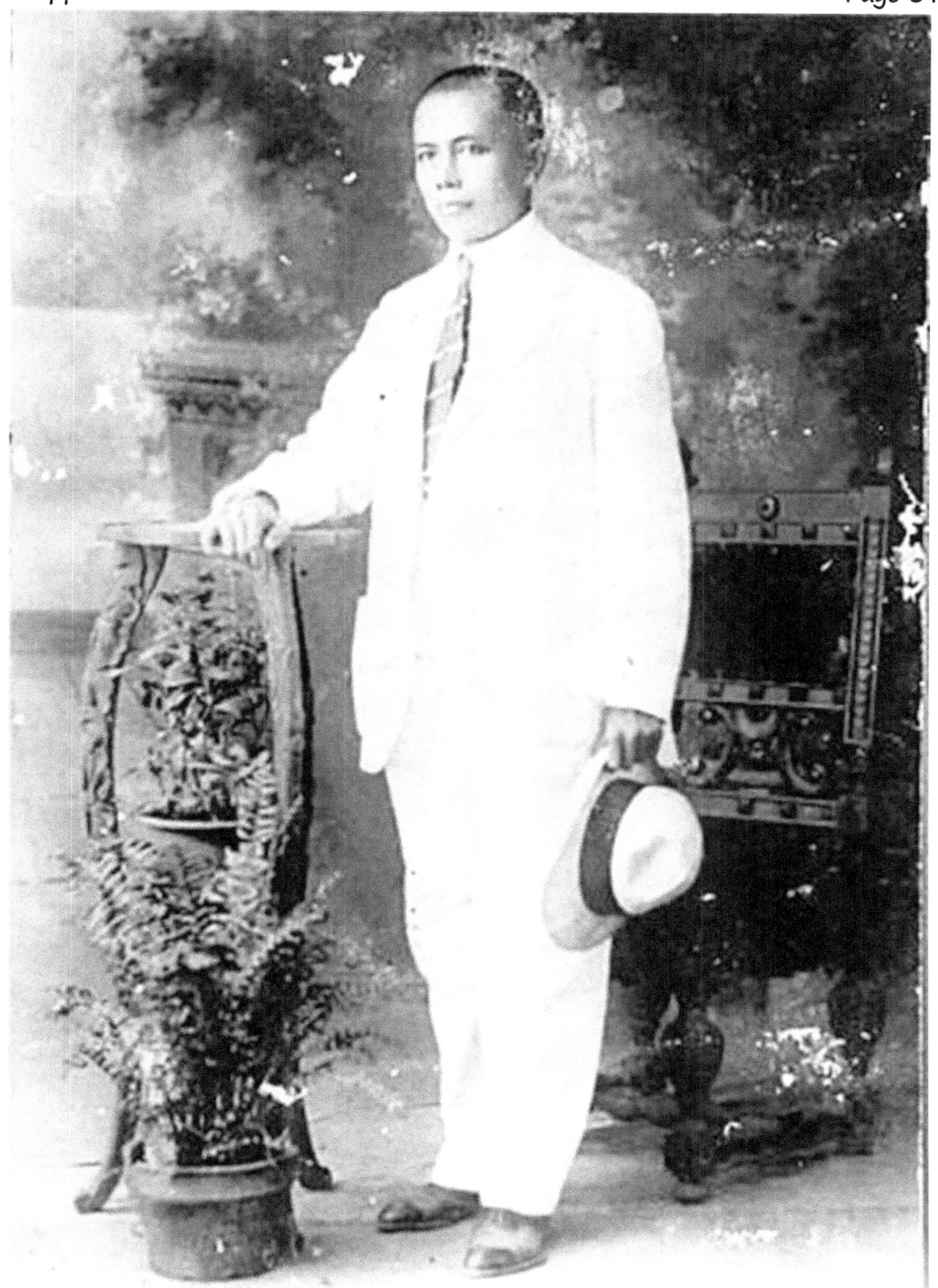

1905 Ambrosio Elizes, my grandfather, 1875-1936 – formal attire (Editor Note)

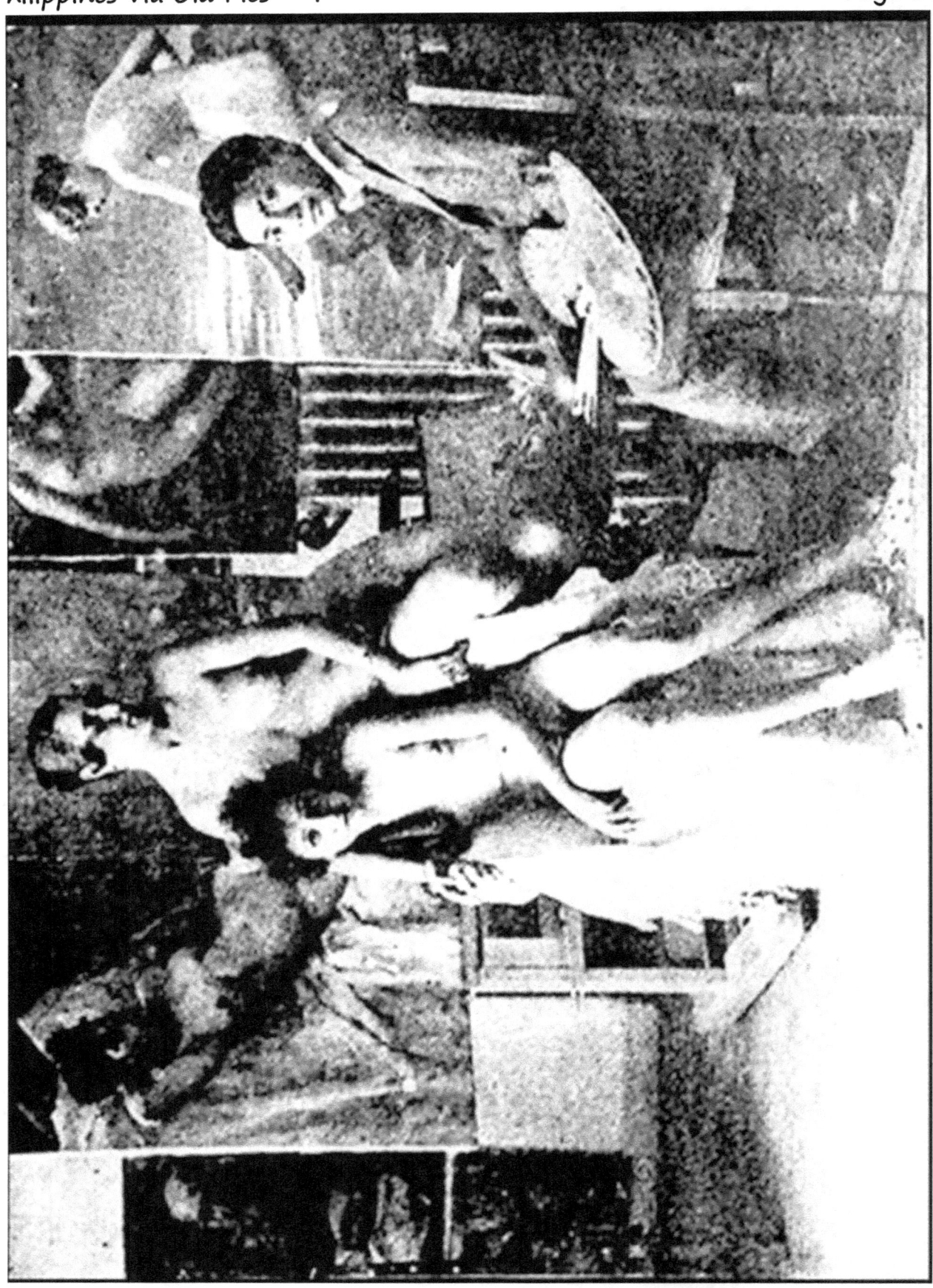

**Amorsolo era – From artistic point of view, without malice –
Fernando Amorsolo at his art studio – (source, internet)**

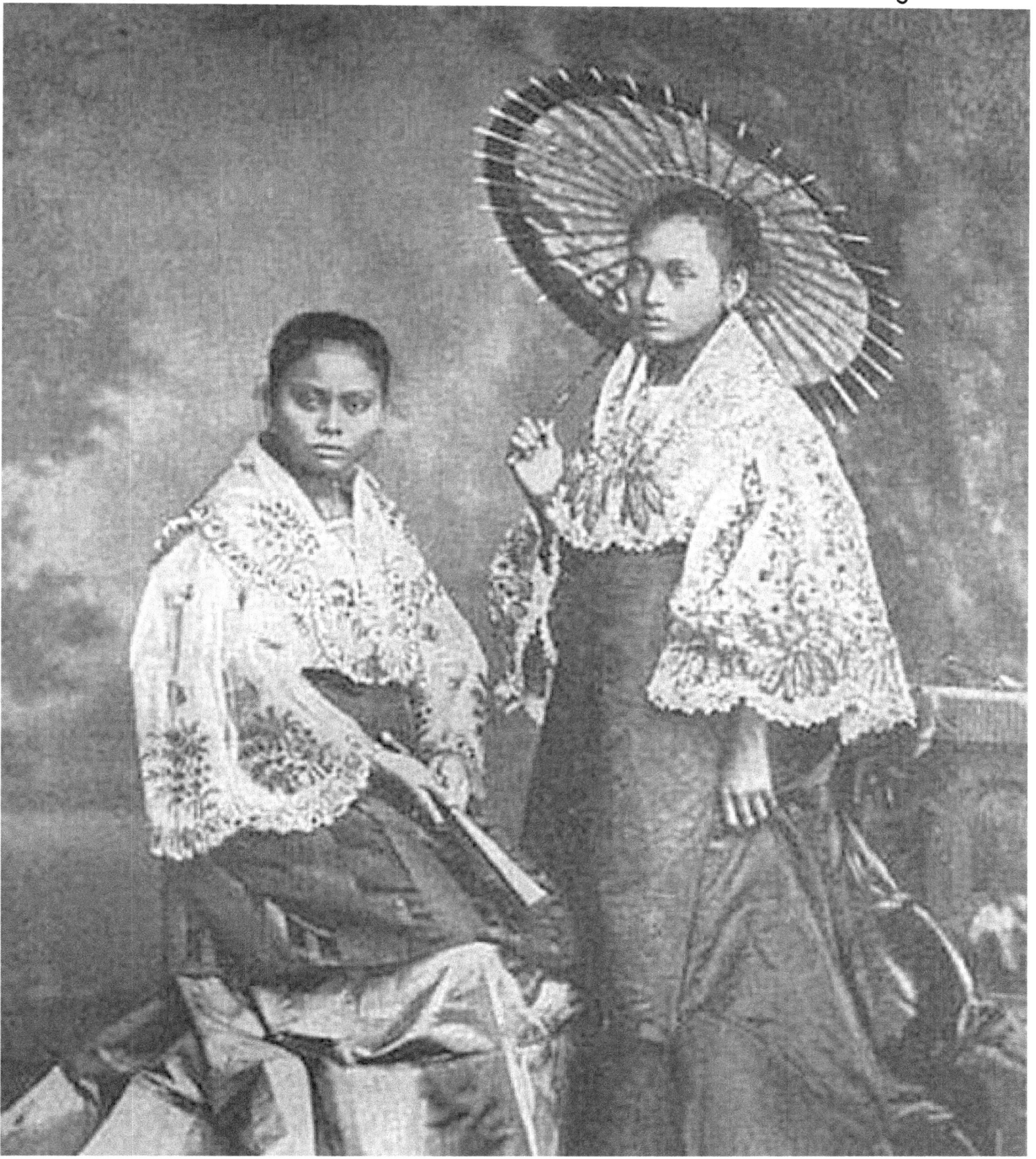

1880s Manila Ladies wearing traditional Maria Claras (internet source)

Chinese Mestizo clothes, 1880's:

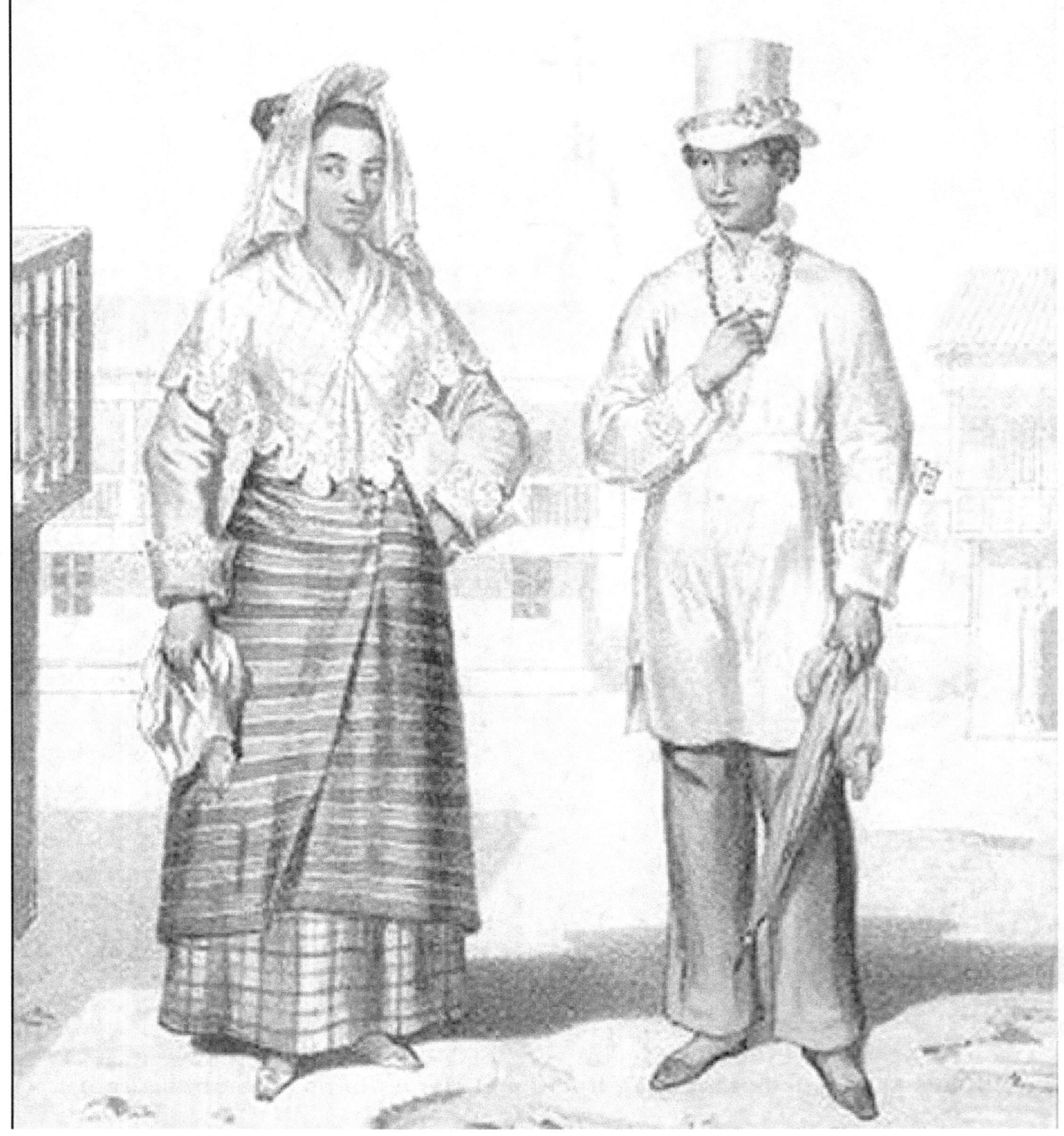

1880s Chinese Mestizo clothes in Manila (internet source)

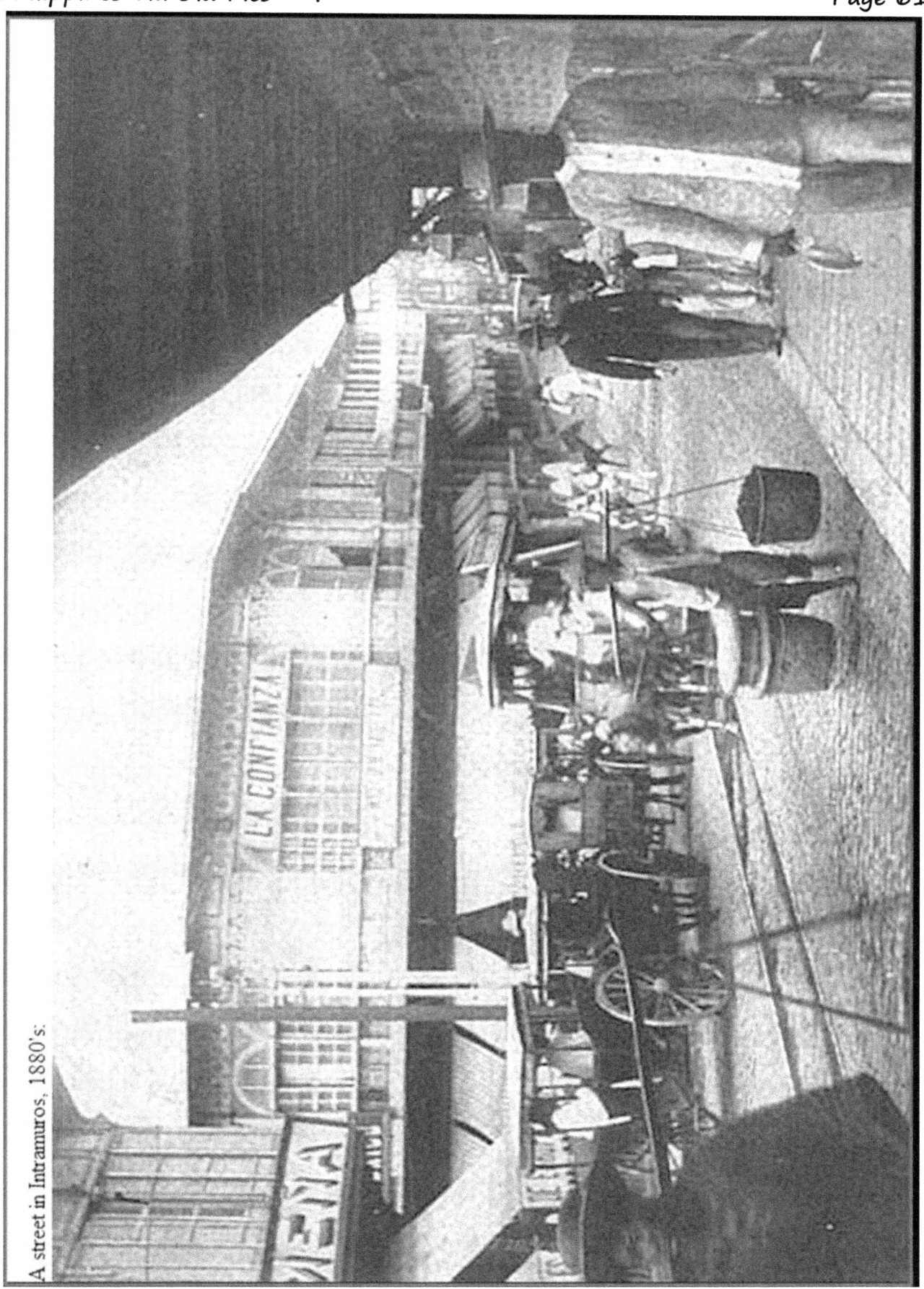

A street in Intramuros, 1880's:

1880s A Street in Manila or Intramuros (internet source)

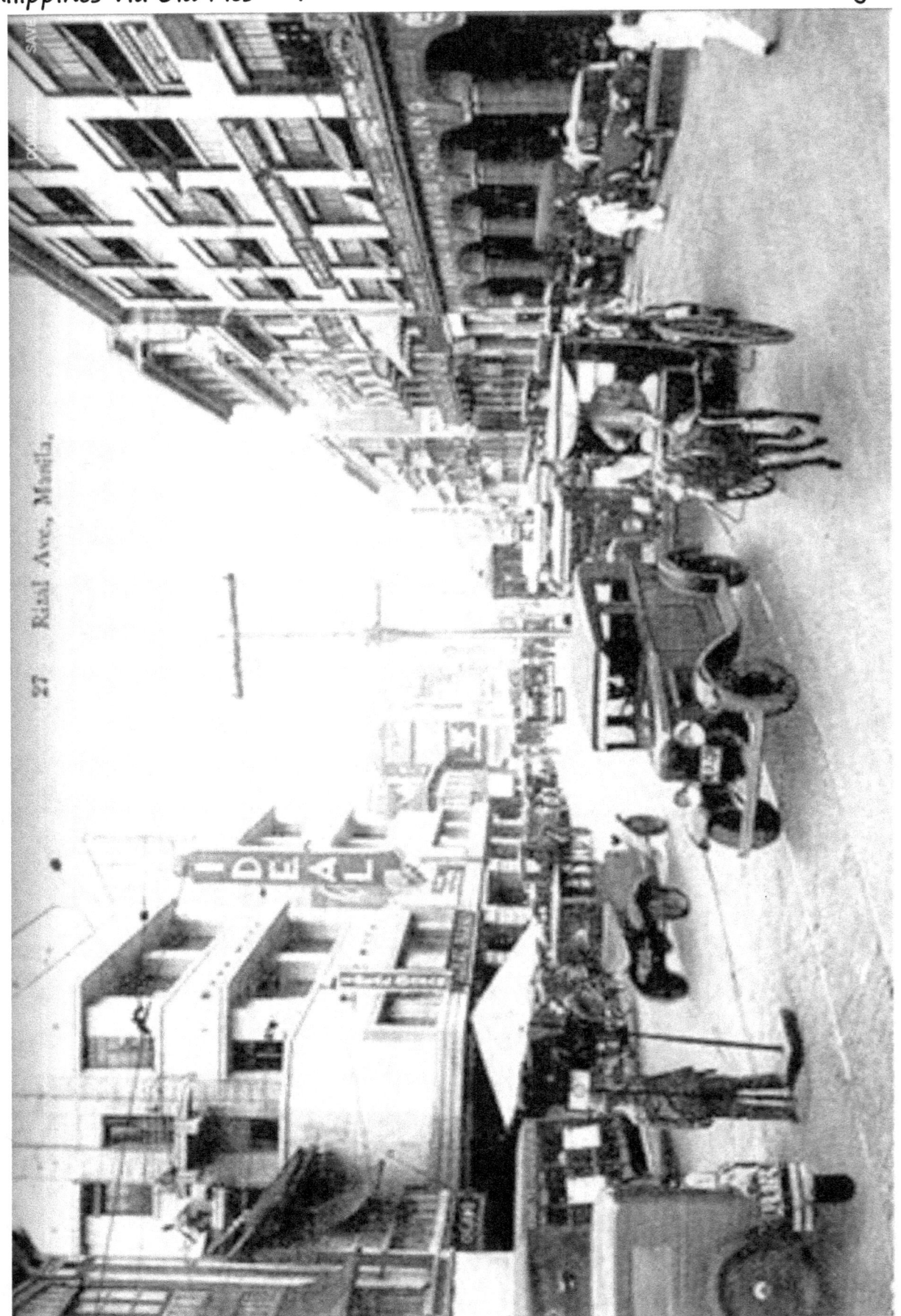

1900s Avenida Rizal – T-Fords and Carromatas (internet source)

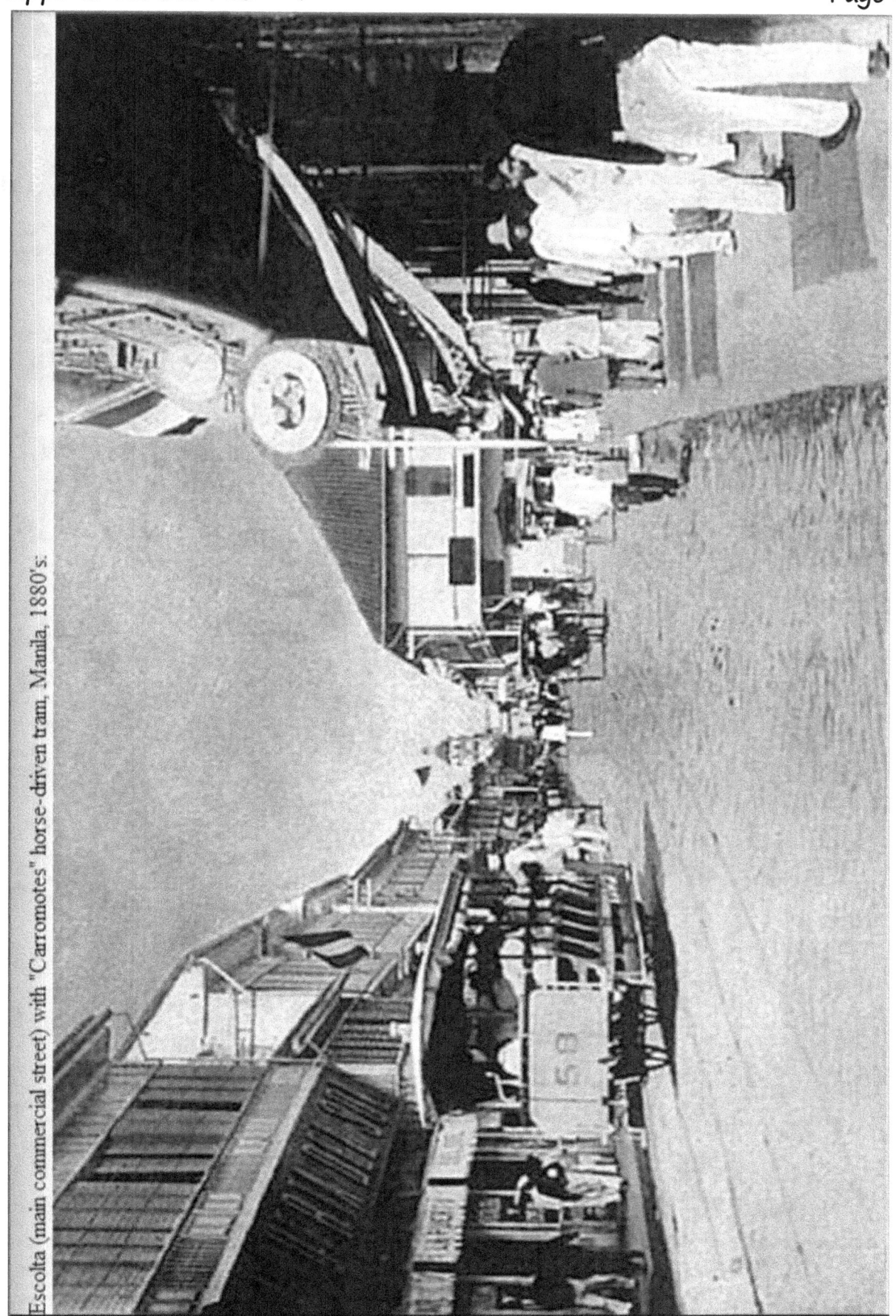

Escolta (main commercial street) with "Carromotes" horse-driven tram, Manila, 1880's.

1880s Escolta (internet source)

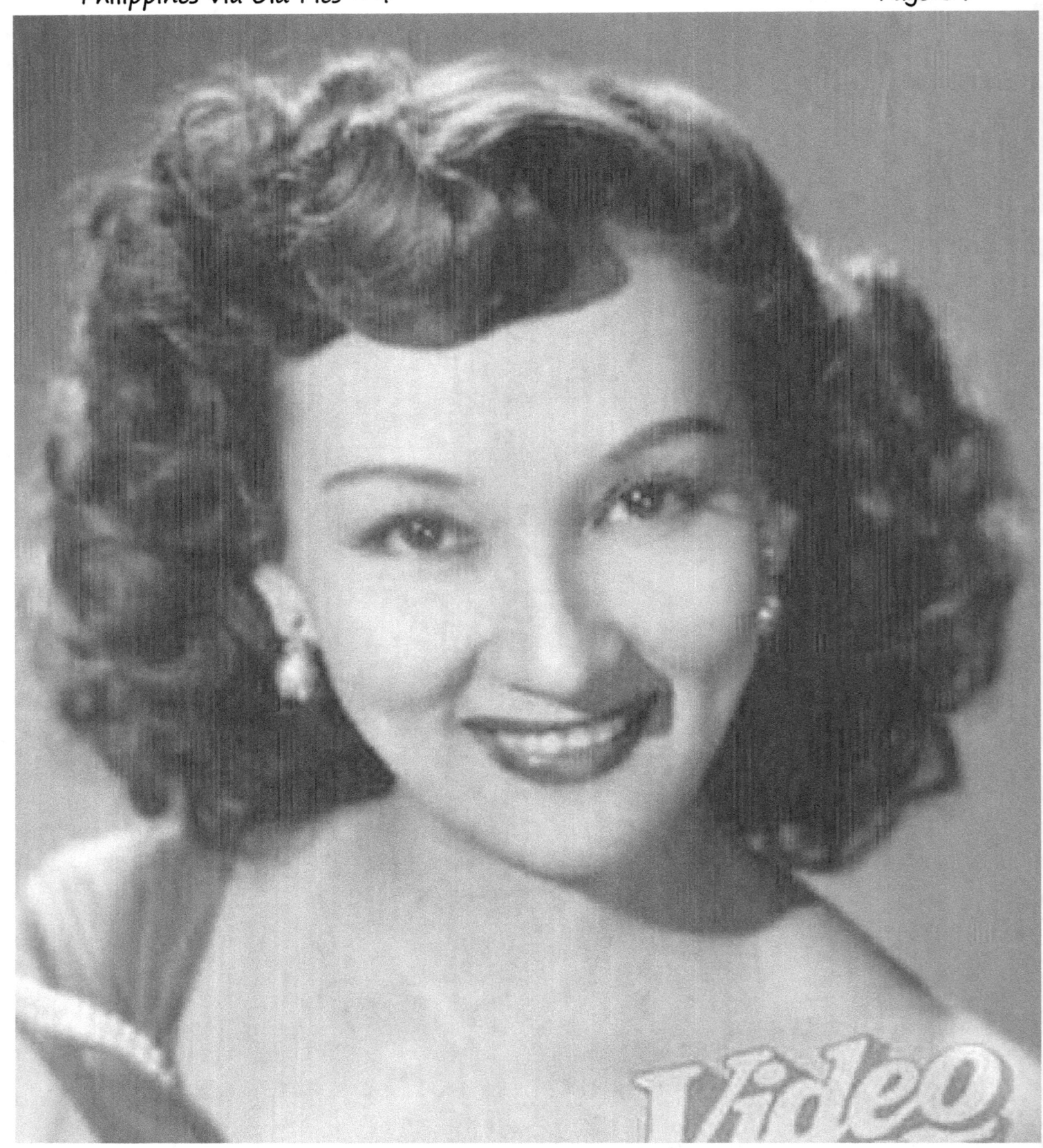

Carmen Rosales – Famous Movie Star of yesteryears (internet source)

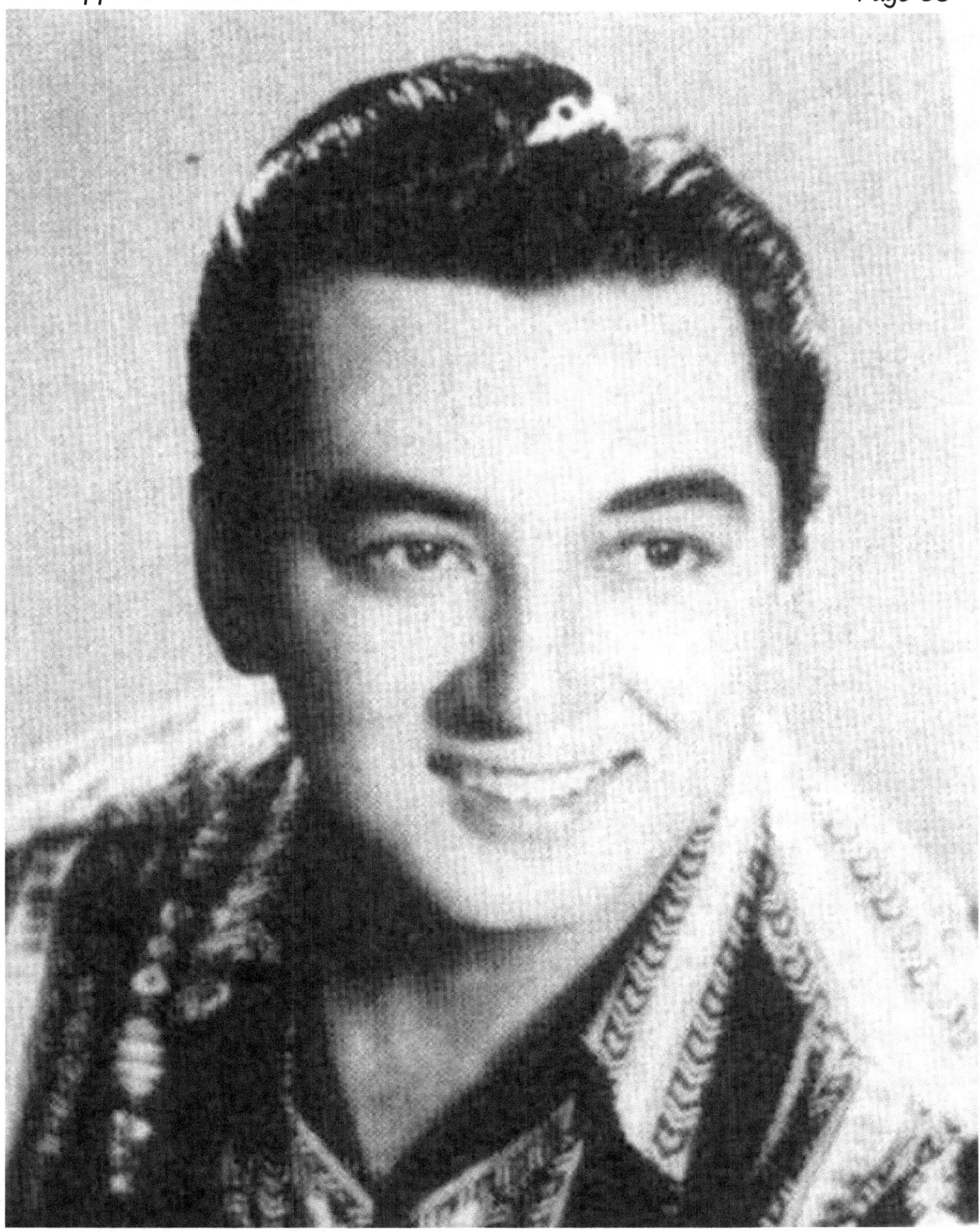

Rogelio dela Rosa – Famous Movie Star of yesteryears – became Senator & Ambassador – (Internet source)

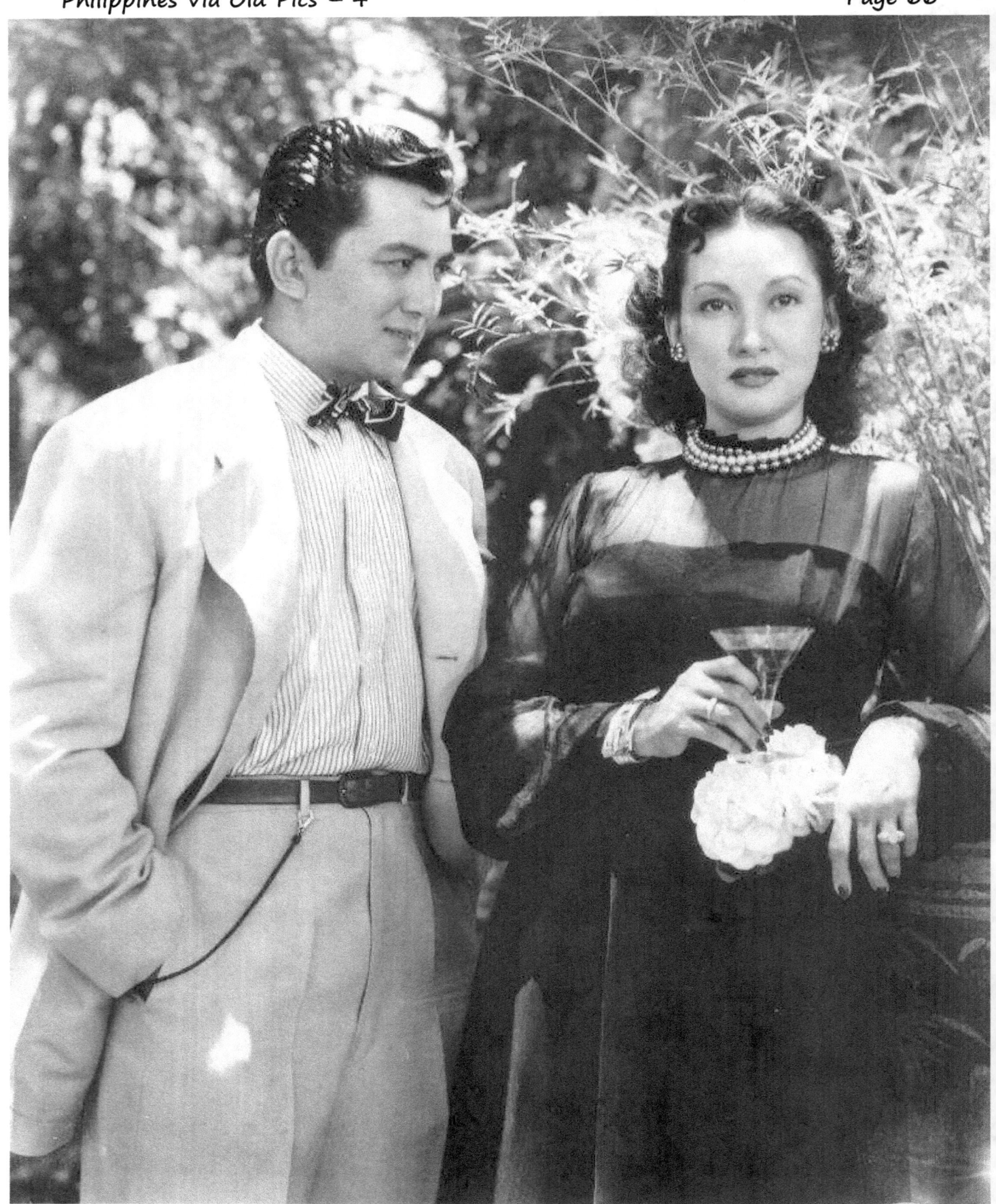

Rogelio dela Rosa & Carmen Rosales – Movie star-team of yesteryears

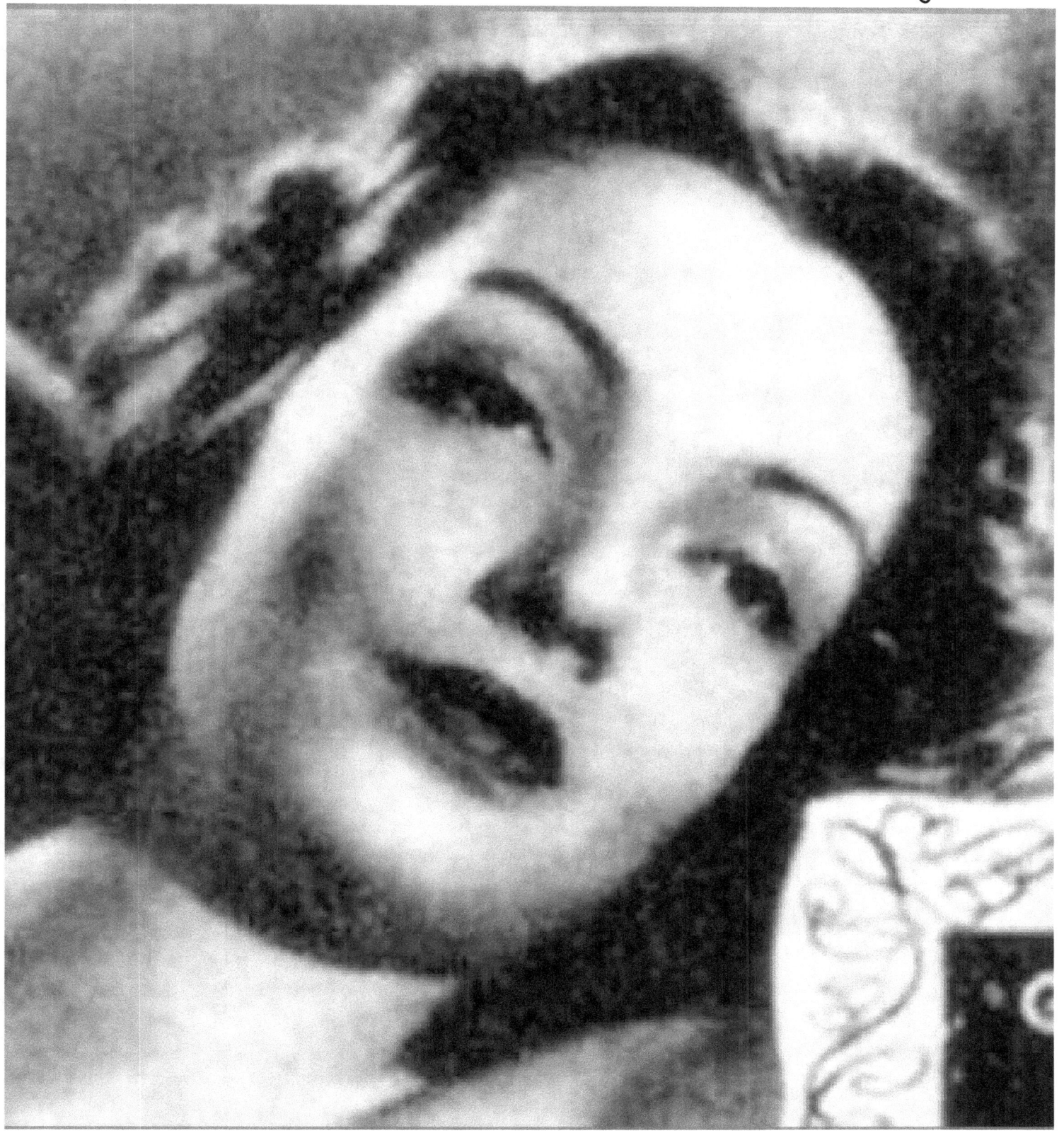

Paraluman – Famous Movie Star of yesteryears – (internet source)

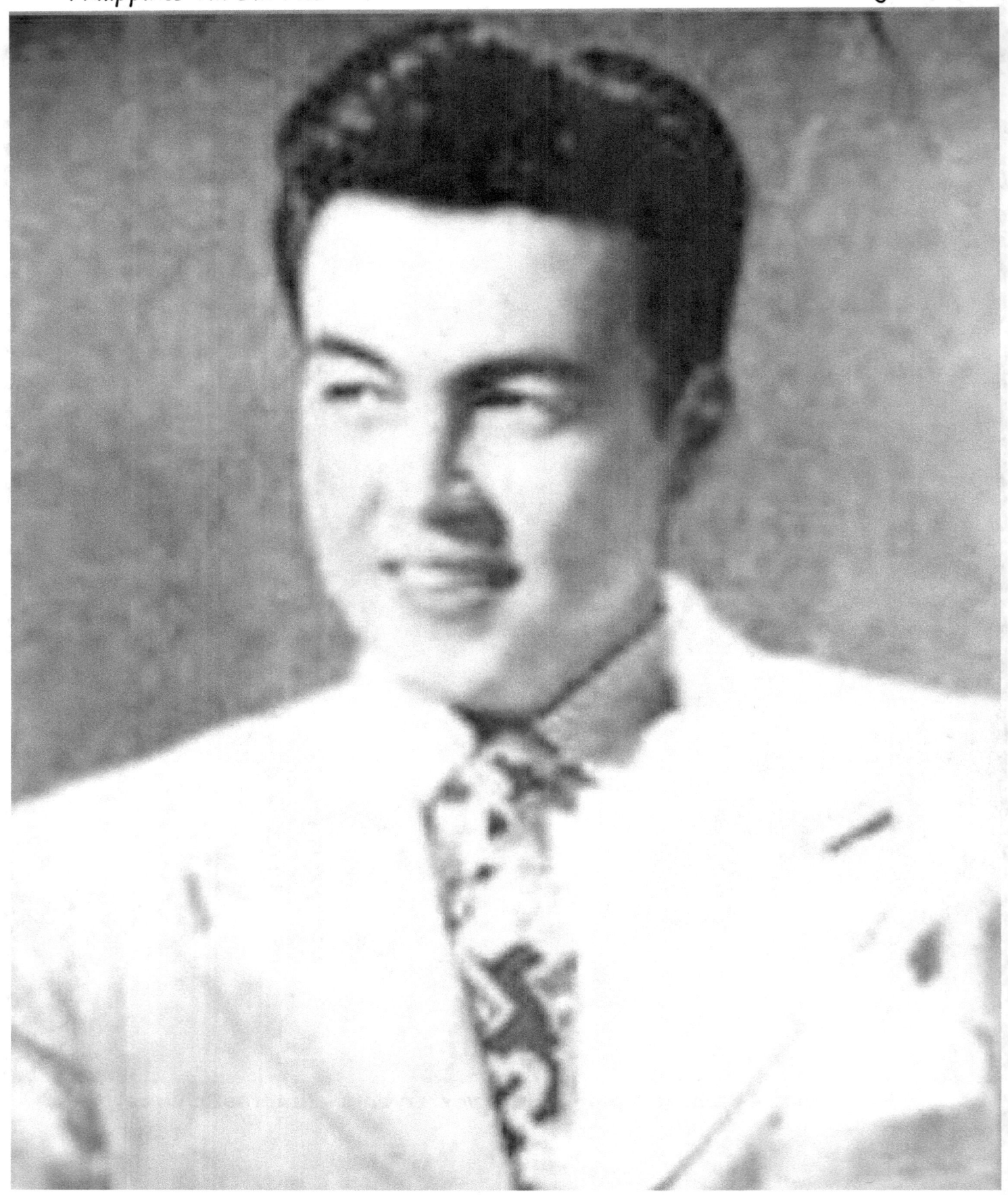

Oscar Moreno – Famous Movie Star of yesteryears – (internet source)

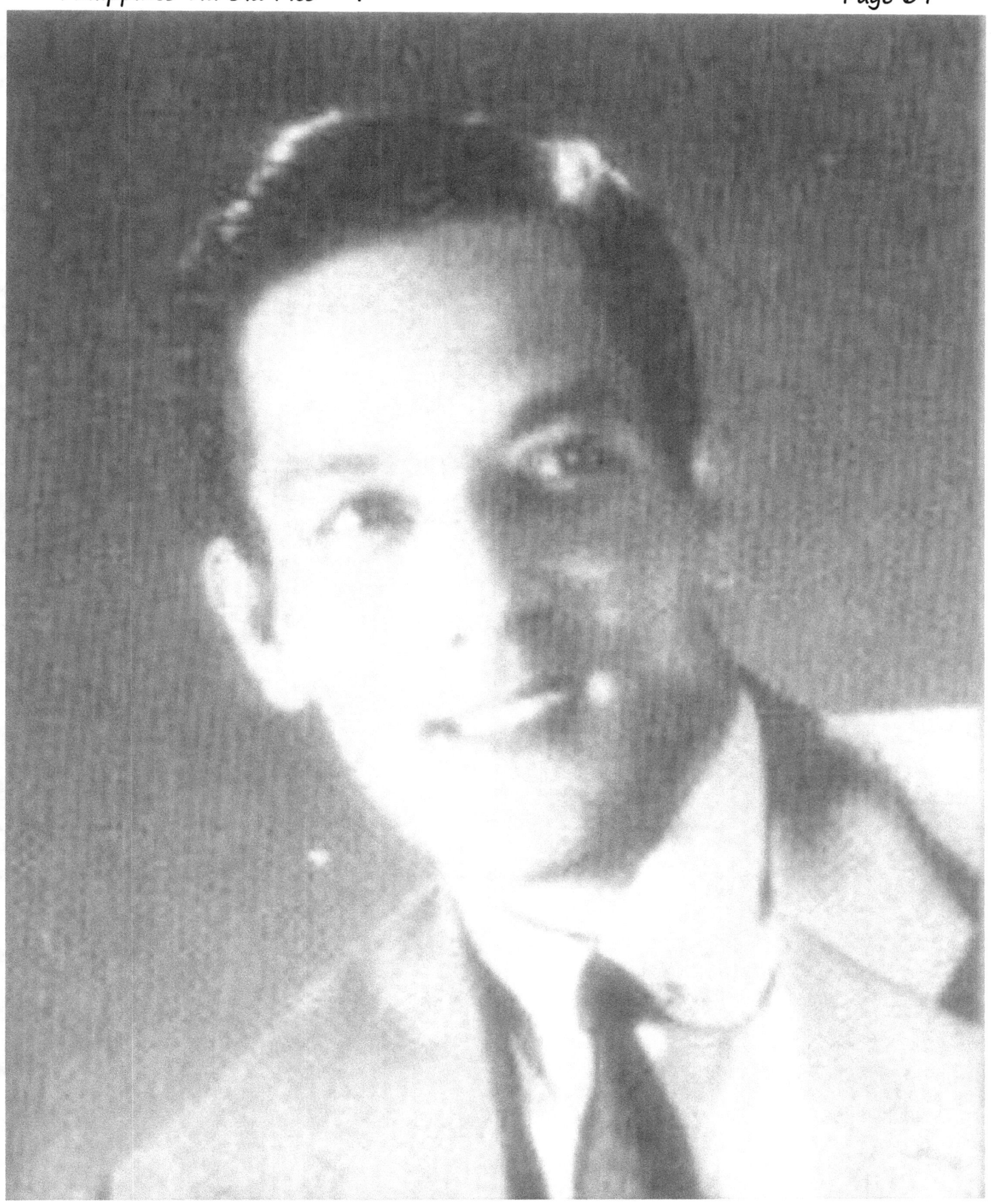

Leopoldo Salcedo – Famous Movie Star of yesteryears – (internet source)

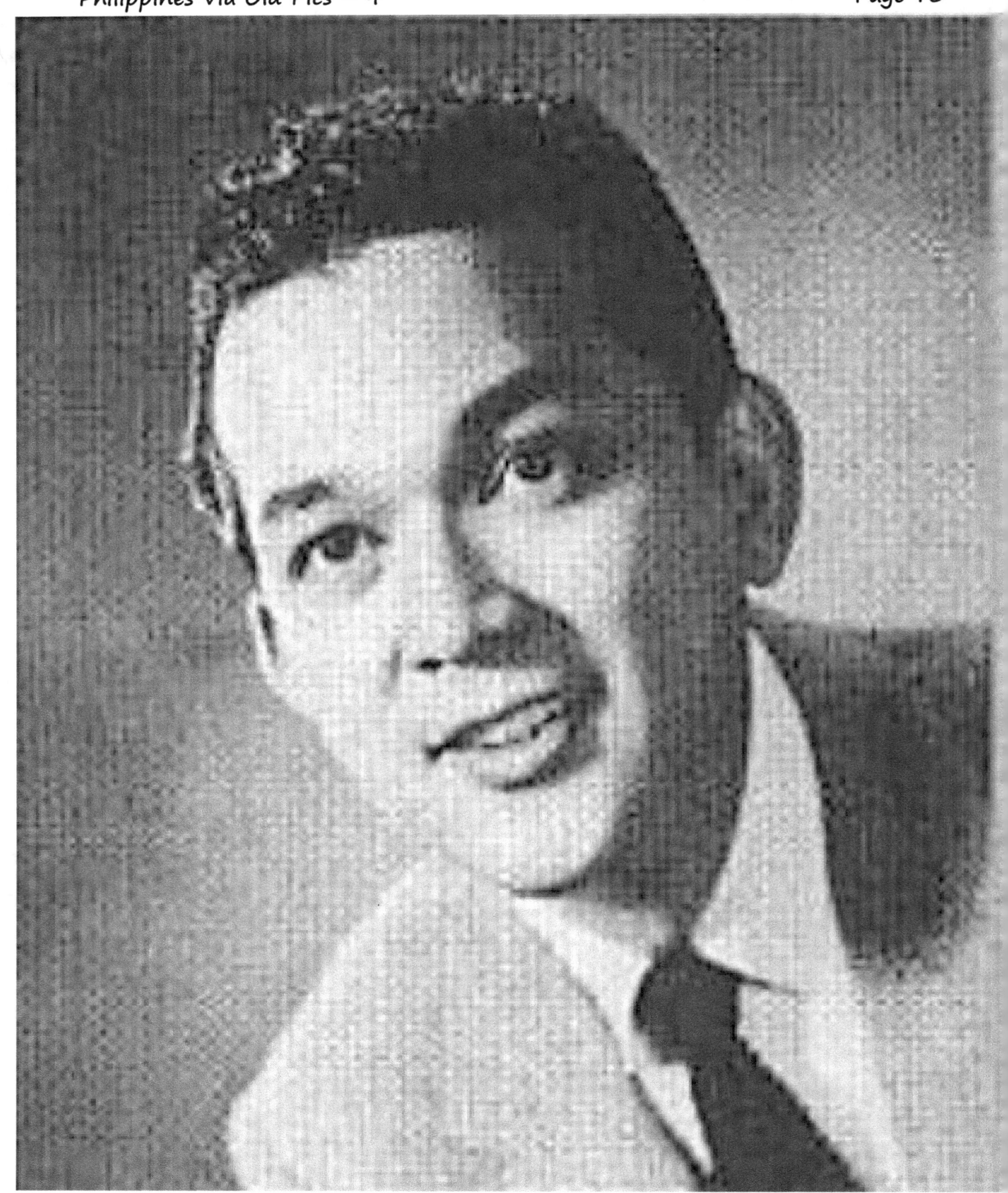

Pancho Magalona – Famous Movie Star of yesteryears – (internet source)

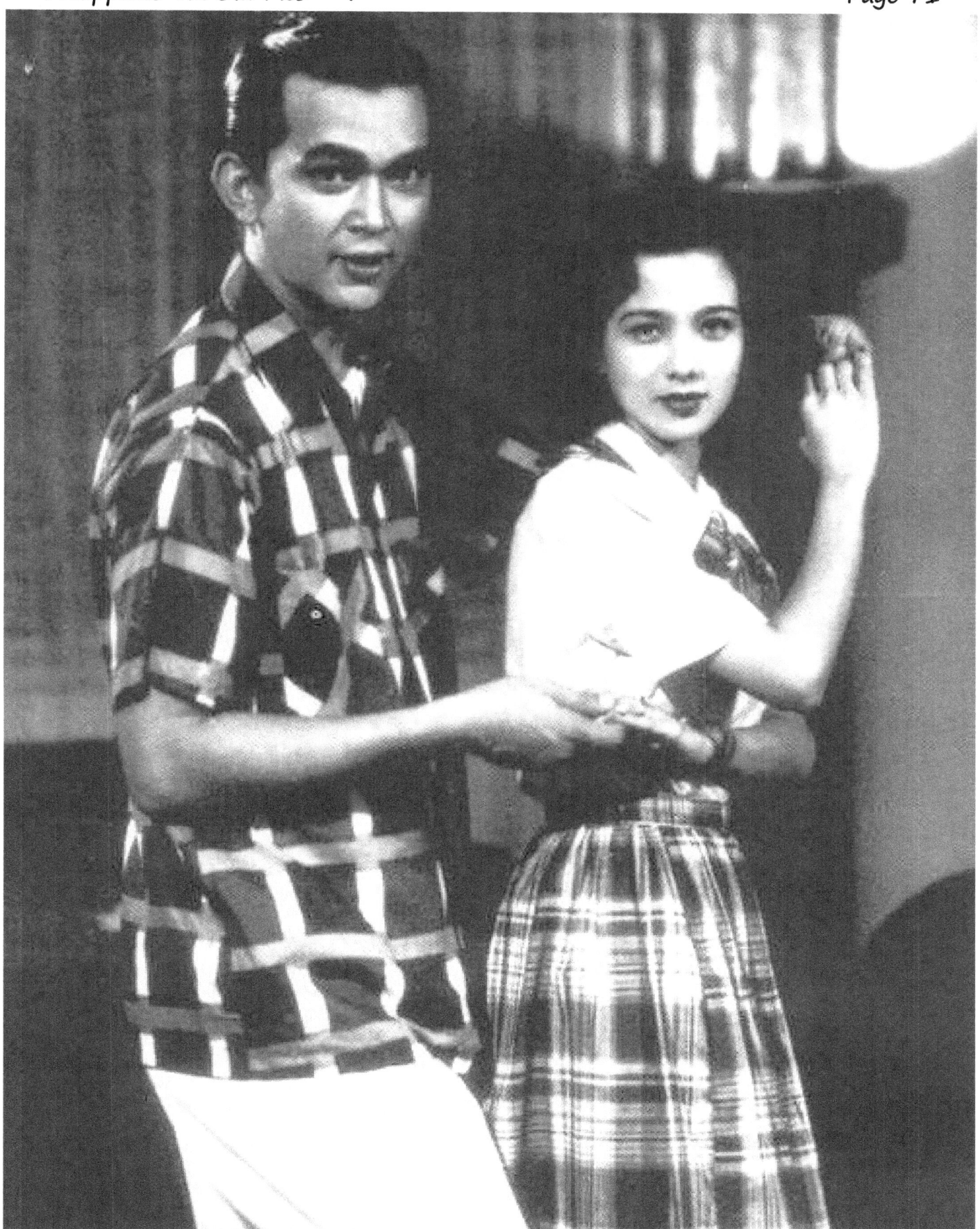

Movie star team of Pancho Magalona & Tita Duran – (internet source)

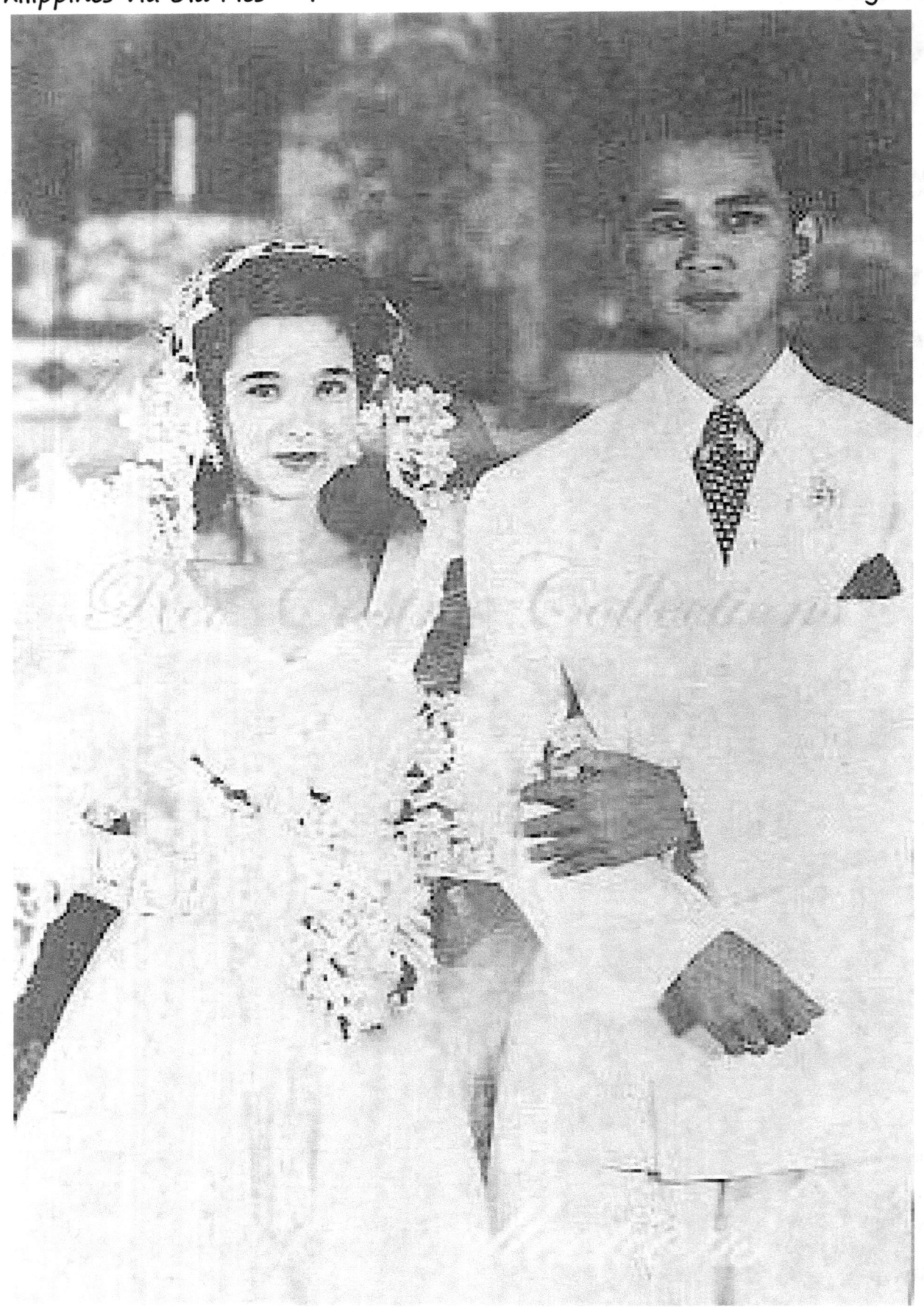

Real Life Wedding of Pancho & Tita – Famous Movie Love Team

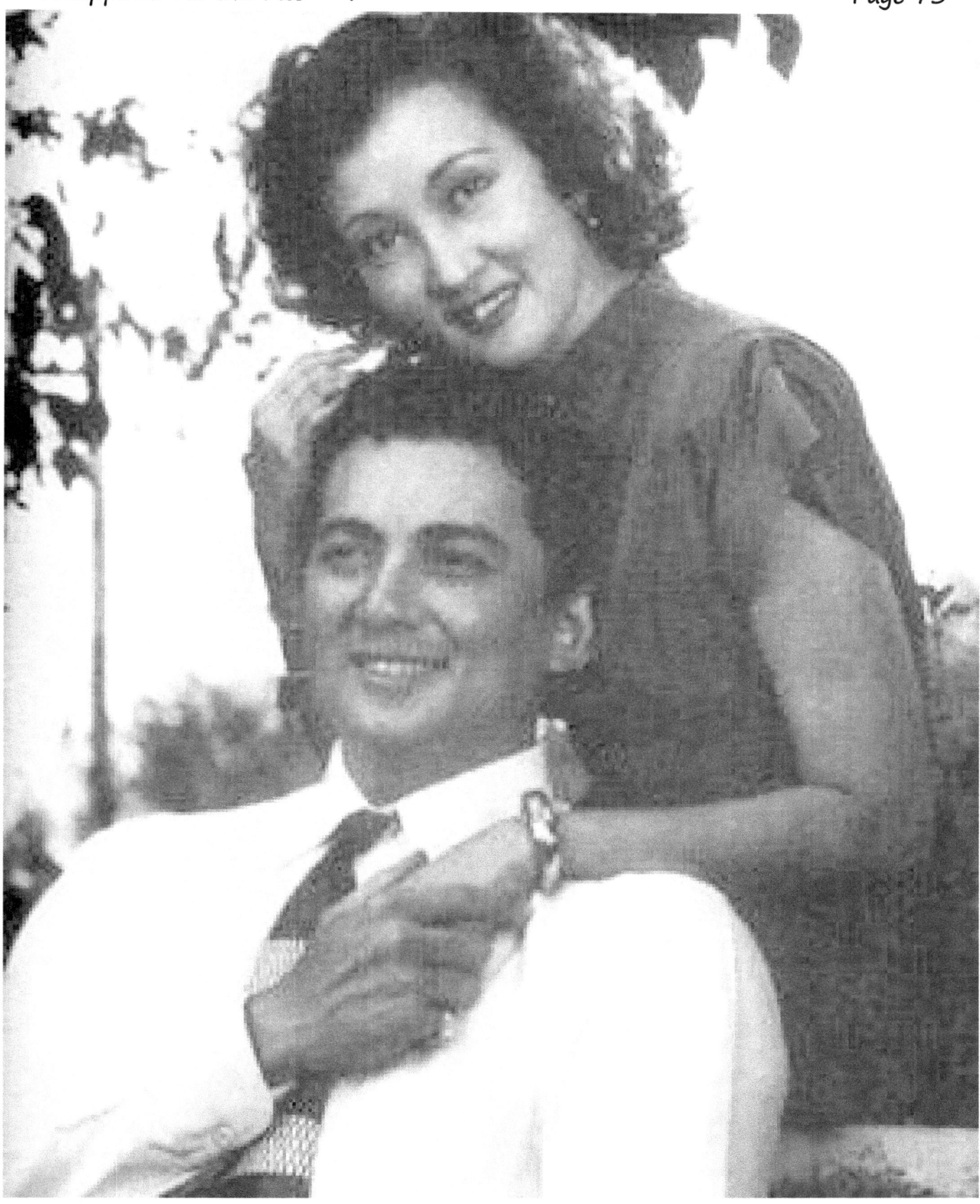

**Famous Movie Love Team of Rogelio dela Rosa & Carmen Rosales of
Yesteryears – (internet source)**

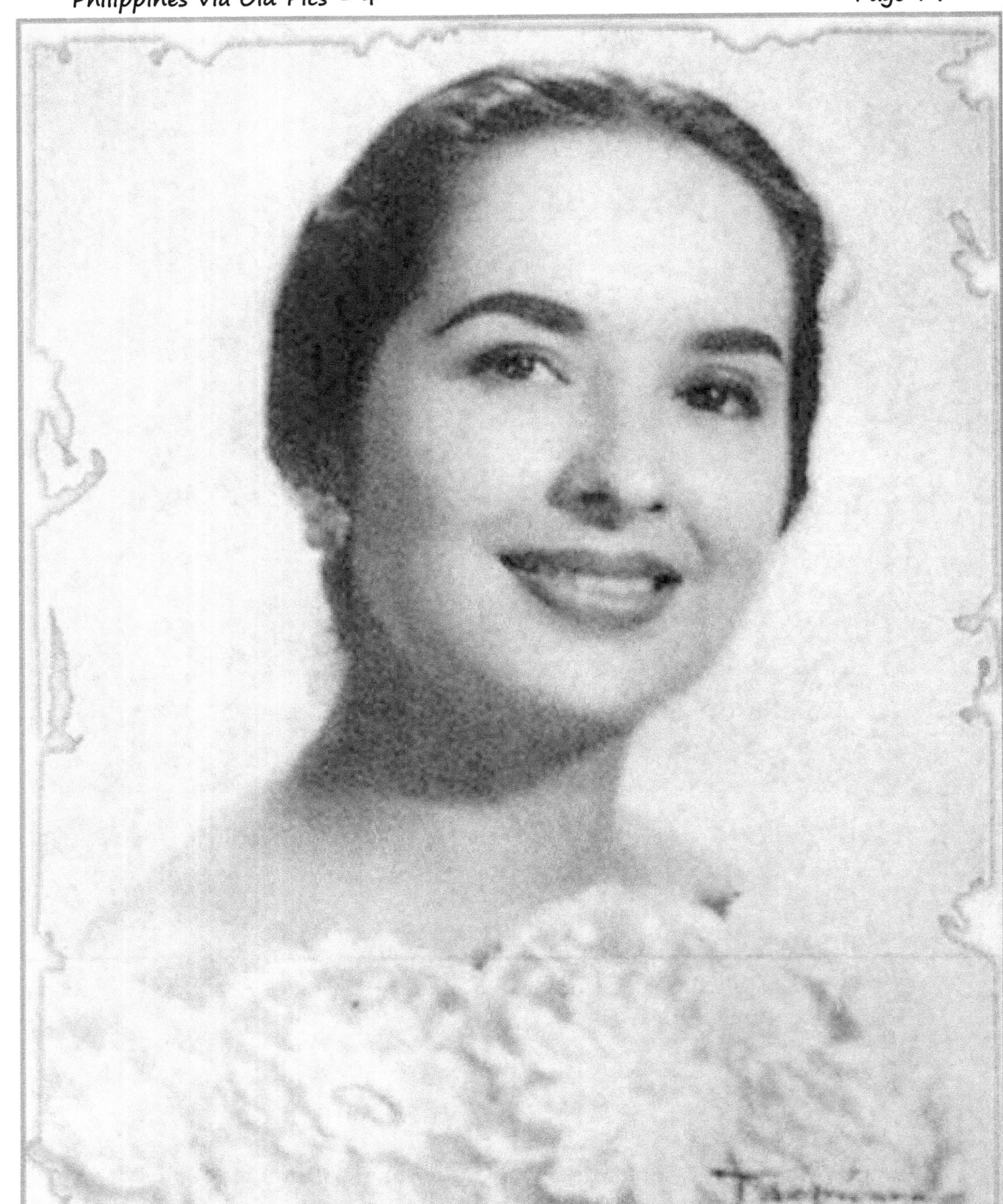

Gloria Romero – Famous Movie Star of yesteryears – (internet source)

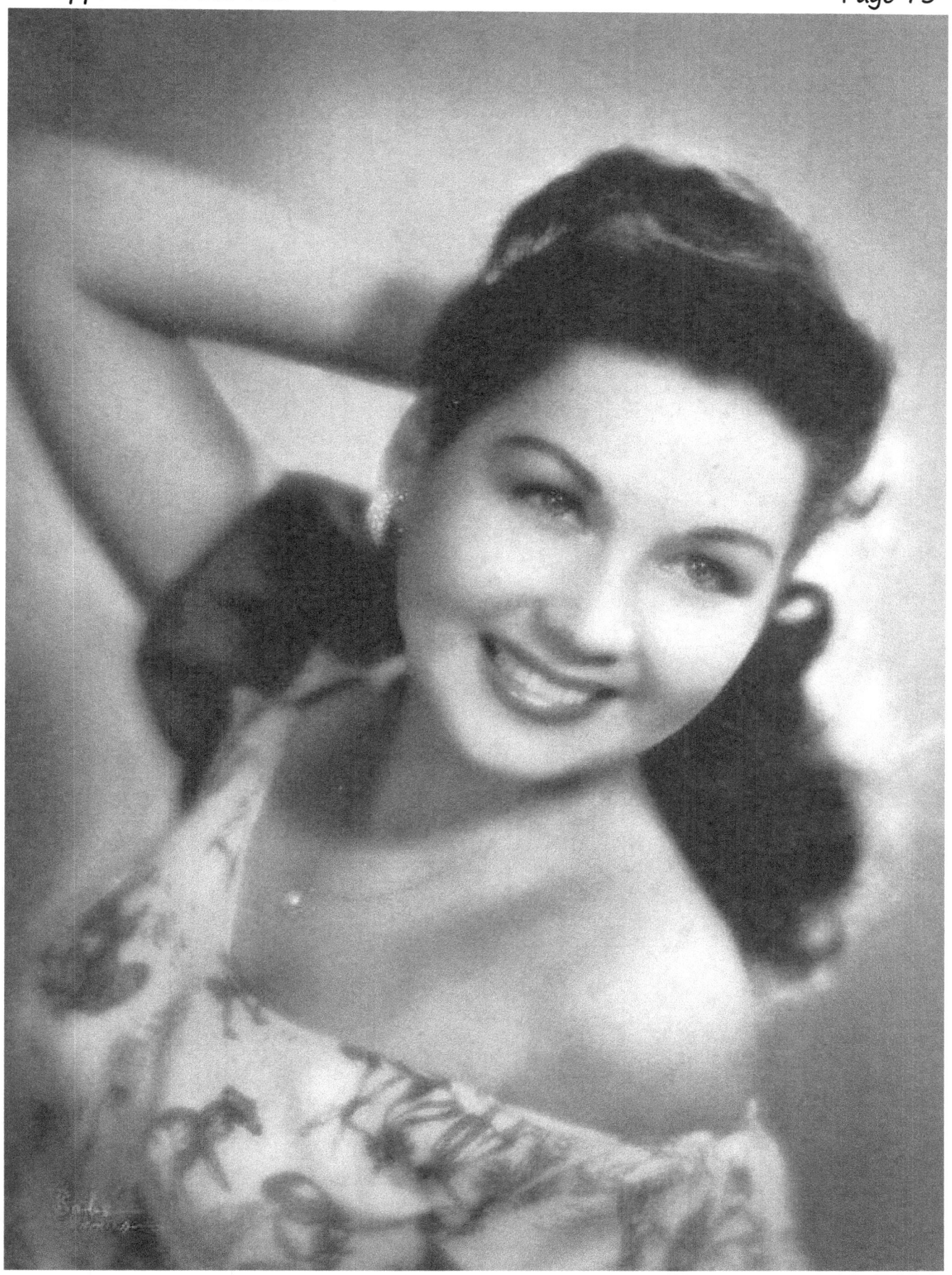

Rosa del Rosario – Famous Movie Star of yesteryears – (internet source)

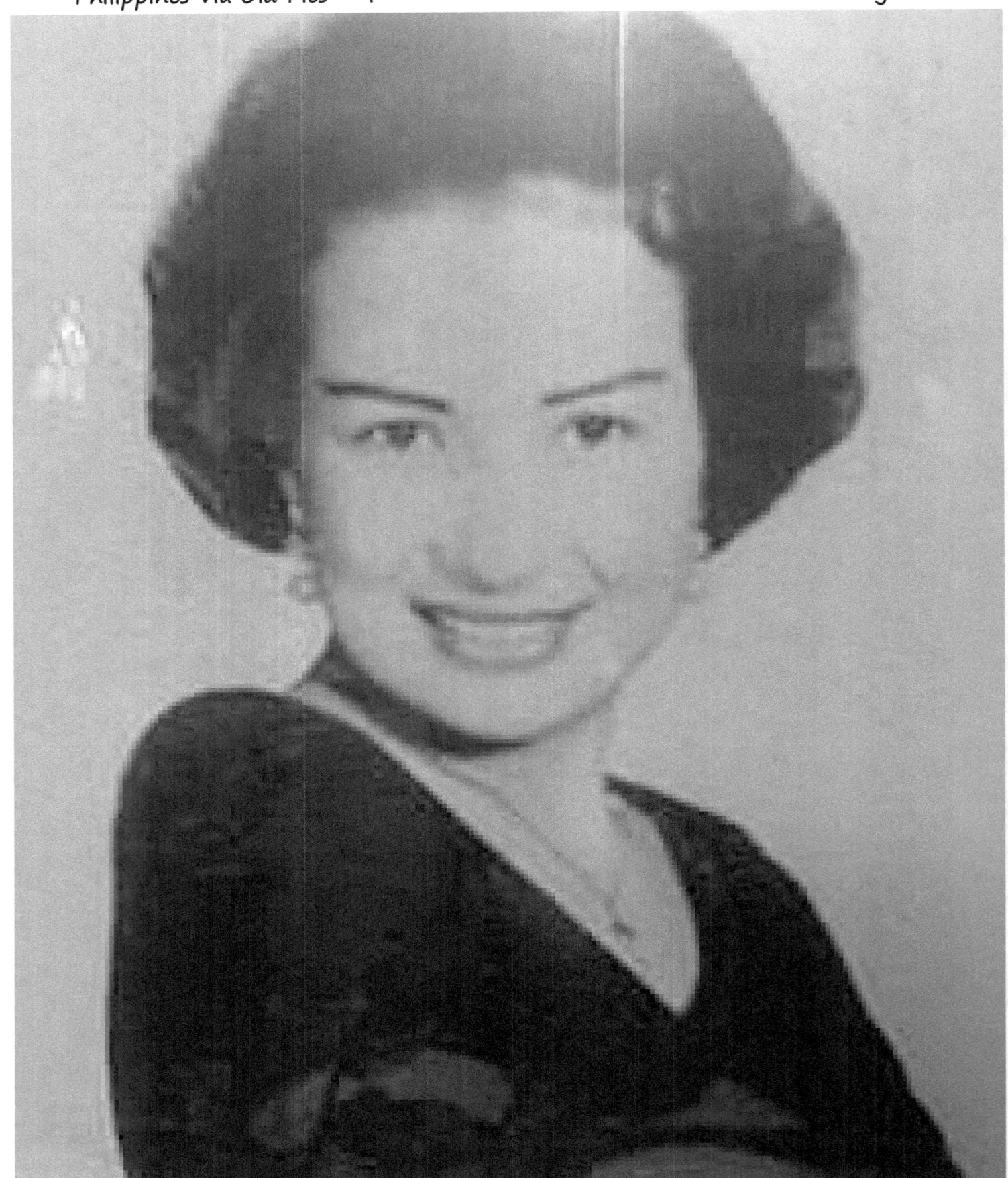

Mila del Sol – Famous Movie Star of yesteryears – (internet source)

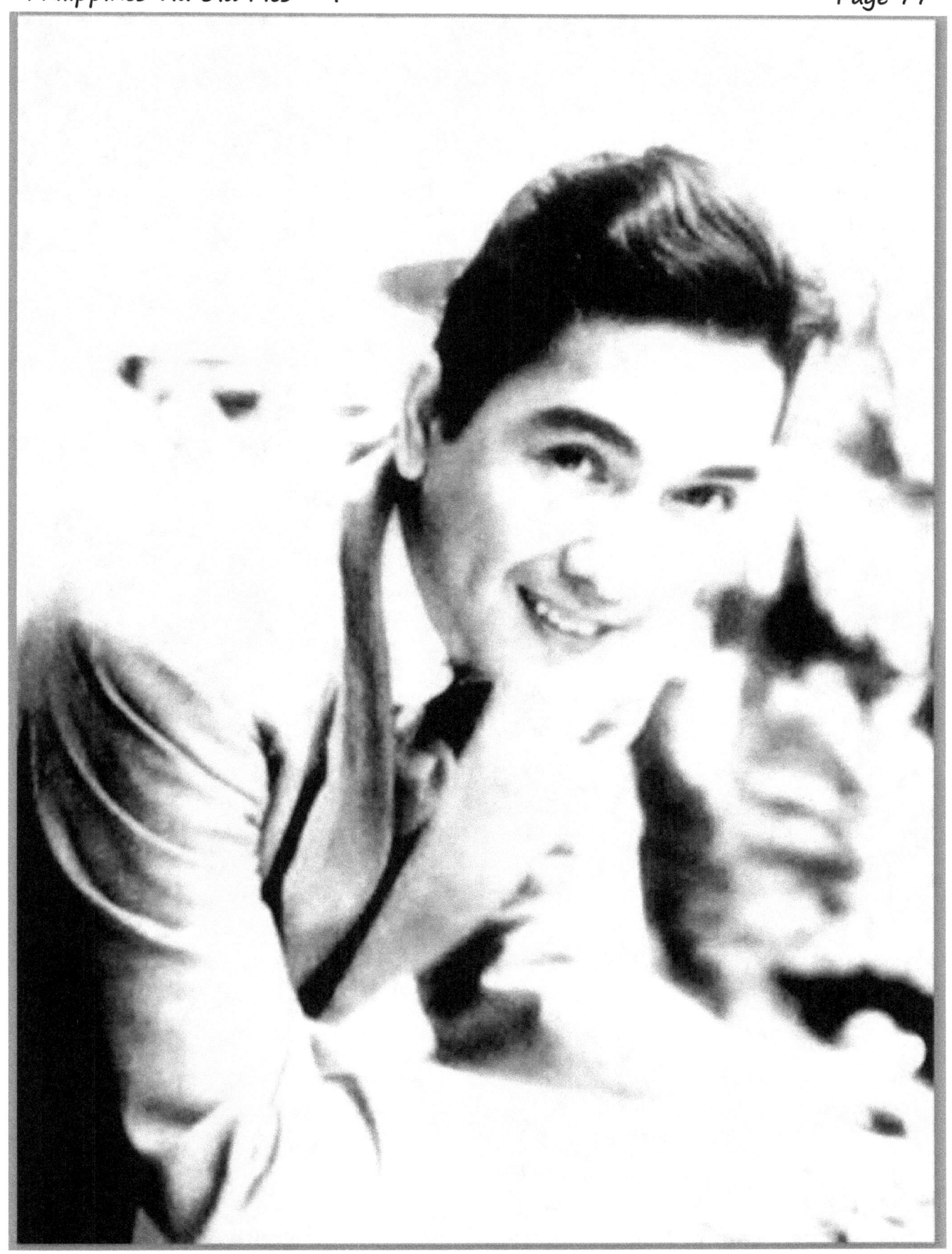

Angel Esmeralda – Famous Movie Star of yesteryears – (internet source)

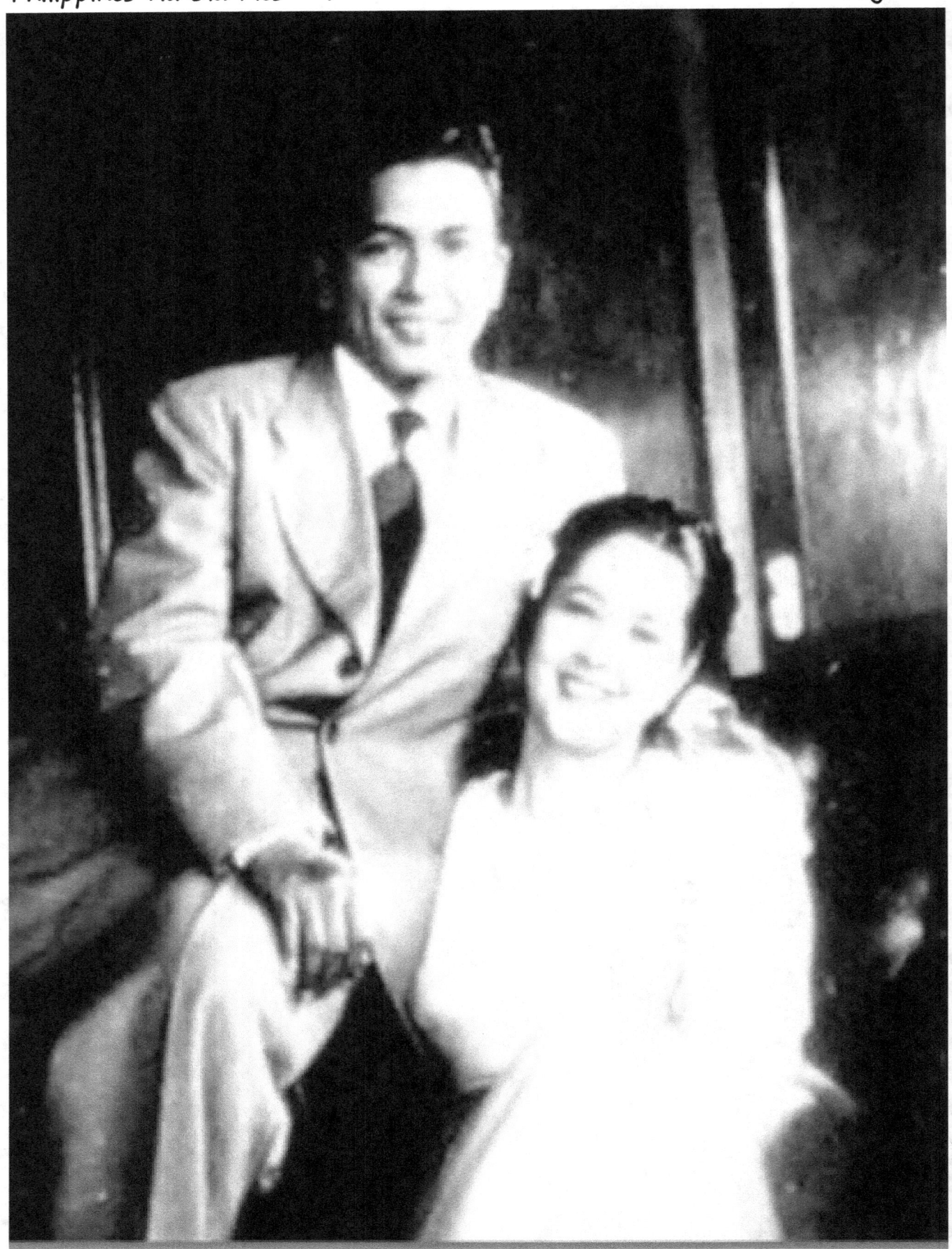

**Movie Love Team of Angel Esmeralda and Corazon Noble of yesteryears –
Married in real life, parents of Jay Ilagan. – (internet source)**

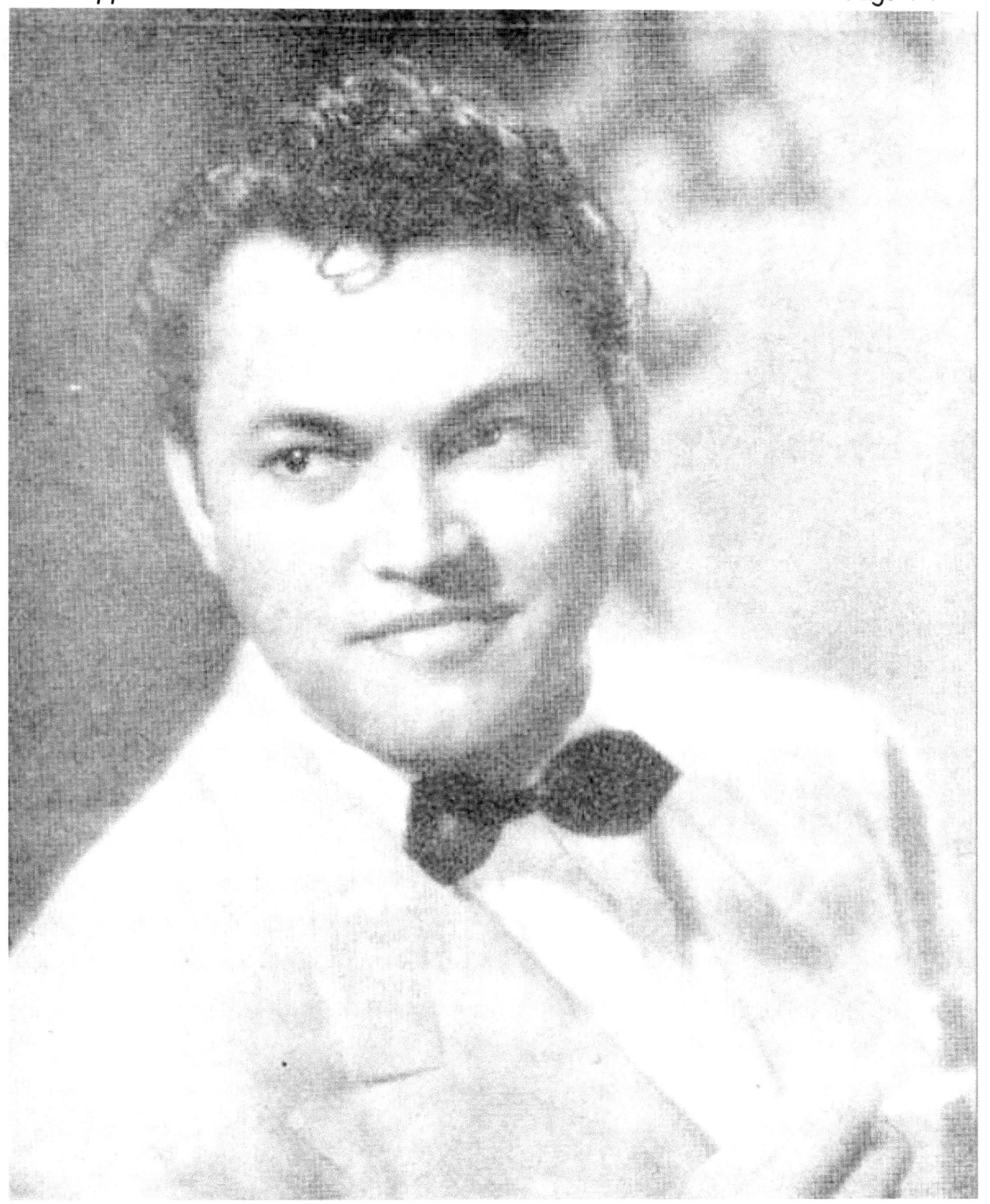

**Fernando Poe Sr. (father of Fernando Poe Jr.) - Movie Idol of yesteryears –
(internet source)**

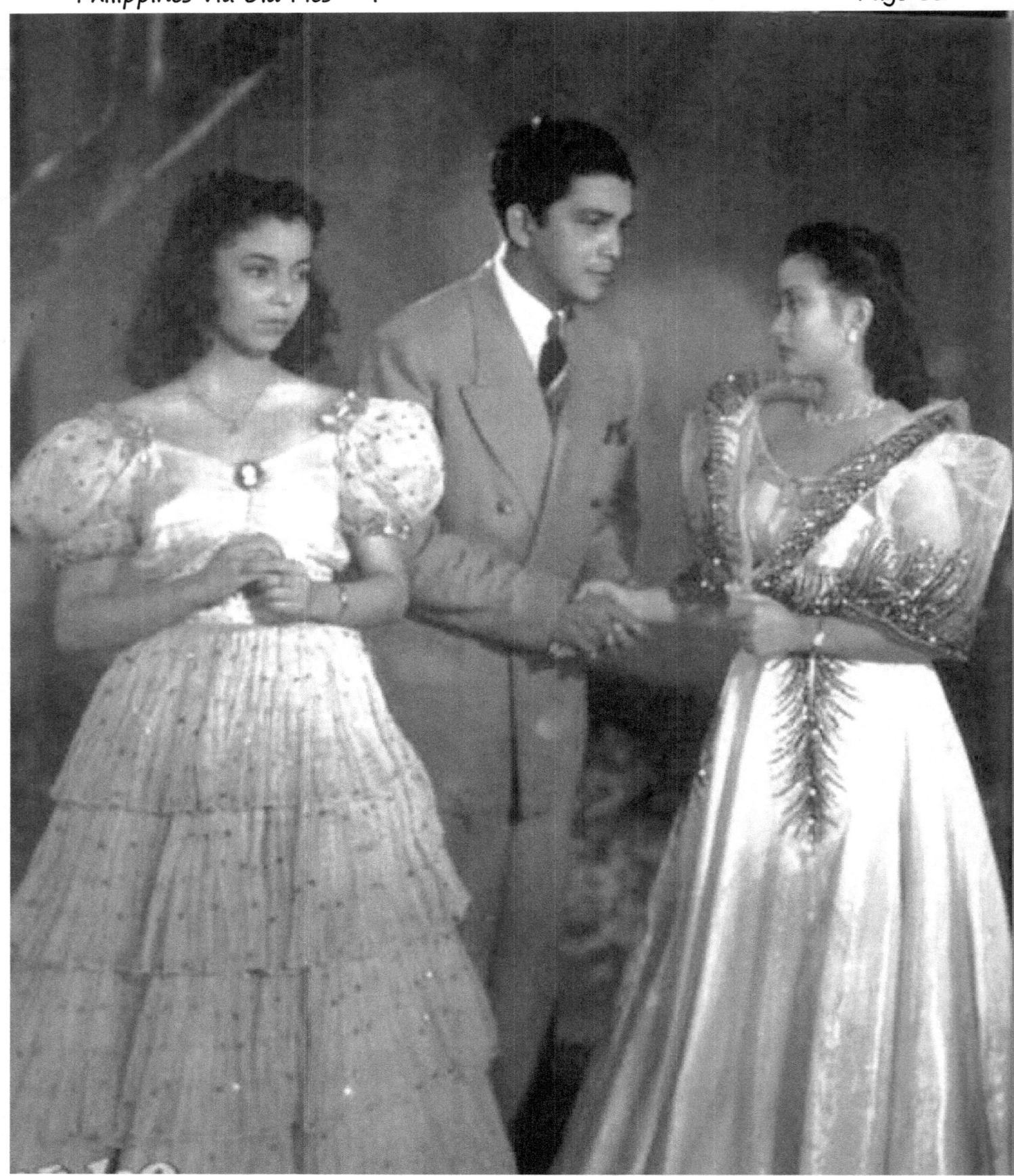

Fleur de Liz + Ely Ramos + Mila Del Sol in one movie of yesteryears –
(internet source)

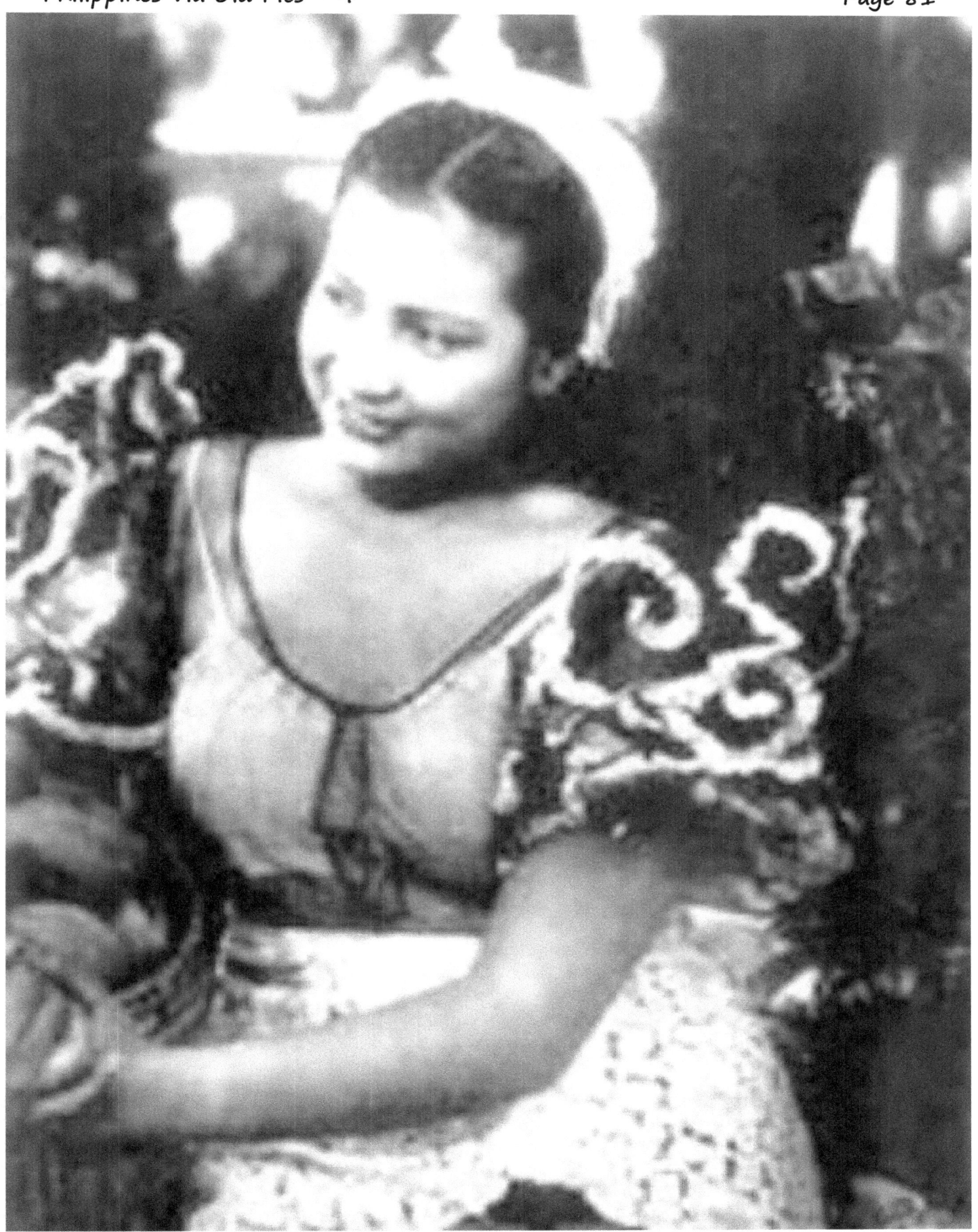

Mila del Sol – Famous Movie Star of yesteryears – (internet source)

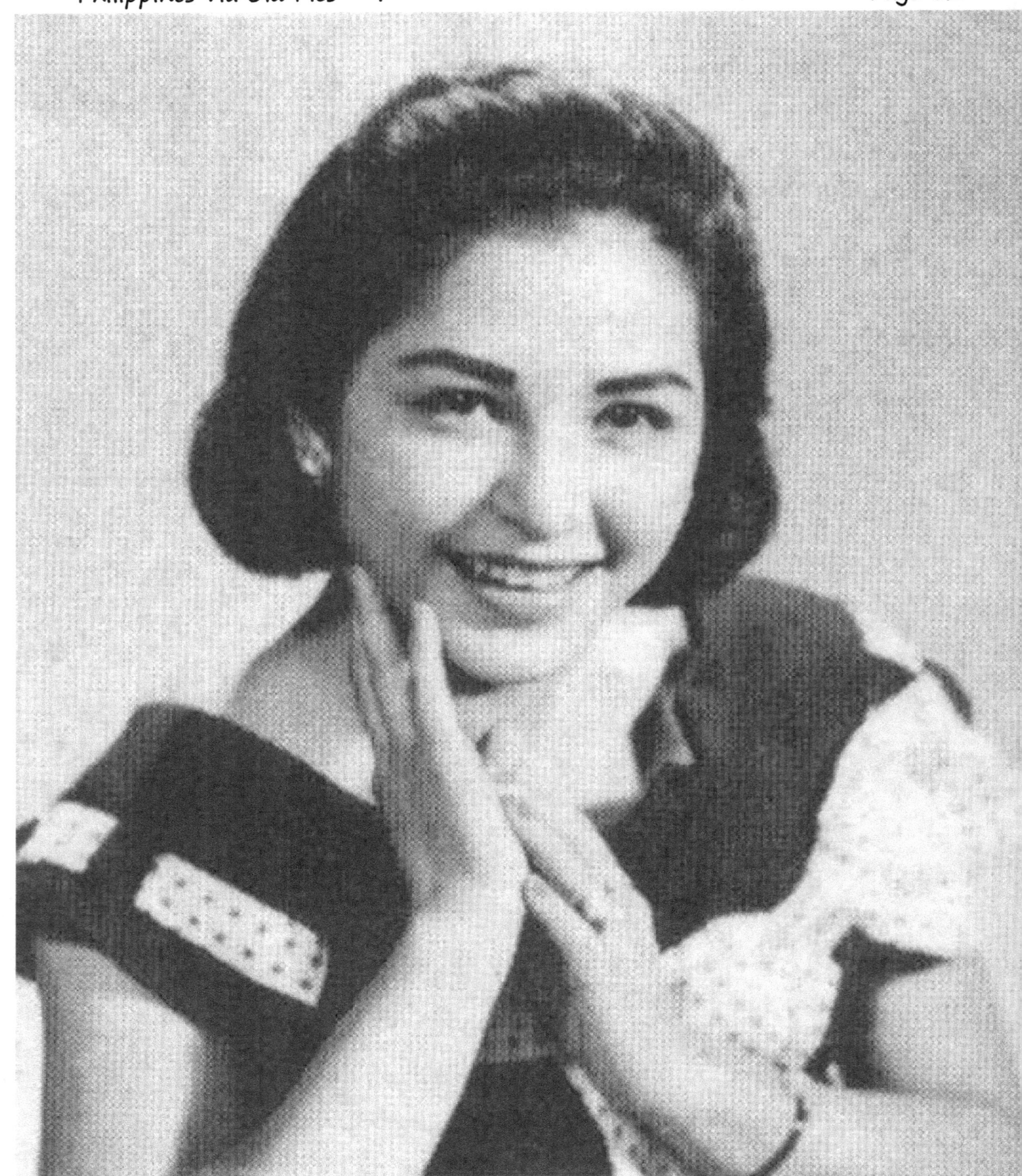

Nida Blanca – Famous Movie star of yesteryears – (internet source)

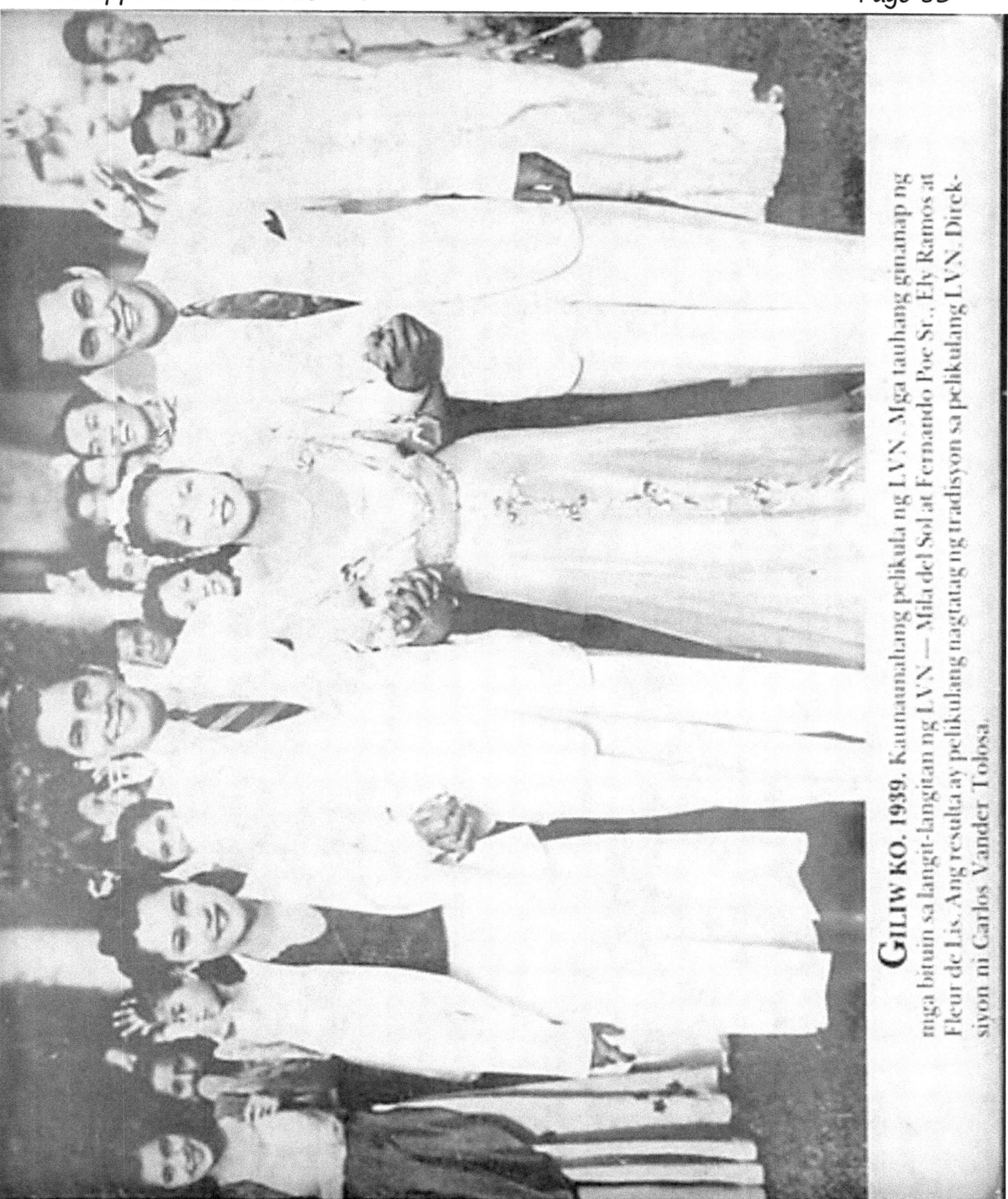

GILIW KO. 1939. Kaunaunahaang pelikula ng LVN. Mga tauhaang ginamap ng mga bituin sa langit-langitan ng LVN — Mila del Sol at Fernando Poe Sr., Ely Ramos at Fleur de Liz. Ang resulta ay pelikulang nagtatag ng tradisyon sa pelikulang LVN. Direksiyon ni Carlos Vander Tolosa.

1039 Movie cast of GILIW KO, with Fleir deLiz+ Ely Ramos + Mila del Sol + Fernando Poe Sr – famous stars of yesteryears – (internet source)

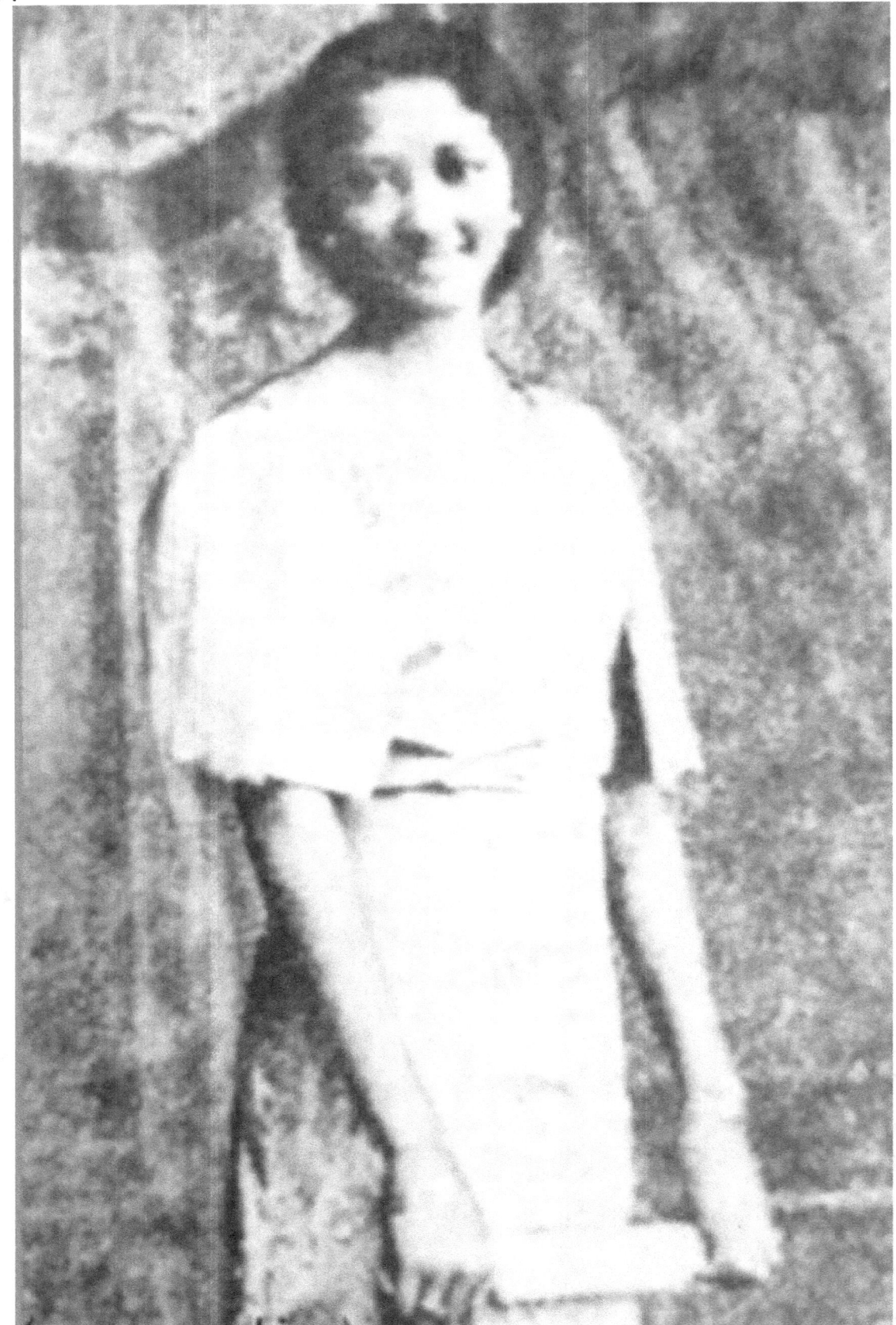

Carmen Rosales – Earliest Photo as Ms. Januaria Constantino Keller, her birth name, until she became a famous actress in Philippine cinema in 1930s-1960s – (internet source)

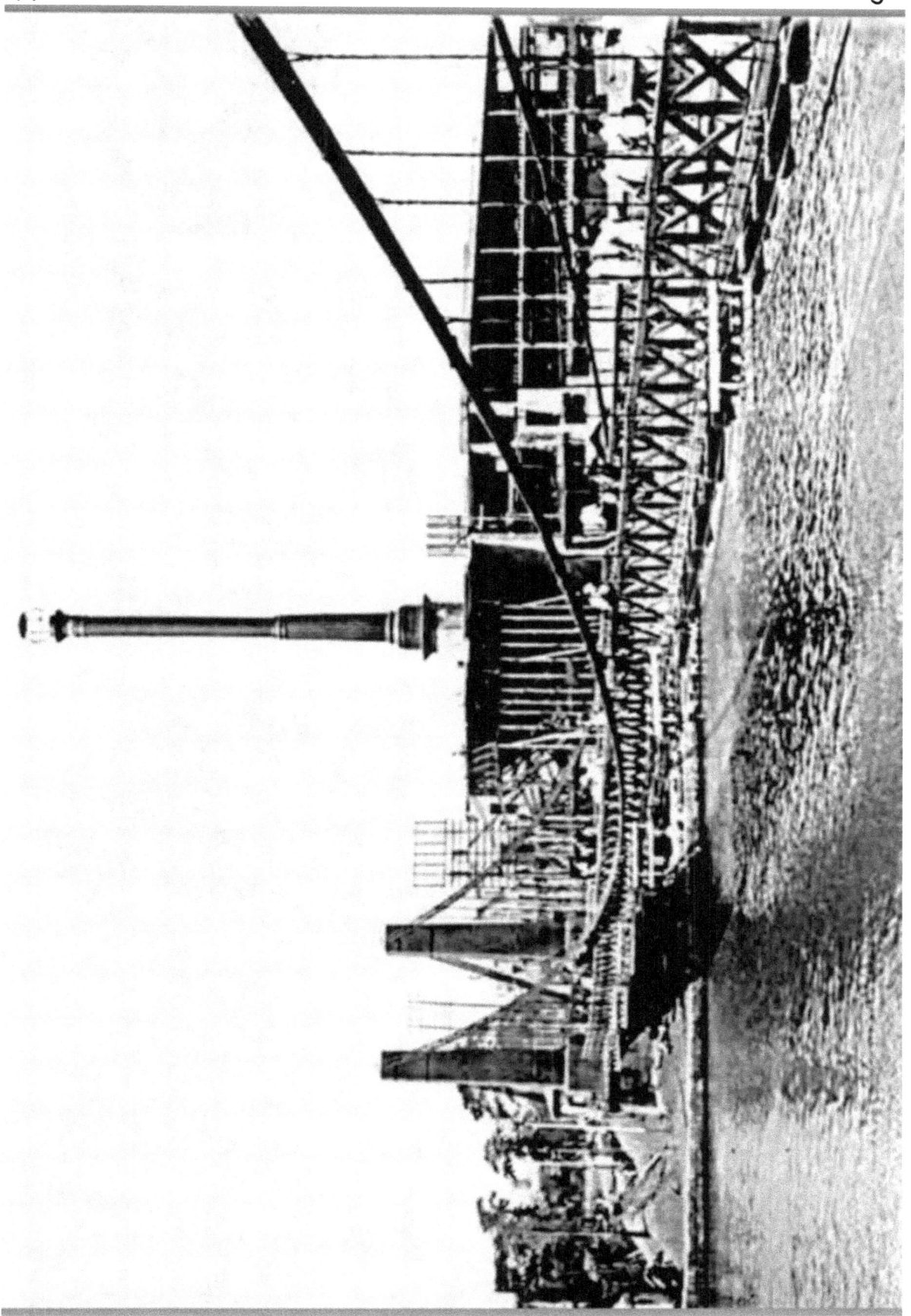

1900 A Foot Bridge across Pasig River, replaced by vehicles bridge. –
(courtesy of Philippines My Philippines FB site)

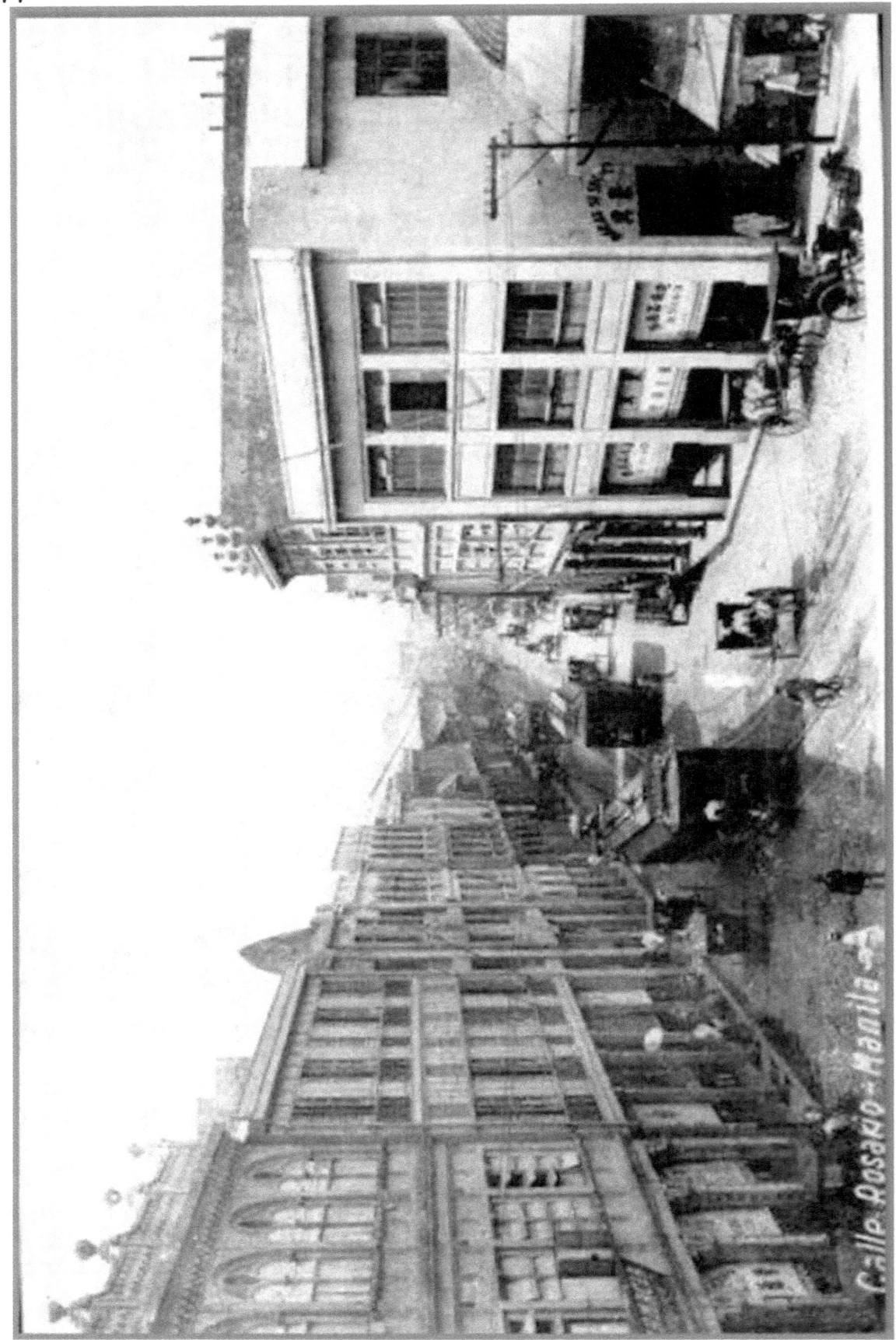

1900s Calle Rosario, Manila – Carromatas + Tranvias (courtesy of Philippines My Philippines FB site)

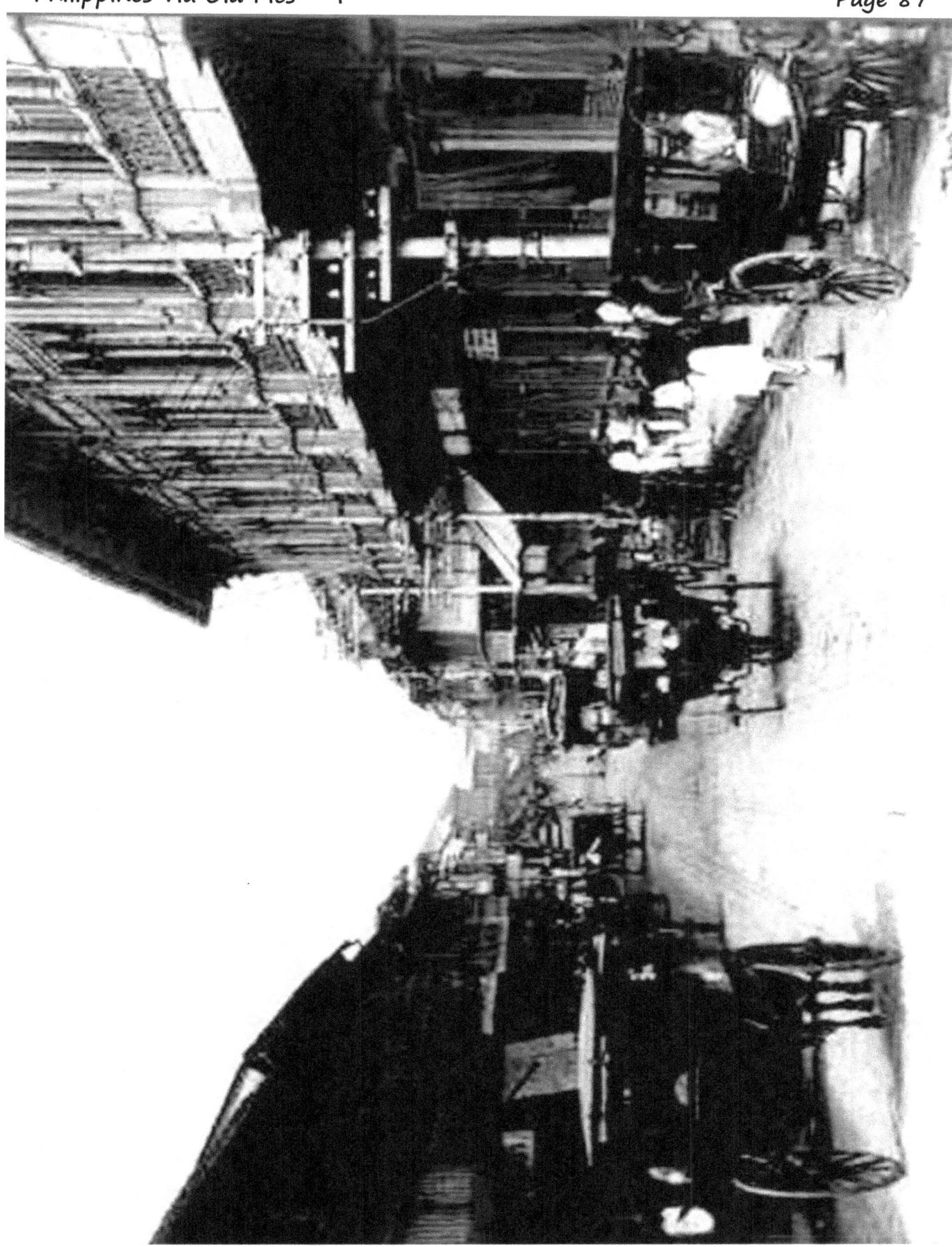

1900s Escolta, Manila – No cars (courtesy of Philippines My Philippines)

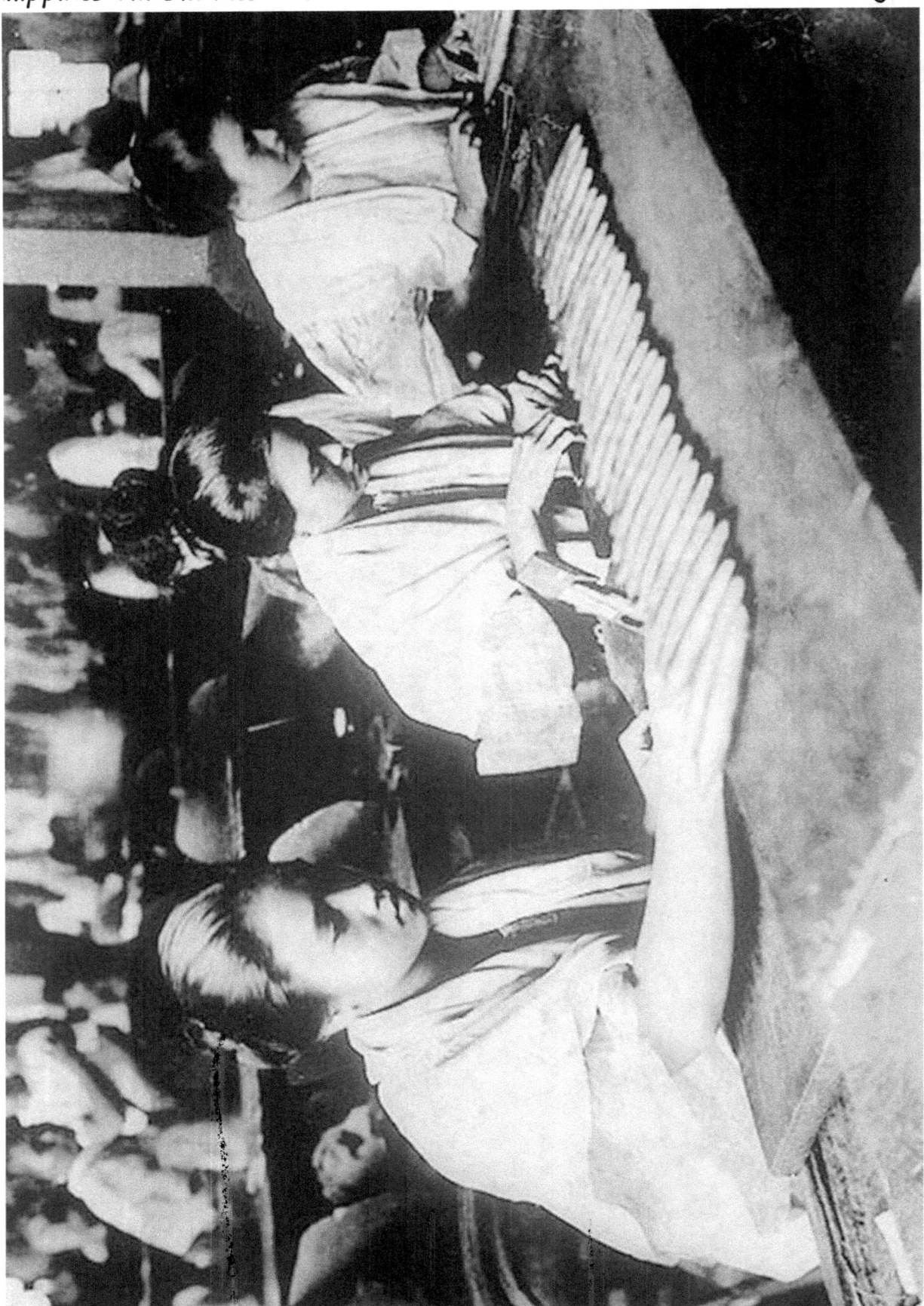

1920-30 – Alhambra Factory, women making cigars – (courtesy of Philippines My Philippines FB site)

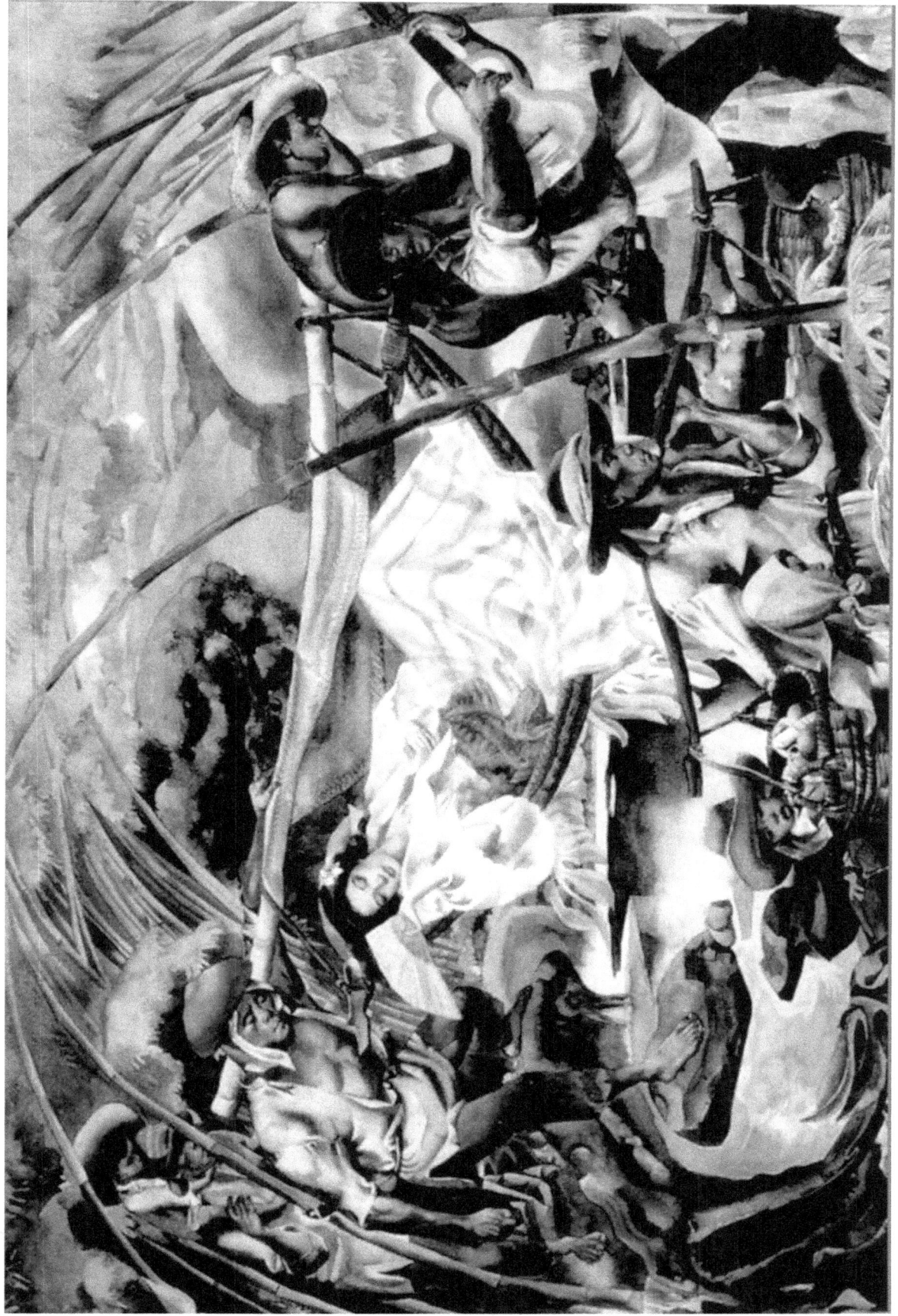

**1960 Botong Francisco, Famous Painter – Antipolo Pilgrimage theme –
(courtesy of Philippines My Philippines FB site)**

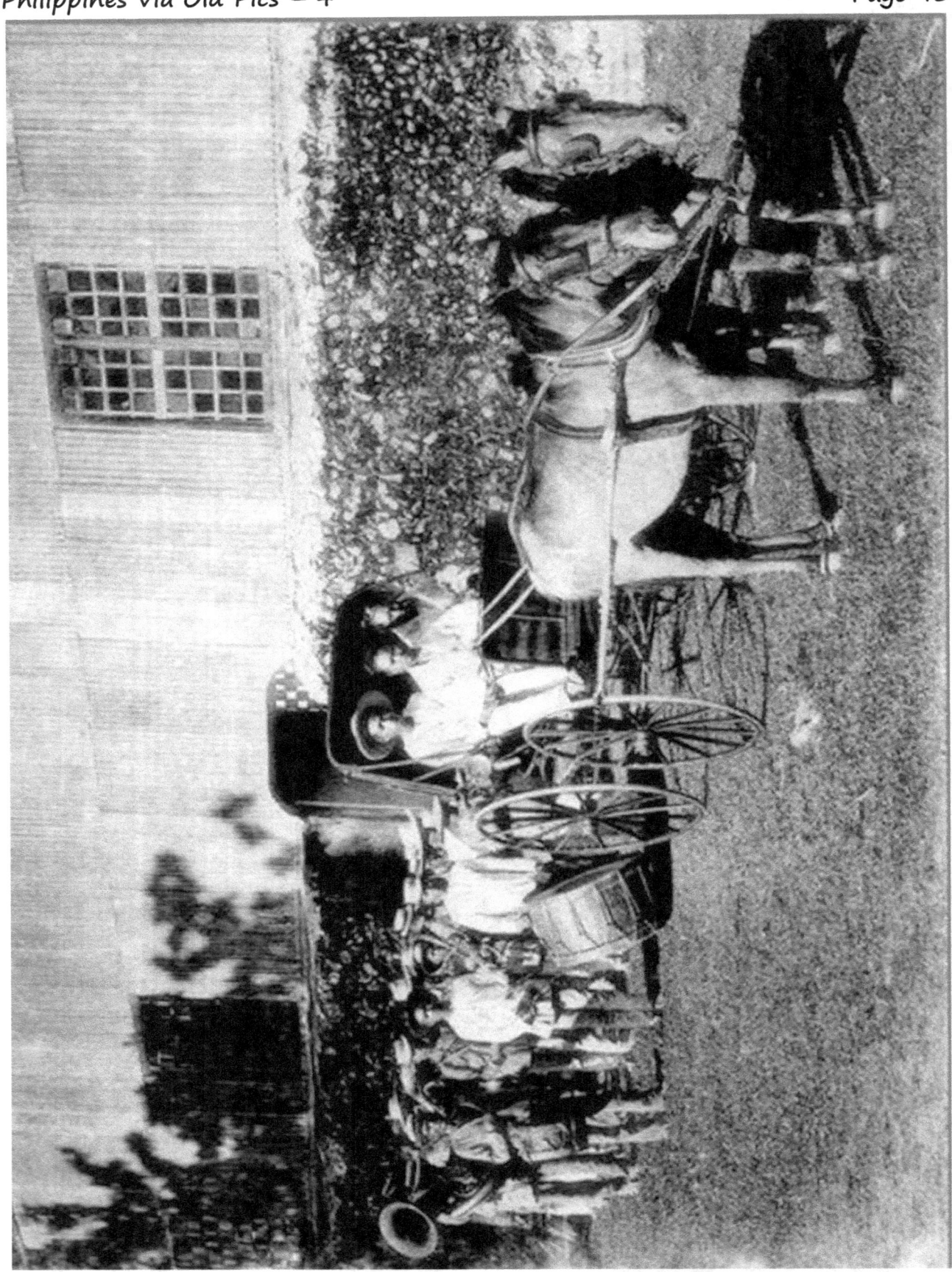

1900s – Musical Band Parade + Carromata – (courtesy of Philippines My Philippines FB site)

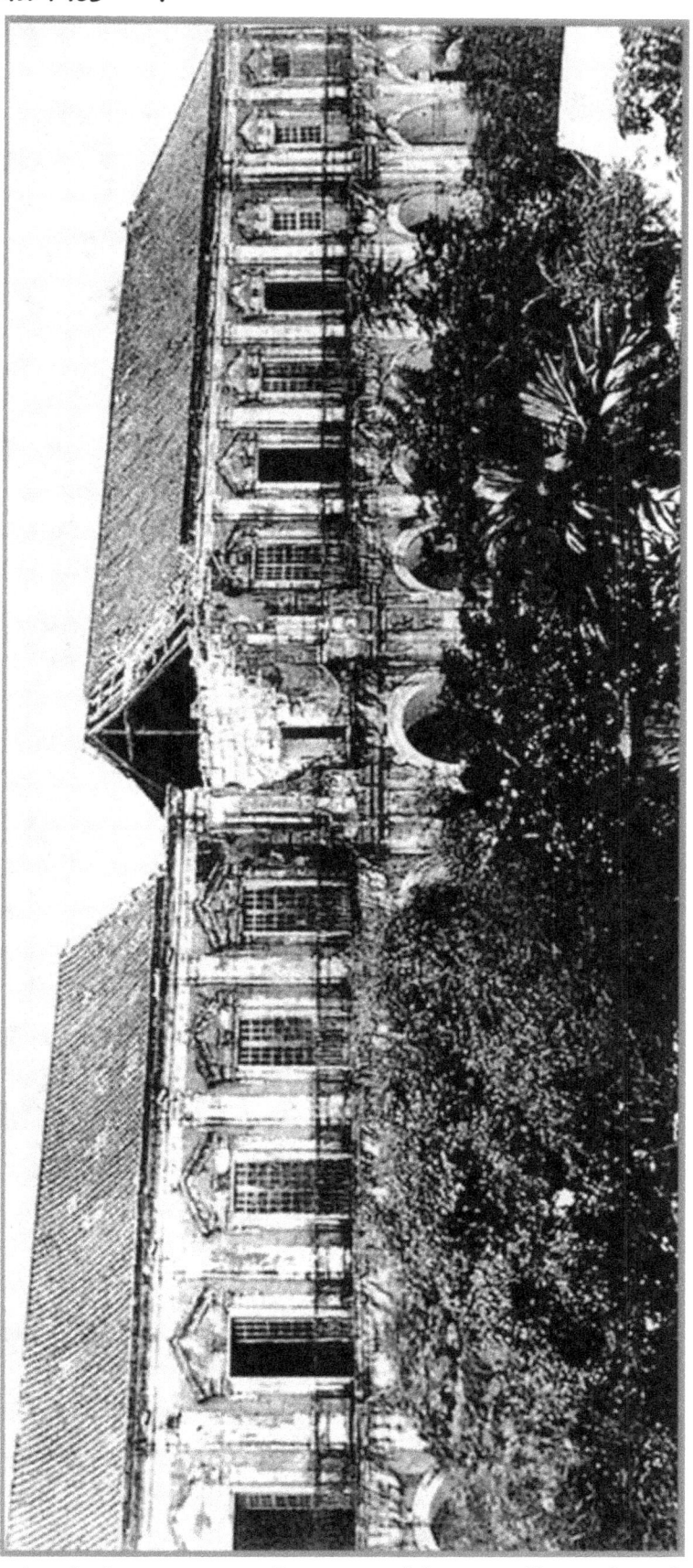

1863 Ayuntamiento, Intramuros, damaged by earthquake, later re-built with Palacio Del Gobernador on one end, bell tower in middle, and Ayuntamiento on another end - (courtesy of Philippines My Philippines FB – David Stanley Cooper)

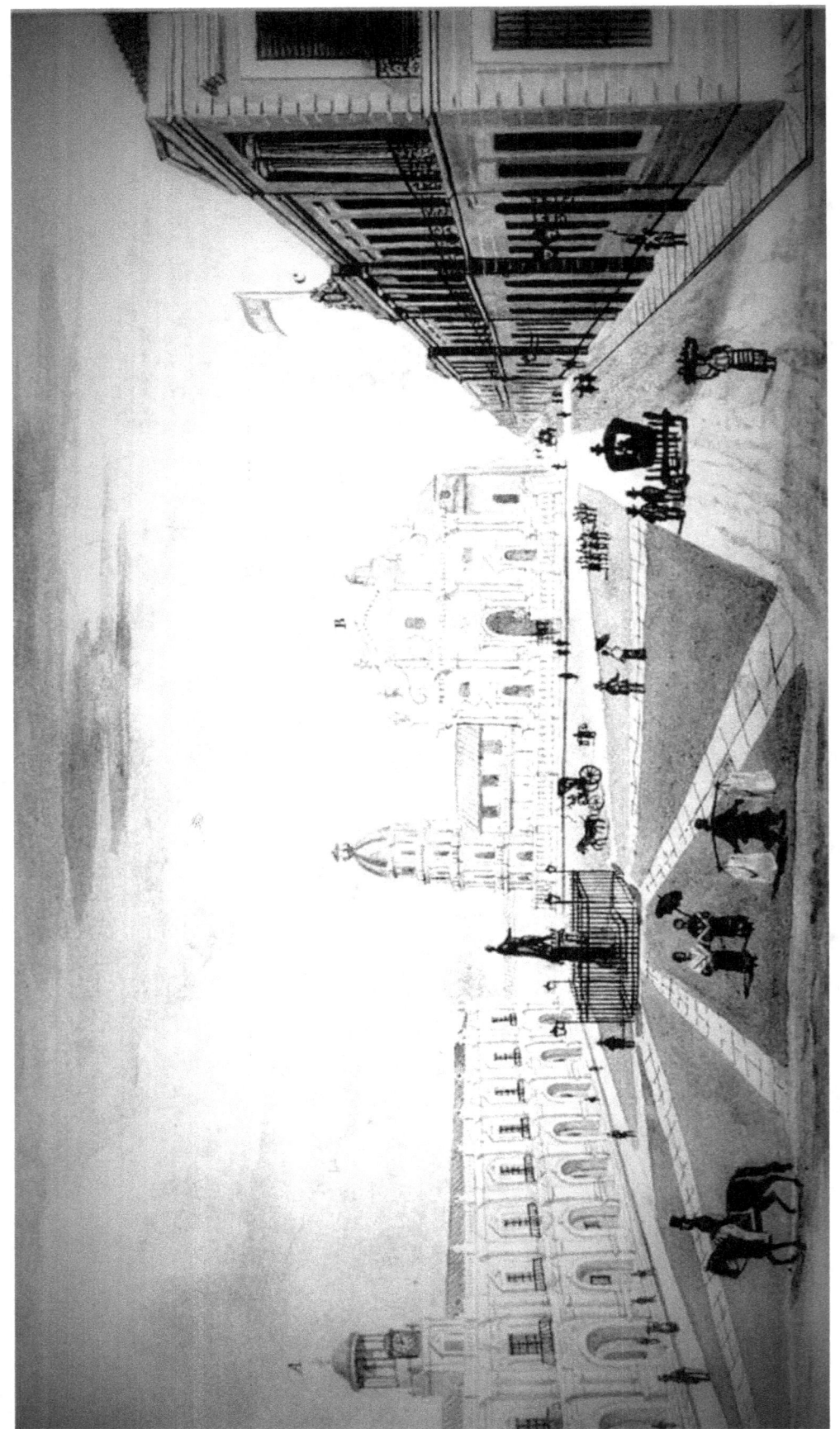

1880s – Old Ayuntamiento on the left with clock tower. All structures are non-existent now. (courtesy of Philippines My Philippines FB site)

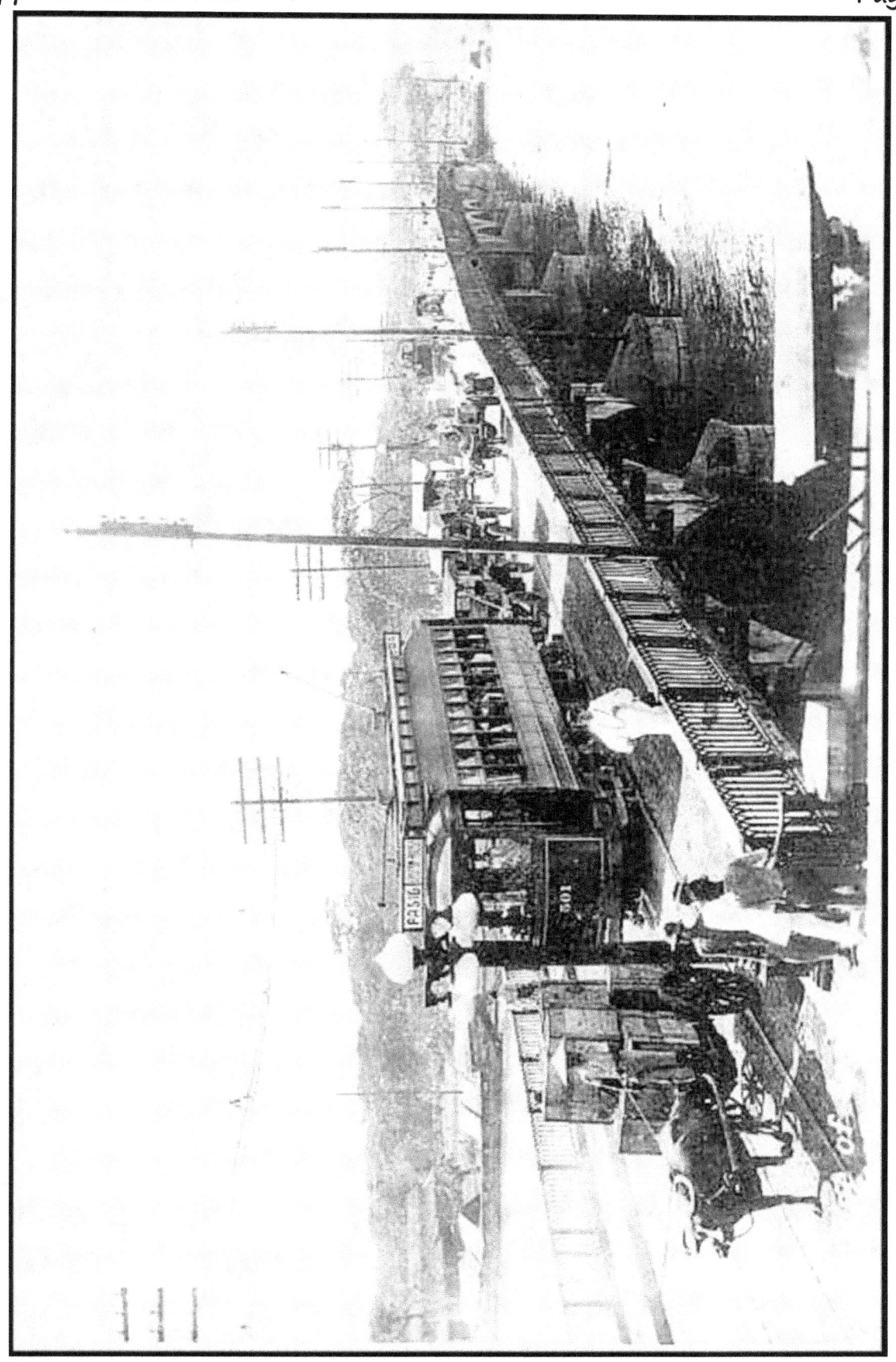

1910 Bridge of Spain in Pasig (Fort Bonifacio). See carromatas and tram –
(courtesy of Philippines My Philippines FB site – Maria Llanderal)

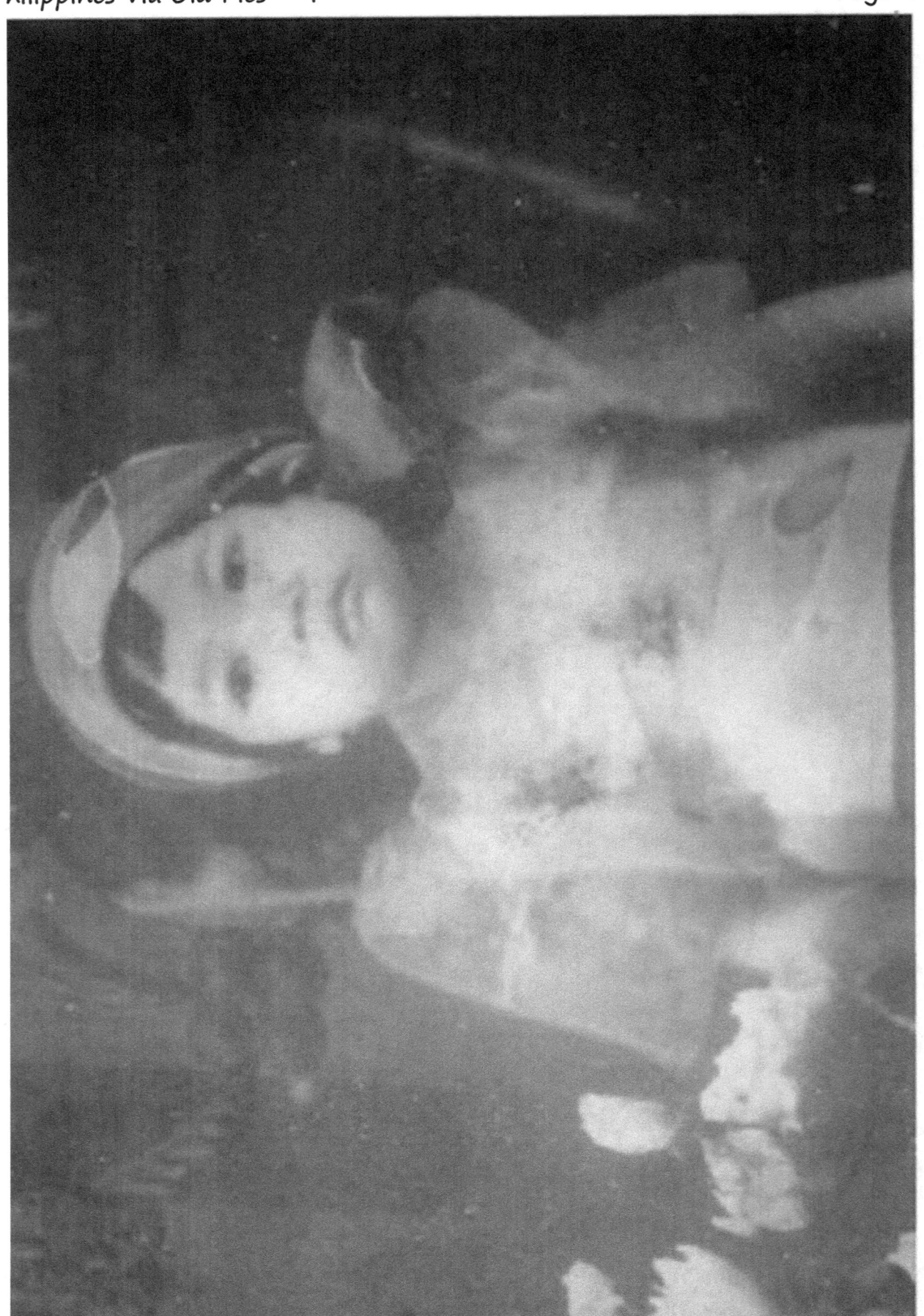

1930s Young girl dressed in Pilipina saya-dress

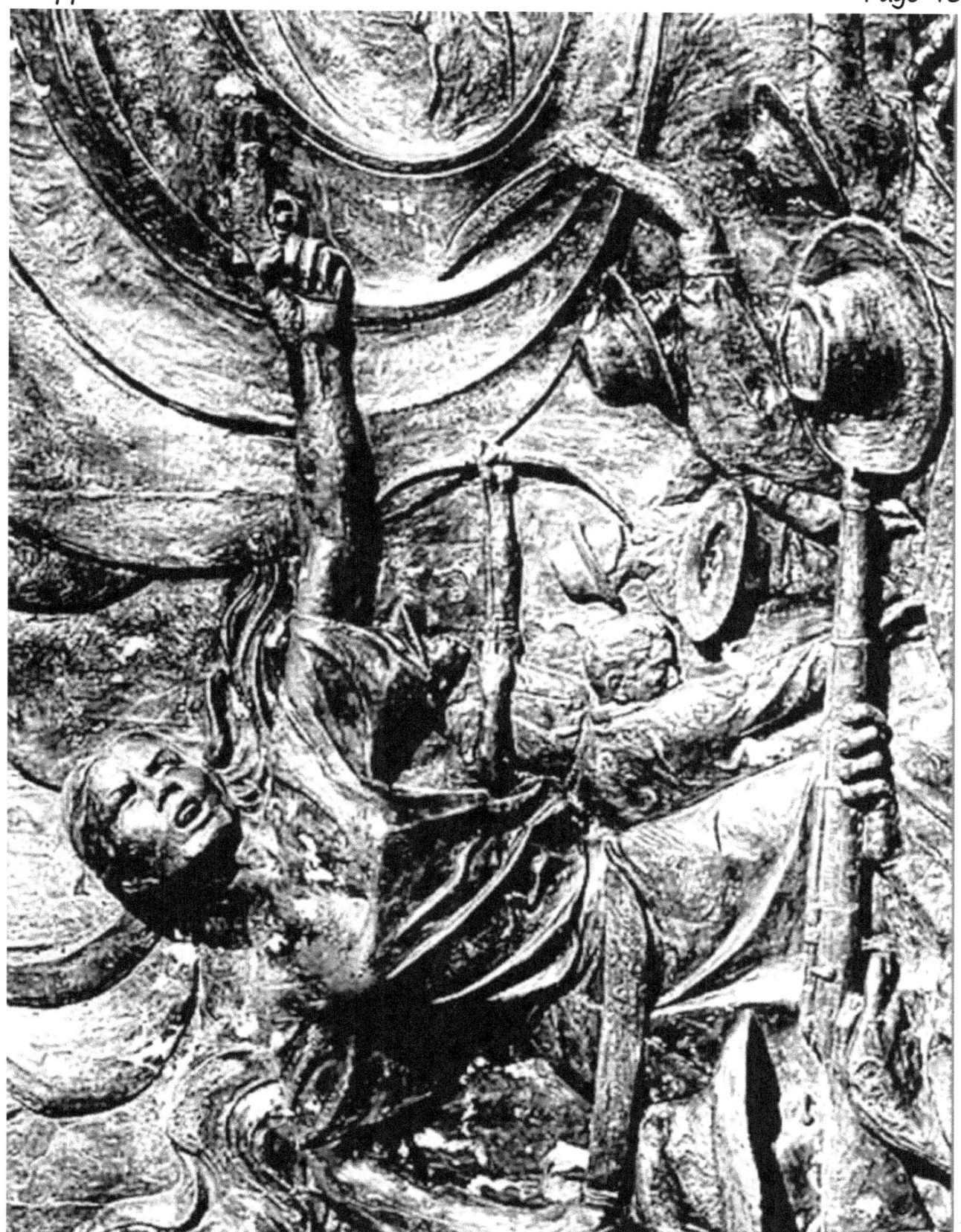

1898-1902 General Teresa Magbanua, Philippine Revolutionary Army against Spain and the United States. Despite opposition from her husband, Alejandro Balderas, a wealthy landowner from Iloilo, Magbanua followed her two younger brothers and joined the revolution (courtesy of Bobby Manasan)

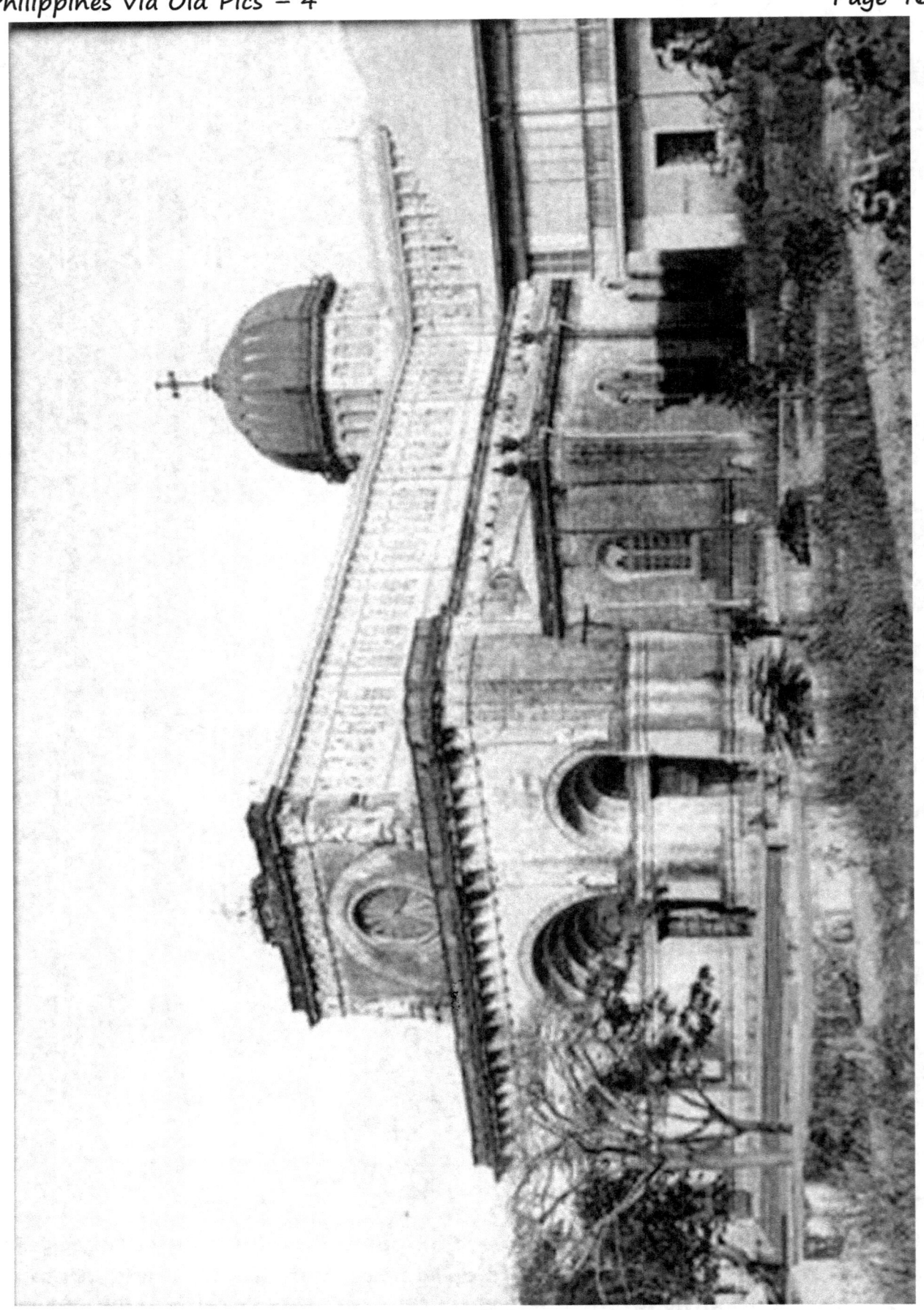

1900 Manila Cathedral (source internet)

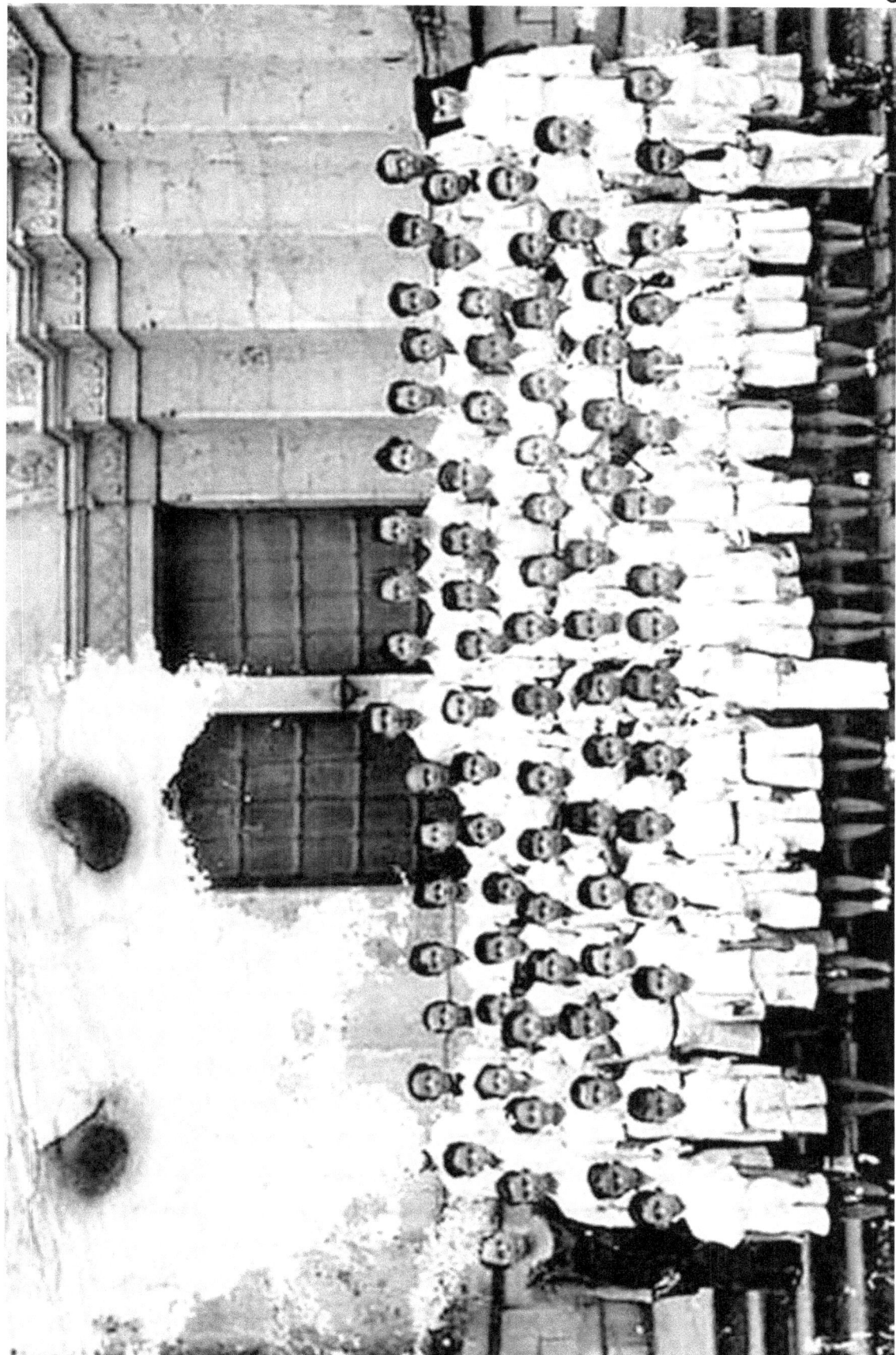

**1941 Manila Cathedral – I was in Grade 2 at the primary school
In this cathedral. Pls see checkmark of boy in second row. Editor's note.**

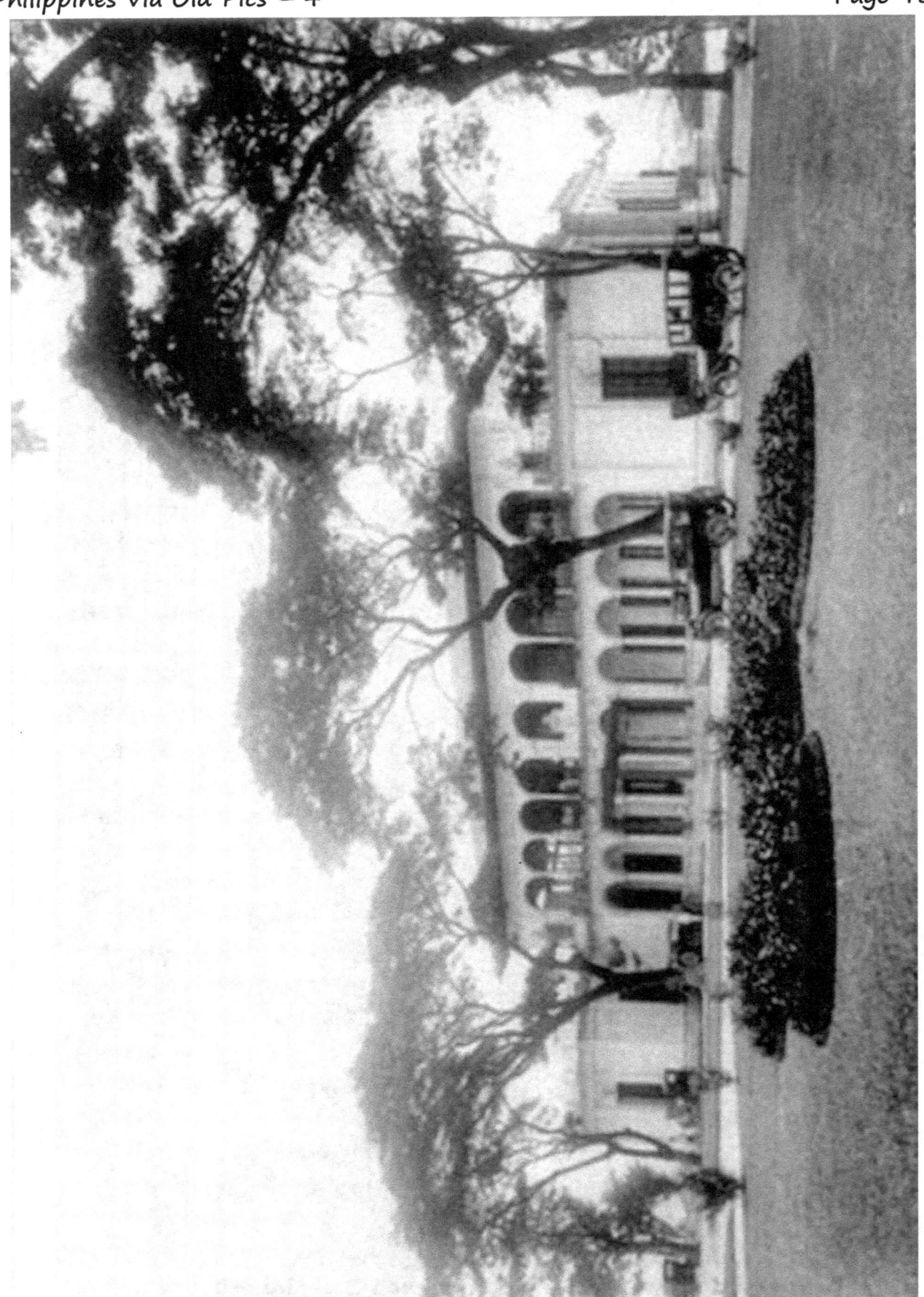

1926 Malacanang Palace (source internet)

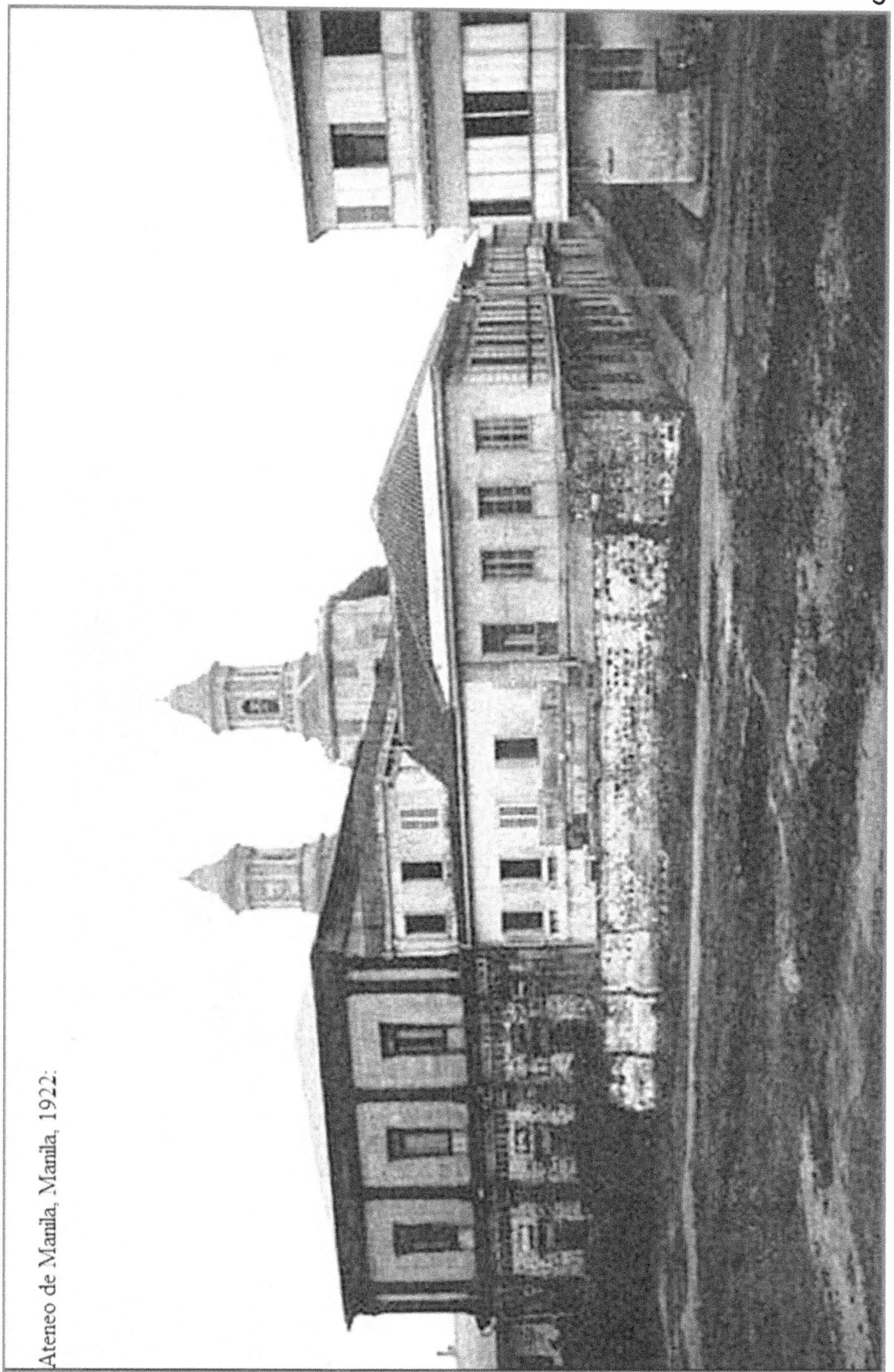

Ateneo de Manila, Manila, 1922.

1922 Ateneo de Manila in Intramuros (source internet)

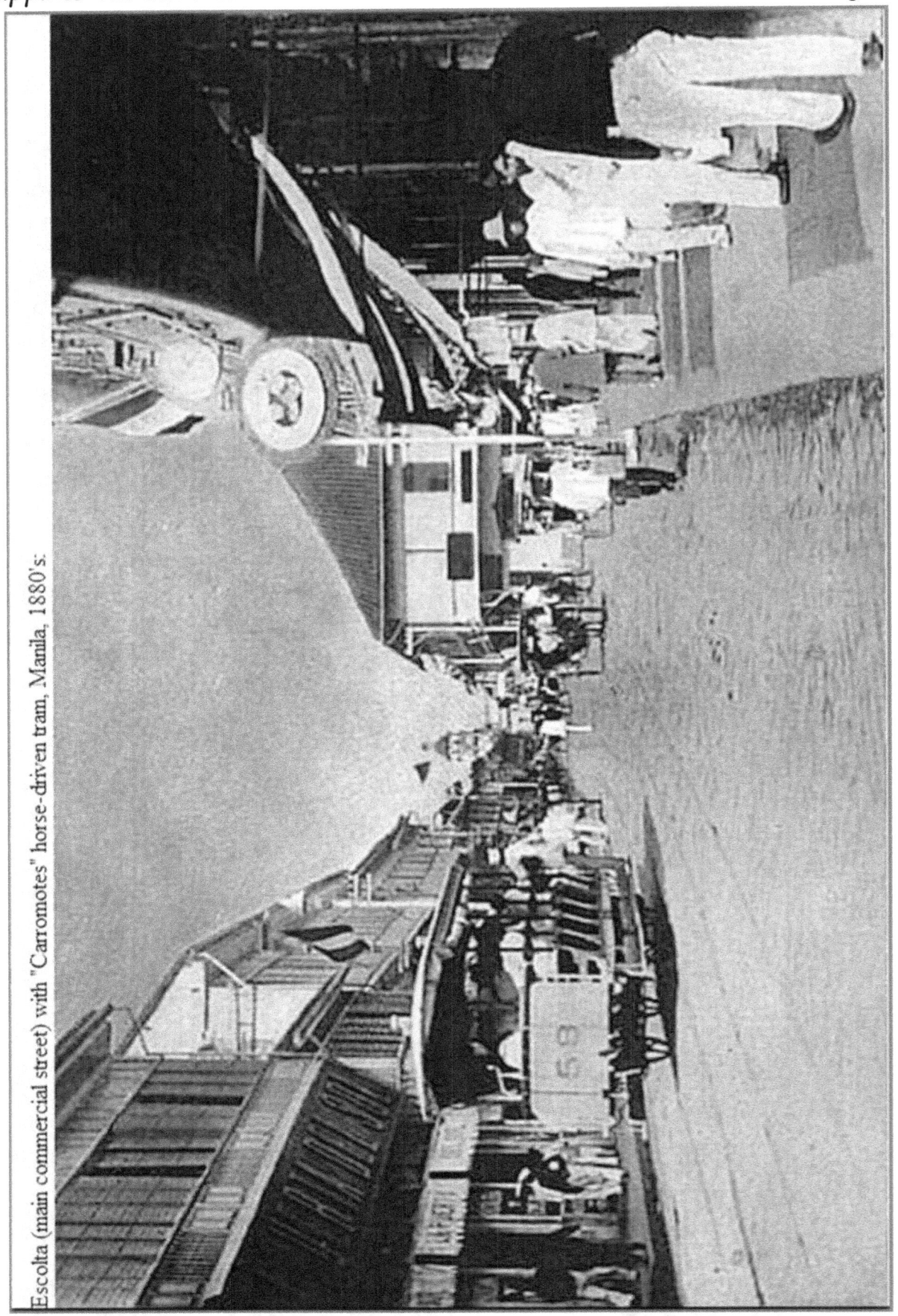

Escolta (main commercial street) with "Carromotes" horse-driven tram, Manila, 1880's:

1880s Escolta Manila + carromatas horse-driven tram (source internet)

Manila women wearning traditional Maria Clara, 1880's:

1880s Manila Women in Maria Clara dress – (source internet)

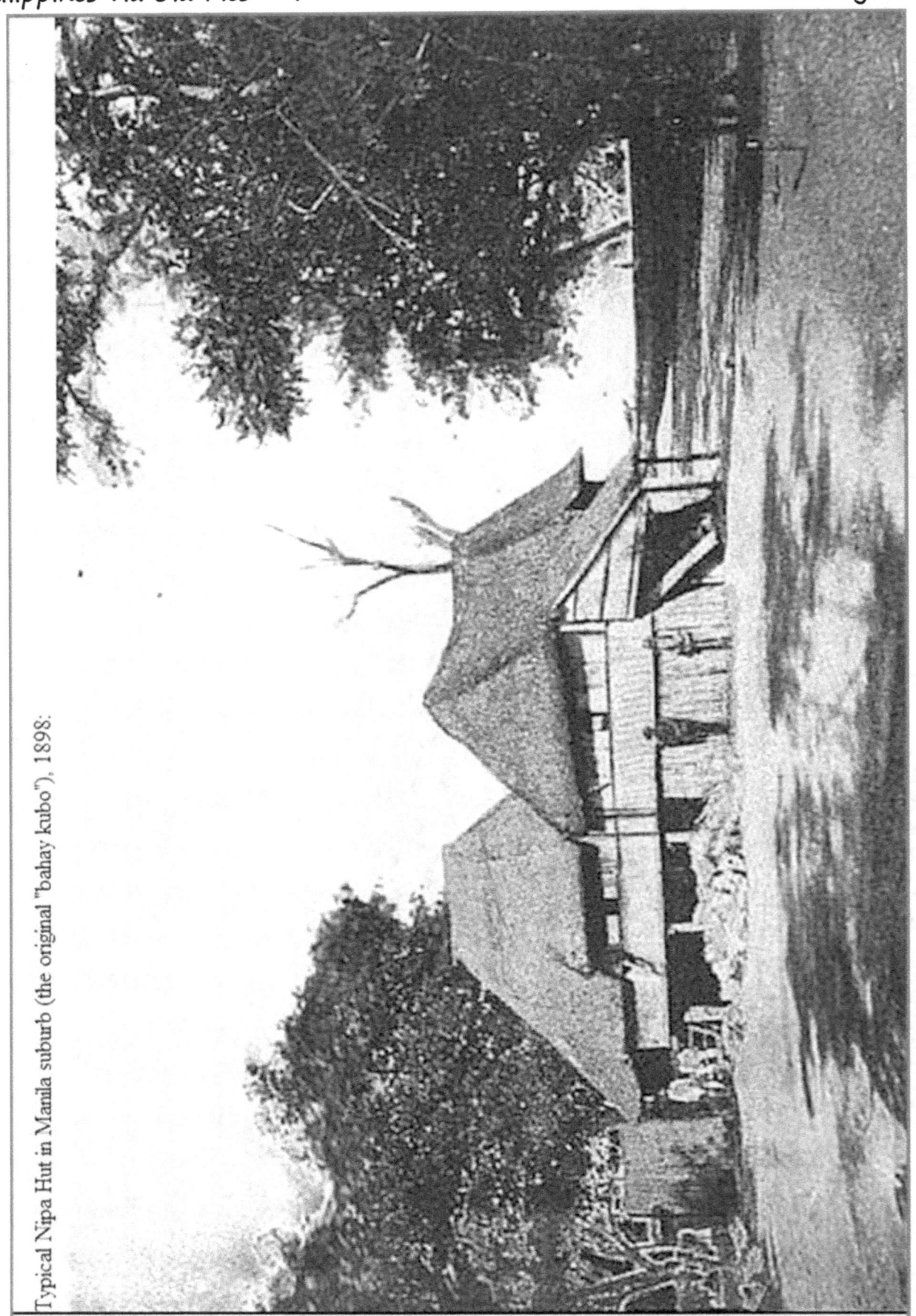

Typical Nipa Hut in Manila suburb (the original "bahay kubo"), 1898:

1898 Typical Nipa Hut in Manila suburb – (source internet)

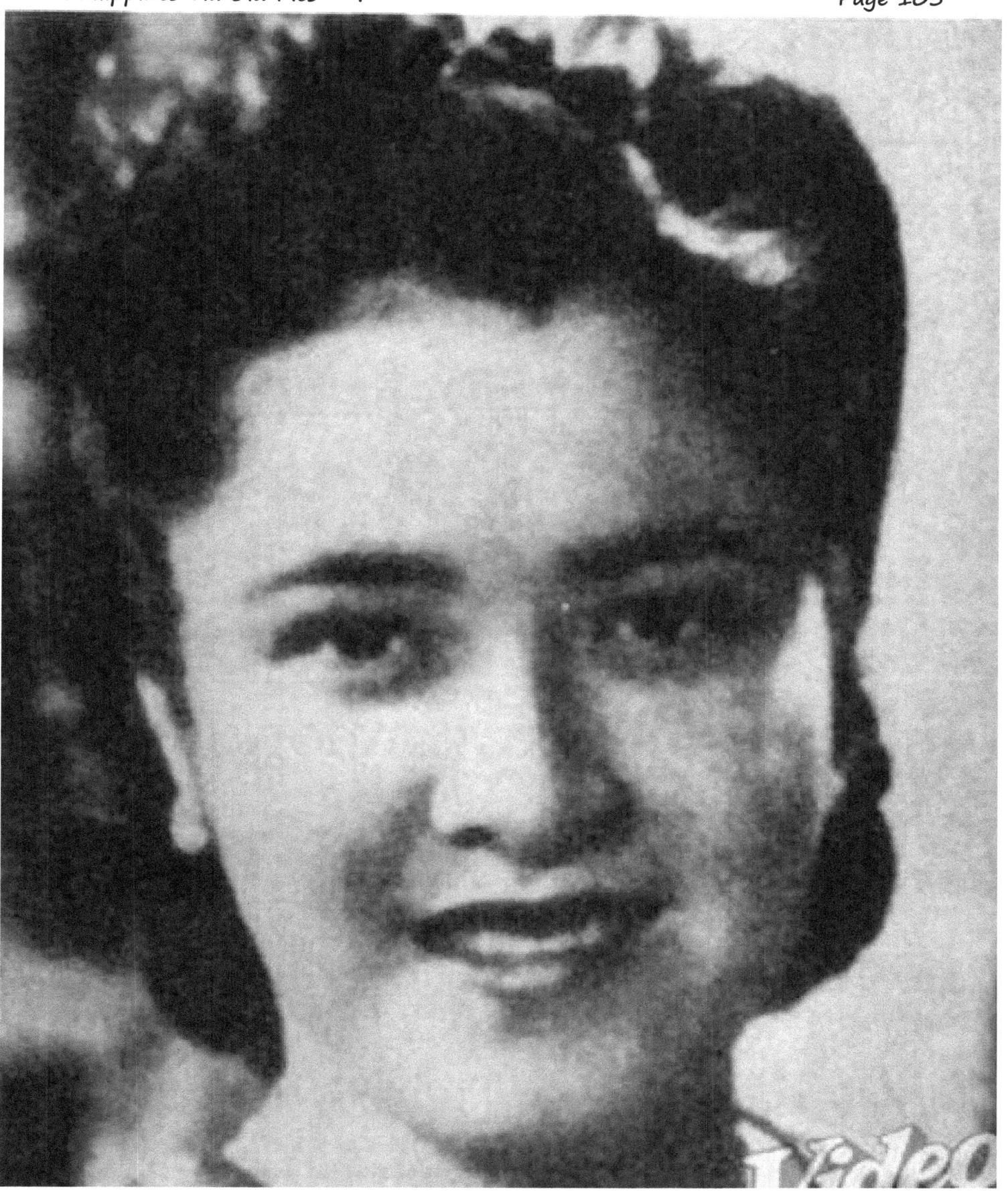

Corazon Noble – Famous Movie star of yesteryears (source internet)

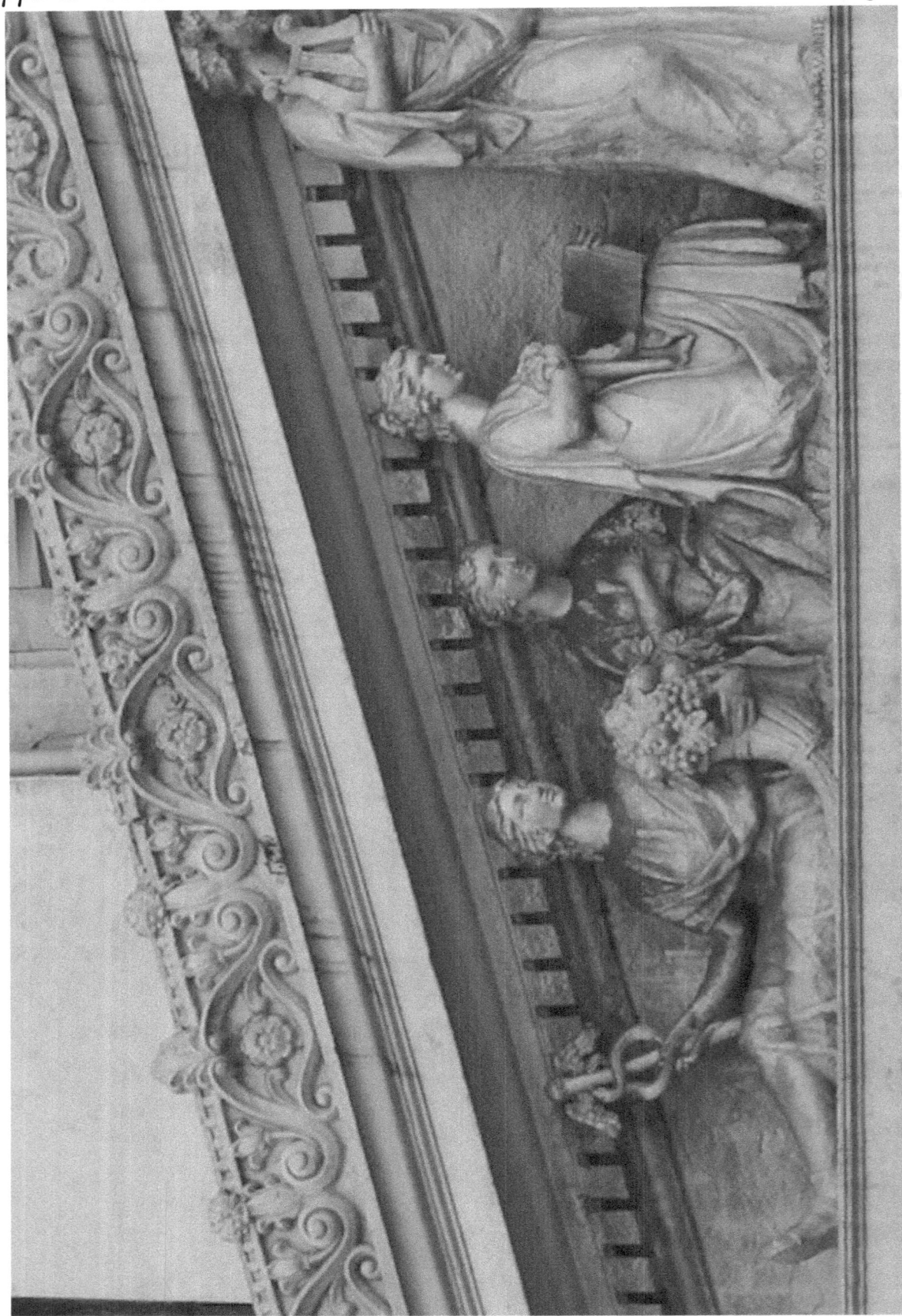

Nice Sculpture at Don Roman Santos Bldg at Plaza Goiti, (courtesy of Philippines My Philippines FB site – Paolo Bustamante – Inang Laya – Eric deGana deRamos)

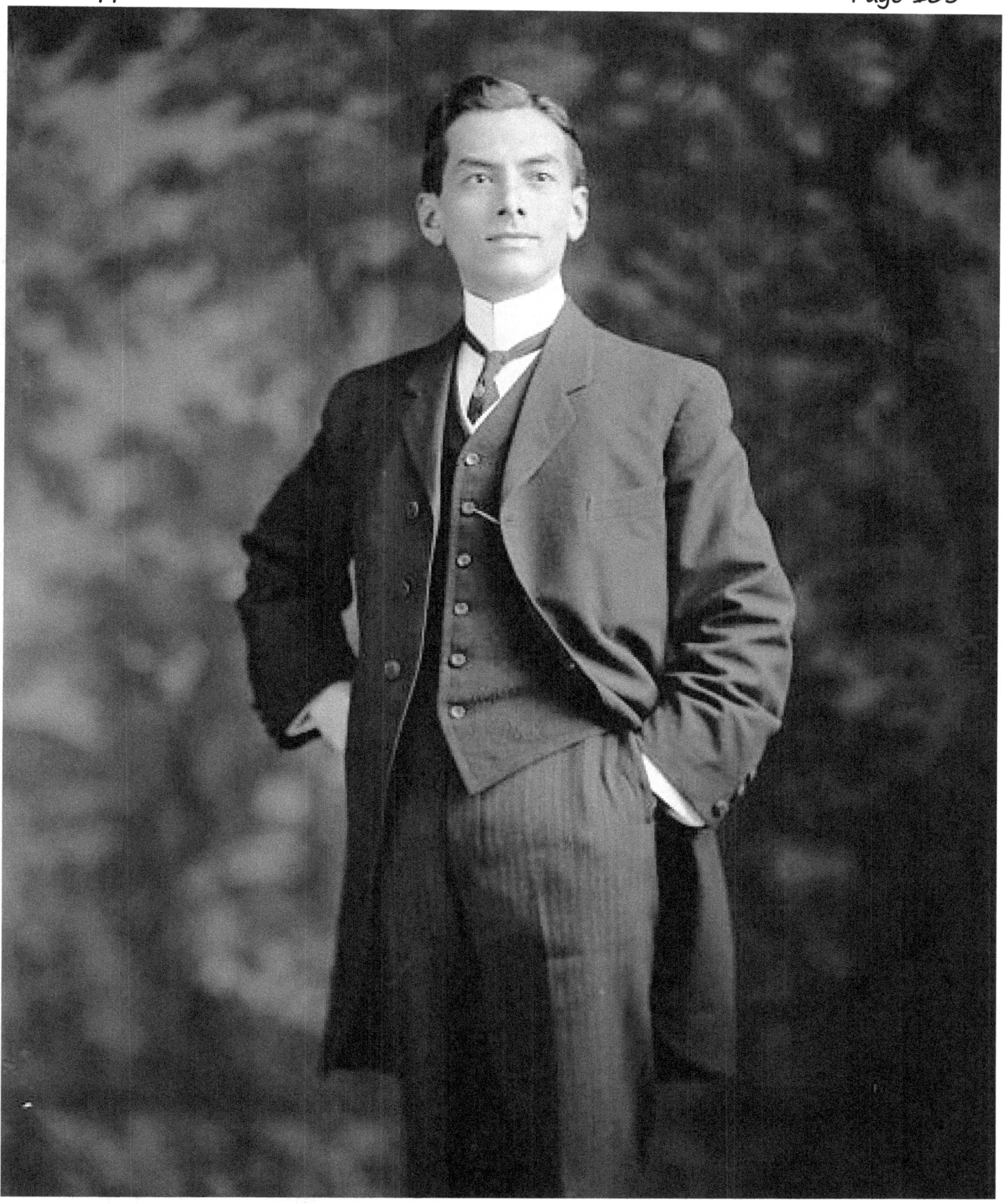

1910s Young Manuel L. Quezon, early political life (courtesy of Philippines My Philippines FB site)

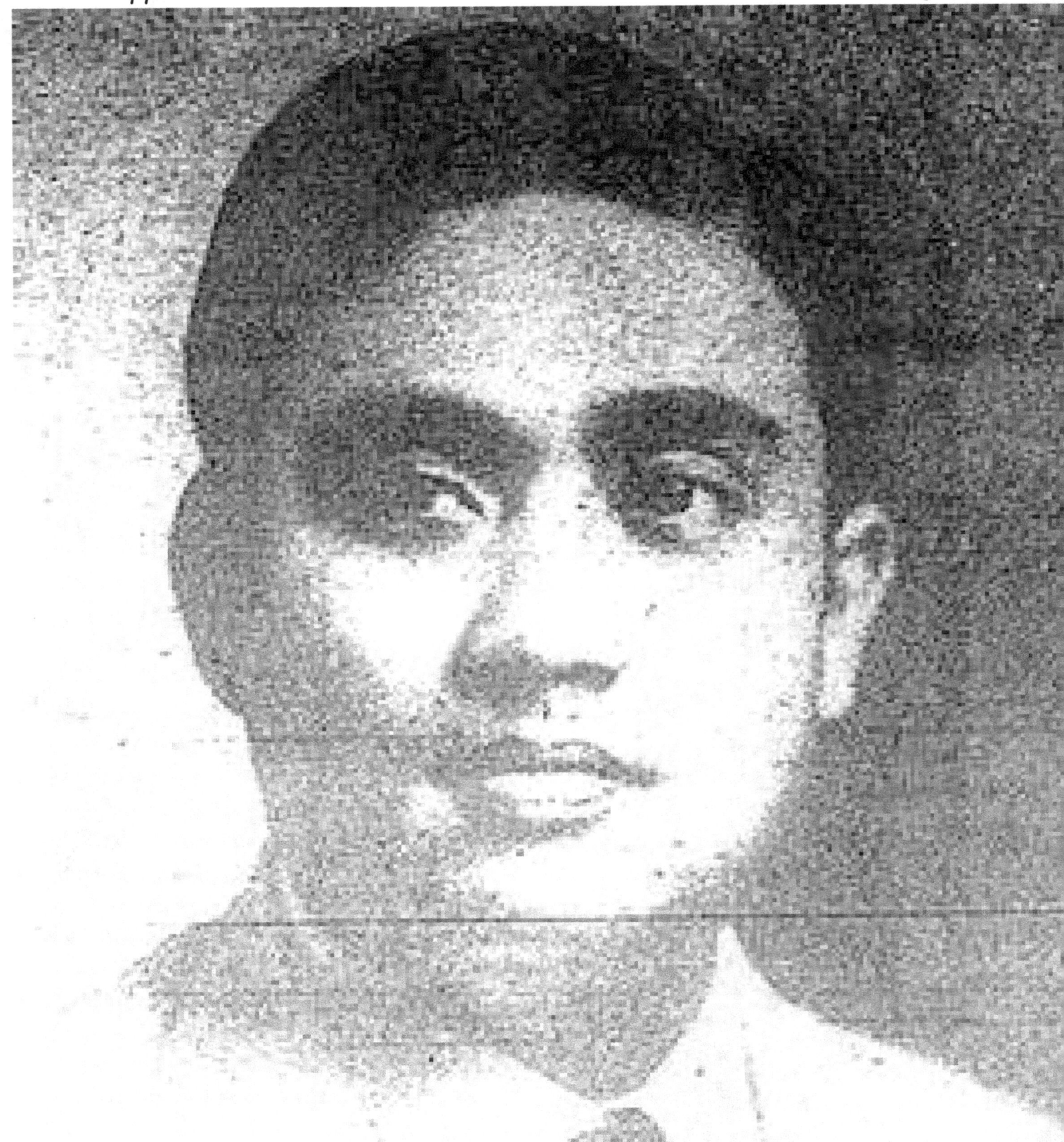

B.1910 – D.1942 – Wenceslao Vinzons, student leader-activist, youngest 1934 Constitution Convention, a governor, congressman, heroic death in hands of Japanese occupation forces

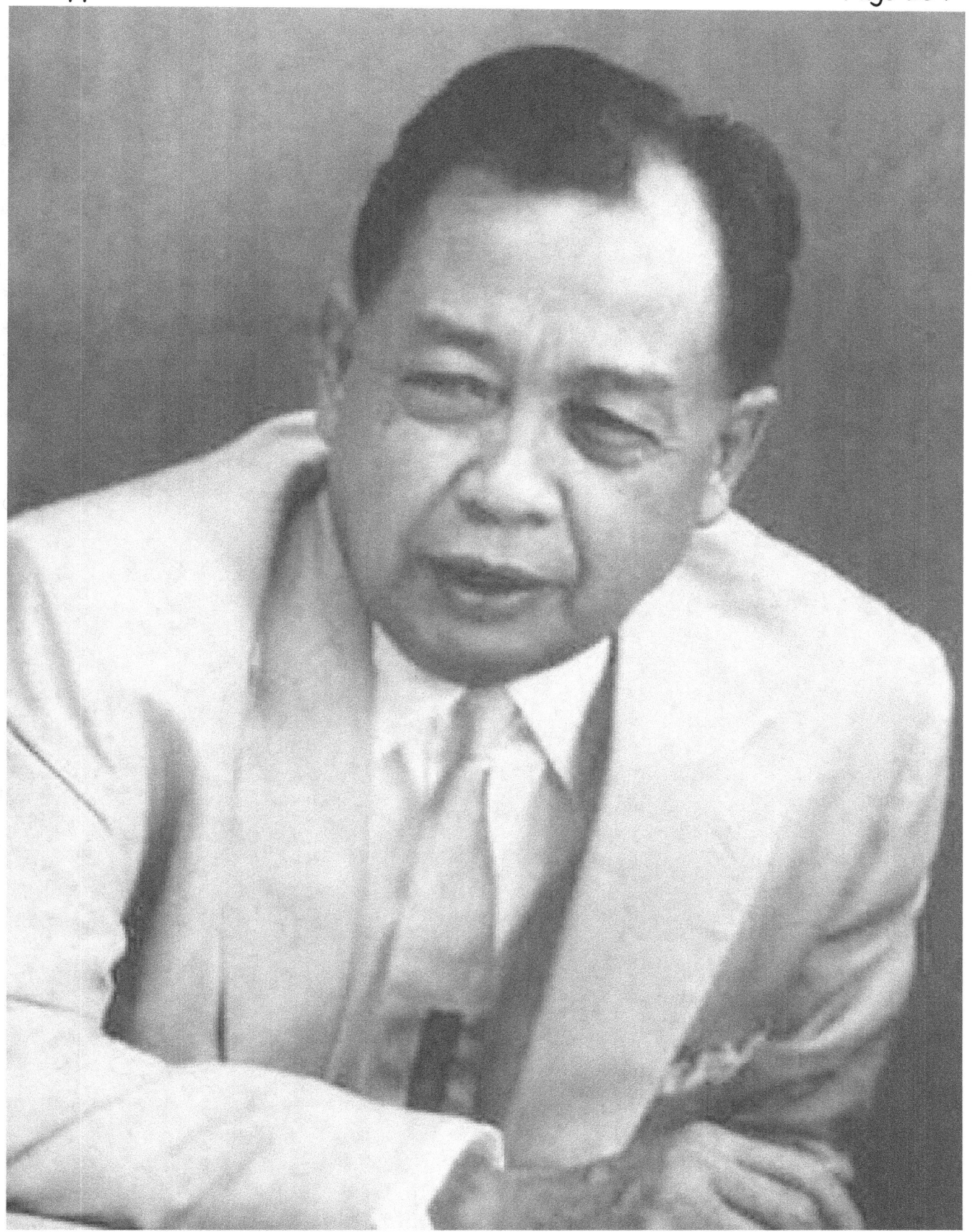

Don Claro Recto - 1934 Constitution Convention President, famous nationalist, senator, writer, giant in political circles up to 1960s.

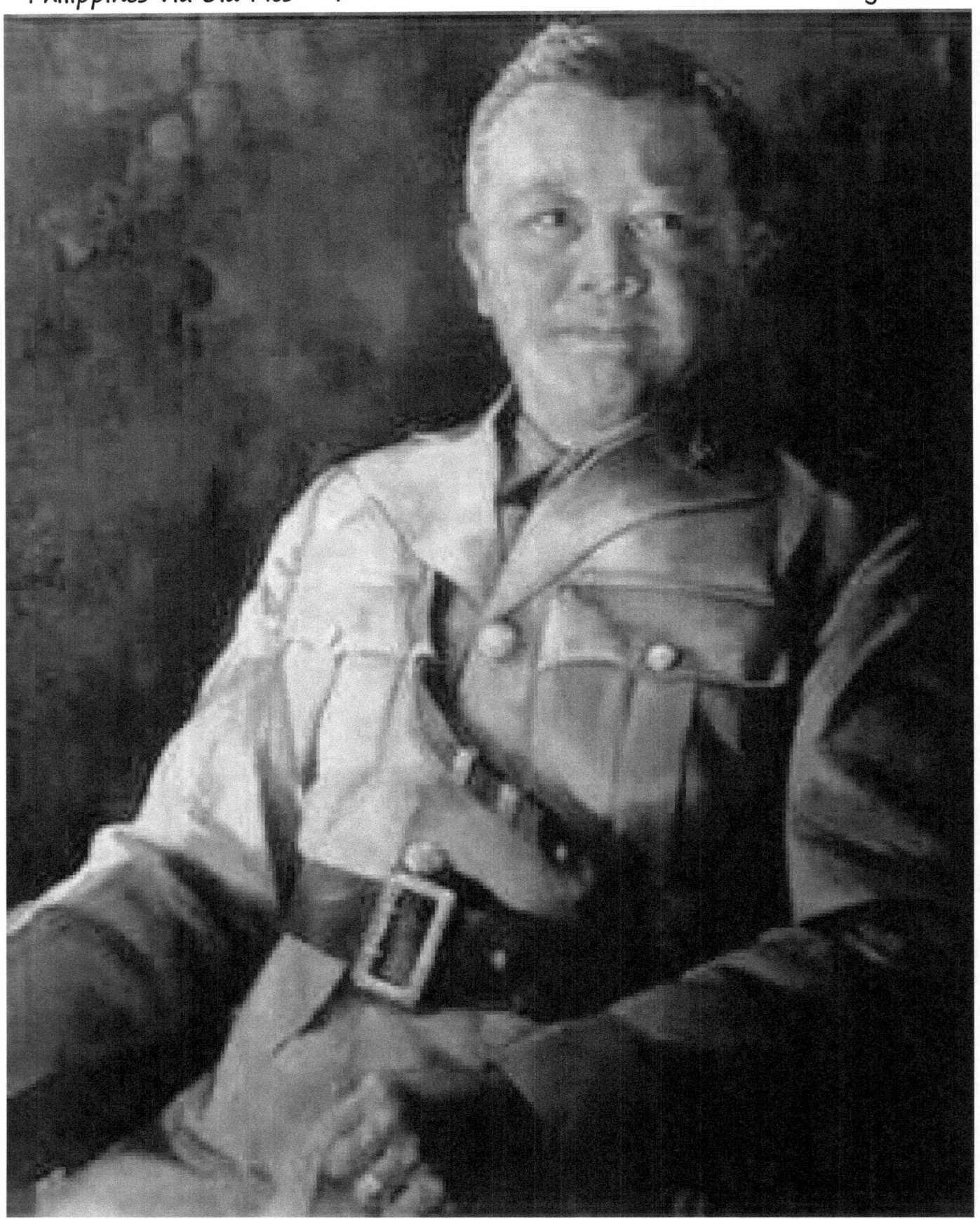

Gen. Vicente Lim – Head of the Philippine Army Division under Pres. Quezon and Gen. MacArthur during Japanese War or WWII. (internet source)

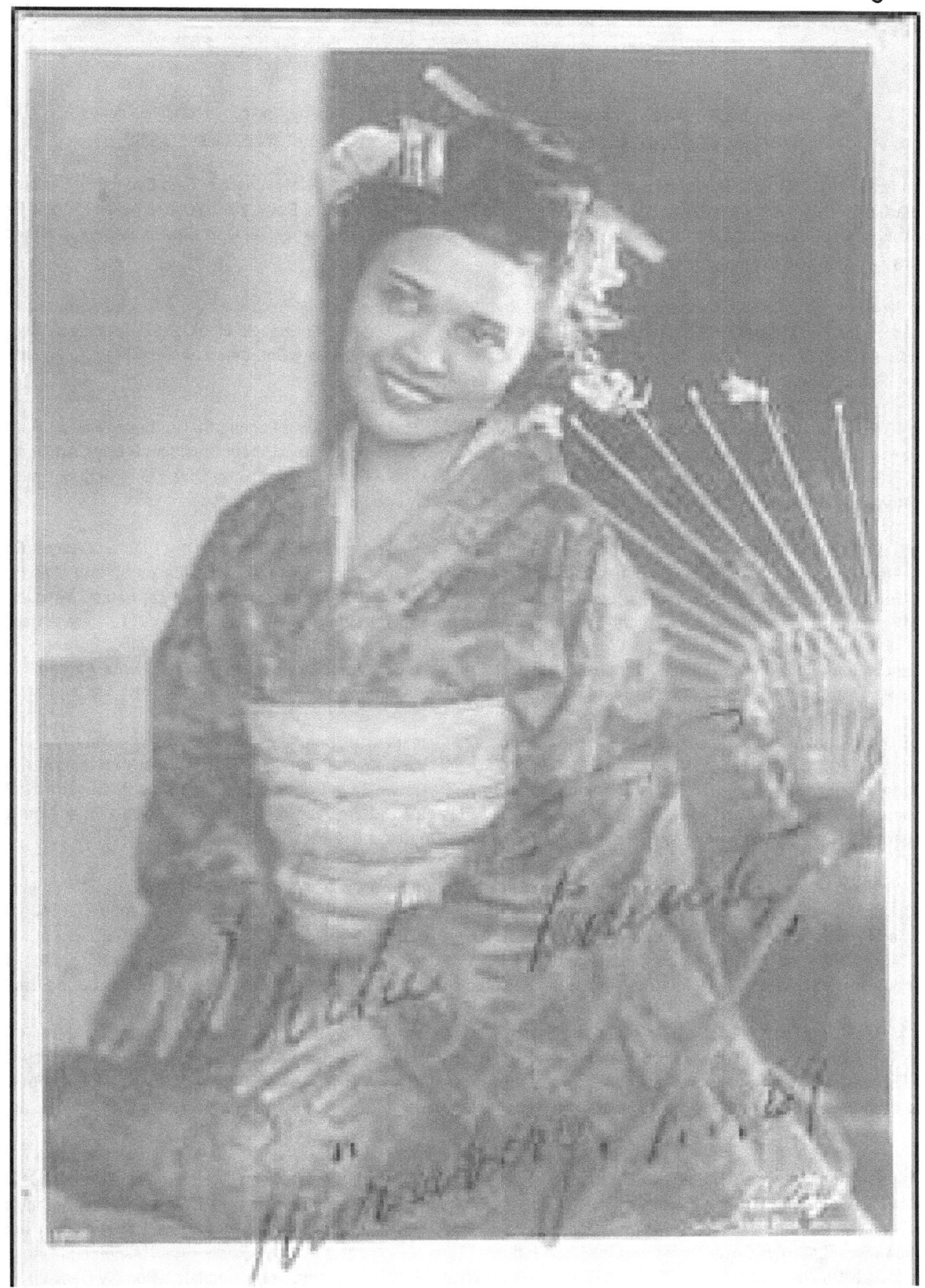

1930s -1940s - Jovita Fuentes – Famous Filipina opera singer – sang Madam Butterfly by Puccini in famous theatres abroad. (internet source)

Published in July 2016 by

Self-Publisher - Tatay Jobo Elizes
Printed, January, 2016, in the United States of America under ISBN codes below.
ISBN-13: 978 - 1522740223 +   ISBN-10: 1522740228

Book List - Buy online as paperback or kindle - Contact: job_elizes@yahoo.com, tatay@usa.com
Websites: http://tinyurl.com/mj76ccq + www.jobelizes.webs.com + www.tatayjobo.com

Writings 1 Book, 2012 , Articles by Bambi Harper + Butch Jiimenez + Dr. Phil Stack + Noel Alegre + Toto Causing +_ Melanie Ferrer + Susie Barbieri _ Rodel Ramos + Sylvia Salvador + Tatay Jobo Elizes + + Writings 2 Book, 2012, Artices by Gov. Grace Padaca + Melanie Aquino + Toto Causing + Rodel Rodis + Cesar Torres + Joey Concepcion + Charity Guides + Cesar Lumba +_ Casiano Mayor Jr. + Sonny Coloma + Anonymous.+ +

Writings 3A Book, 2012, Articles by Norman Madrid + Dr. Rene Azurin + Ernie Delfin + Toto Causing + Dr. Jose Abueva + MarVic Cagurangan + Casiano Mayor Jr + Rod Garcia + Roy Gaane + Tatay Jobo Elizes + + Writings 3B Book, 2012, Articles by Ceres Busa + John Reyes + Bert Guiang. + + Writings 4A Book, 2012, Articles by Dr Jose Abueva + Col. Dennis Acop + Fred Natividad + Irineo P. Goce, KaPule2 + Miguel Reynadlo + Marjorie Ann Elizes Reyes+ +

Writings 4B Book, 2012, 1. Mi Ultimo Adios (My Last Farewell), *Dr. Jose P. Rizal* + 2. Aling Pagibig Sa Tinubuang Bayan, *Gat. Andres Bonifacio* + Articles by Irineo P. Goce or KaPule2 + + Writings 5 Book - "Best Hopes" 2010 (About President P-Noy), Articles by Tony Meloto + F.SionilJose + Juan L. Mercado + OFWs Letter + Marcelo Tecson + Cesar Torres+ Perry Diaz + Dr. Philip S. Chua + Ernie Delfin + Atty. Ted Laguatan + Frank Wenceslao Jaileen F. Jimeno + Tatay Jobo Elizes + +

Writings 6 Book, 2010 + I. SONA - State Of Nation Address - English - *Pres. Benigno Aquino III* + II. SONA - State of Nation Address - Pilipino - *Pres. Benigno Aquino III* + III. First 100 Days peech - Pilipino - *Pres. Benigno Aquino III* + *Artiucles by Bert Guiang + Tony Meloto + Felicito or Tong C. Payumo + Cesar Lumba + Flor Lacanilao + Juan DelaCruz or Txtmanika + Dr. Ramon Marquez + Joey Jamito + Percival Cruz + Rod Garcia + Orion Perez Dumdum + Sarah Raymundo.* + + Writings 7 Book, 2010 - My Vintage Pics - Pictorials & Family, Tatay Jobo Elizes + + Writings 8 Book, 2010, Articles by Gel Santos Relos + Ms.Mike Portes + Jose Ma. Montelibano + Tony Meloto + Dr. Philip S. Chua + Dr. Cesar D. Candari + Dr. Eliseo Serina + Greg B. Macabenta + Irineo P. Goce or KaPule2 + Percival Cruz + Juan DelaCruz or Textmani + Demosthenes B. Donato. + +

Writings 9 Book, April 2011, Articles by Judge Simeon dumdum Jr + Gemma Cruz Araneta + Larry Henares Jr + Tony Joaquin + Allen Gaborro + Atty. Toto Causing + Mar-Vic Cagurangn + Emily Espanol Derry, Poet + Elyn Jean Felarca, Poet + Naysan A. Albaytar + Laura Wade, Blogger + Perter Allan Mariano + Marge Trajeco-Aberasturi + Julia Carreon Lagoc + Irineo P. Goce or KaPulle2 + Anonymous. + + Writings 10 Book, July, 2010, Articles by Atty.Ted Lagutan + Percival C. Cruz + Allen Gaborro + Peter Allan Mariano + M.L. Munoz + Alvib T. Tabaniag + Resty Odon + Dr. Phili S. Chua + Dr. Cesar D. Candari + Anonymous. + +

Writings 11 Book, August, 2011 + 1, SONA In English and Filipino, by President Benigno Aquino III (P-Noy) + 2, Telltale Signs: SONA and the Dogfight Over Spratlys, by Rodel Rodis + Atty. Ted Laguatan + Tatay Jobo Elizes + Jeremiah M. Opiniano + OFW Journalists + Bob & Carol Hammerslag + Roger P. Olivares + Rob Ceralvo + Anonymous + Irineo P. Goce or KaPule2 + Random. + + Writings 12 Book, April 2012 + Articles By Orion Perez Dumdum + Julia C. Lagoc + Honorio M. Cruz, MD + Ben Gonzales, MD + Mar-Vic Cagurangan + Marisa Lerias + Gerry Partido + Dr. Cesar D. Candari + Erwin De Leon + Jovelyn B. Revilla + Tatay Jobo Elizes + +

Writings 13 Book, July 2012 + Articles by Raymundo E. Narag + M.L. Munoz + Sonia Barbara gl Munoz + Pamela Joy Agtoto + Percival C. Cruz + Tatay Jobo Elizes + Jhakie Eslit Bayobay + Reygel Saplad Perales. + + Timely Writings 14, 2013 + Articles by Cesar F. Lumba + Eugenio Pulmano + Late Jesse Robredo + Antonio Nievera + Alvin T. Tabaniag + Kevin L. Nadal + Anonymous + Fred Natividad + Anonymous + Ellen Tordesillas + Lat Capt. Rene N. Jarque + +

Timeless Writings-15 (TW15), 2014 + Articles by SC Justice Antonio T. Carpio + Atty Dodel Rodis + Atty. Ted Laguatan + Sona by Pres. Benigno Aquino III + F. Sionil Jose + Dr. Philipi Stack + Racz Kelly, Padilla + Bert Armada.+ + Timeless Writings-16 (TW16), 2014 + Articles about The Martyrs of Camarines Norte + by Rodel Rodis + R.A.Gubalane + Robert Bernardo + Pres. Aquino's SONA 2014 + + Timeless Writings-17 (TW17), 2014 + Articles by Rodel Rodis+ Jose P. Rizal+ Irineo Goce+ Julia Lagos + Alvin Tabaniag+ Ragubalane + Red Butterfly+ Cesar Torres + + Timeless Writings-18 (TW18) + Articles by Rodel Rodis + Raul Manglapus + Ragubalane + Allen Gaborro + Manuel Vergara + + Timeless Writings-19 (TW19) + Articles by Atty. Ted Laguatan + Romely Bacsain + Charlie Chaplin + Orlando Carvajal + Allen Gaborro + Rodel Rodis + Primitivo Mijares + Krip Yuson + + Timeless Writings-20 (TW-20) + Excerpts from Primitivo Mijares Book, Conjugal Dictatorship + +

Solo Authored Books: + + +

Book A, Turning Points, *Job Elizes Sr,1968 (Reissue 2009)* + + + Book B, Be Considerate For Once, *Tatay Jobo Elizes (Jr), 2013* Book C, Piglets Unlimited - Wealth, *Tatay Jobo Elizes, 2009* + + + Book D, Out of the Misty Sea We Must, *Cesar Lumba, 2010* + + + Book E, Fulfilled – *Gonzales Reynaldo, Editor, 2010* + + + Book F - Reflections - *Bert Guiang, 2010* + + + Book G, Writings 7 - My Vintage Pics, *Tatay Jobo Elizes, 2010* +

Book H, May Bagwis Ang Pag-ibig, *Percival C. Cruz* + + + Book I, Letters To Matrimony, *Irineo P. Goce, Ka Pule2, 2011* + Book J, Songs I Wish You Knew, *Soledad R. Juan, 2011* + + + Book K, Make My Day, *Larry Henares Jr., 1993, Re-issue 2011* + Book L, Our Guerrero Family, *Tatay Jobo Elizes, 2010* + + + Book M, Handy Jokes, *Tatay J. Elizes, 2011* + Book N, FaveArt 1, *Tatay Jobo Elizes, 2011* + +

Book O, Beyond idle thoughts, *MLMunoz, Sept,2011* + + + Book P, Cracks In The Armor, *Mariano Ngan, Oct 2011* + + + Book Q, FaveArt 2, *Tatay Jobo Elizes, 2011* + + Book R, Balitang Kutsero, *Perry Diaz, Jan 2012* + + + Book S, FaveArt3, *Tatay Jobo, 2011* + + Book T, FaveArt4 ,2012, Tatay Jobo* + + + Book U, Stack Family Journals, *Phil & Fe Stack, 2012* + + + Book V, Emily, An Adoption Journey, *Romerl Elizes, 2012* + + +

Book W, Hermes Alegre Art Gallery, *TJ & Hermes, 2012* + + + Book X, Masaya Din, Malungkot Din, *Jovelyn B. Revilla, 2012* Book Y, Tiis, Sipag At Tiyaga, *Raquel Delfin Padilla, 2012* + + + Book Z, Until I Meet You, *Jhackie Eslit Bayobay, 2012* + + + Book AA, Buhay At Pag-ibig, *Argel Lucero Tamayo, 2012* + + + Book AB, Hail to the Second Best, *Dr. Philip Stack, 2012* + + + Book AC, Life Bus, *Mommy Joyce Pineda-Faulmino, 2012* + + + Book AD, My Candid Musings, *Monette Dioquino Calugay, 2012* + Book AE, Tickets to Life, *Maria Lourdes Jesalva, 2012* + + + Book AF, The Dove Files, *Mike Portes, 2012* + + + Book AG, Nursing Vignettes, *Jocelyn Cerrudo Sese, 2012* + Book AH, Poor Ba Us, *R.A. Gubalane, 2012* + + +

Book AI, Summer Idyll, *Avelina Gil, 2012* + + Book AJ, Legacy (Pamana), *Rachel Astrero, 2012* + + Book AK, Narratives Old & New, *Avelina J. Gil, 2013* + + Book AL, Buhay Saudi, *Adele J. Esic, 2013* + + Book AM, Buhay Ofw Atbp, *Jessica Napat, 2013* + + Book AN, Mga Tula Ng Buhay, *Angelita C. Esguerra, 2013* + + Book AO, Not by Bread Alone, *Judge Lily V. Magtolis, 2013* + + Book AP, Jokes Collection-2, *Tatay Jobo Elizes, 2013* + + +

Book AR, *My Writings Sometimes, Tatay Jobo Elizes, 2013* + + Book AS, Sa 'Yo Na Ako, *Shayne A. Martinez, 2013* + + Book AT, My Kin's Family Trees, *Tatay Jobo Elizes, 2013* + + Book AU, Rizal Family Tree & Others, *Tatay Jobo Elizes, 2013* + + Book AV, Make My Day-2, Nice & Nasty, *L. Henares, 2013 (1993)* + + Book AW, Make My Day-3, Cecilia, Love, *L.Henares, 2013 (1993)* Book AX, Handy Lyrics-1, *Tatay Jobo Elizes, 2013* + +

Book AY, Ang Biblos, *Rev. Dr. Eugenio Guerrero, 2014 (1929)* + + Book AZ, Make My Day-4, *Sweet & Sour, L. Henares, 2014 (1993)* + + Book BA, Life's Journey, True Stories, *Dr. Phil Stack, 2014* + + Book BB, Gerry Gil Writings, 2014, Danny Gil + + Book BC, Mr. President, *Hermie Rotea, 2014* + + Book BD, Nostalgic Pics 1, *Tatay Jobo Elizes, 2014* + + Book BE, MakeMyDay-5, Saints & Sinners, *Henares, 2014 (1993)* + +

Book BF, MakeMyDay-6, Villains & Heroes, *Henares, 2014 (1993)* + + Book BG, Nostalgic Pics 2 (ElizesClan), *TatayJE, 2014* + + Book BH, MakeMyDay-7, Tough & Tender, *Henares, 2014(1993)* + + Book BI, MakeMyDay-8, Light & Shadow, *Henares, 2014(1993)* + + Book BJ, MakeMyDay-9, Give & Take, *Henares, 2014(1993)* + + Book BK, MakeMyDay-10, ToBeOrNotToBe, *Henares, 2014(1993)* +

Book BL,Emily Forever In Love, Poems,*Emily Espanol Derry, 2013* + + Book BM, The Sinatra Songbook, *Henares, 2014* + + Book BN, The Gaborro Reader, *Allen Gaborro, 2010* + + Book BO, Ramon H. Lopez - *Art Gallery, 2014* + + Book BP, Philippines Via Old Pics-1, *Tatay Jobo, 2014* + + Book BQ, Ronna Manansala - *Art Gallery, 2014* + + Book BR, Philippines Via Old Pics-2, *Tatay Jobo, 2014* + + Book BS, Being Good-A Medley Of Love, *Dr. Phil Stack, 2014* + + Book BT, Lifestream Fisherman, A Filipino Odyssey, *Paul Dalde, Jul2014* + + Book BU, Kristina Reed Manansala, Art Gallery-1, *August 2014.* + +

Book BV, Hermes Art Gallery-2, *Sep2014,* + + Book BW, Fave Art-5, *Tatay Jobo, Sep2014* + + Book BX, Cash & Credits, Make My Day-11, *Larry Henares, Sept 2014* + + Book BY, Rise & Fall, Make My Day-12, *Larry Henares, Oct 2014* + + Book BZ, Swans & Swine, Make My Day-13, *Larry Henares, Oct 2014* + + Book CA, Touch & Go, Make My Day-14, *Larry Henares, Oct 2014* + + Book CB, Life & Death, Make My Day-15, *Larry Henares, Oct2014* + +

Book CC, Kiss & Bite, Make My day -16, *Larry Henares, Oct 2014* + + Book CD, Good & Evil, Make My Day-17, *Larry Henares, Oct2014* + + Book CE, Beast & Beauty, Make My Day-18, *Larry Henares, 2014* + + Book CF, Beggar & King, Make My Day-19, *Larry Henares, Oct 2014* + + Book CG, Trash & Treasures, Make My Day-20, *Larry Henares, Oct 2014* + + Book CH, Wear & Tear, Make My Day-21, *Larry Henares, Oct 2014* + + Book CI, Why Blame the President, *Irineo P. Goce, Oct 2014* + + +

Book CJ, Angel & Devil, Make My Day-22, *Larry Henares, Oct 2014* + + Book CK, Pretty Ugly, Make My Day-23, *Larry Henares, Oct 2014* + + Book CL, Salvation & Damnation, Make My Day-24, *Larry Henares, Oct 2014* + + Book CM, Don Daniel Maramba, *Larry Henarez & Edith Perez de Tagle, Oct 2014* + + Book CN, Hilarion G. Henares, *Larry Henares & Edith Perez de Tagle, Oct 2014* + +Book CO, FaveArt-5 ++ Book CP, FaveArt-6, Book CQ, FaveArt-7, Book CR, FaveArt-8 *(All FaveArt books by Tatay Jobo), 2014* + +

Book CS, Minsan May Isang Puta, *Ms.Mike Portes, 2014* + + Book CT, Ramblings A, *Danny Gil, 2014* + + Book CU, Ramblings-B, *Danny Gil, 2014* + + Book CV, Grace Esmeralda Album, by her, 2014* + + Book CW, Secrets of a Romantic Man, *Dr. Phil Stack, 2014* + + Book CX, Ramblings-C, *Danny Gil, 2014* + + Book CY, Ramblings-D, *Danny Gil, 2014* + + Book CZ, Ramblings-E, *Danny Gil, 2014* ++ Book DA, Tenacious Nurse-1, *Gretheline Bolandrina, 2014* + + Book DB, Tenacious Nurse-2, *Gretheline Ramos-Bolandrina, 2015* + + Book DC, Of Words I Have Found, *Dan Jimenez (danmeljim), 2015* + + Book DQ, *PhilippinesViaOldPics-4, Tatay Jobo Elizes, Jan2016* + +

Book DD, Tanjay East Coast Magazine, *Issue 1, Feb 2015* + + Book DE, Tanjay East Coast Magazine, *Issue 2, April 2015* + + Book DF, Catechism Manual, *Dr. Latorre, April 2015* + + Book DG, Tanjay East Coast Magazine, *Extra Issue 2A, April 2015* + + Book DH, Wedding Album, *Anita & Barry, May 2015* + + Book DI, Tanjay E. Coast Magazine, *Poconos, May 2015* + + Book DJ, Baptism Guidebook, *Dr. Latorre, May 2015* + + Book DK, Chita, a Memoir, *Tony Joaquin* + + Book DL, A Journey Unto Peace, *Dr. Phil Stack, June2015* + + Book DM, Jokes Collection-3, *Tatay Jobo Elizes, July2015* + + Book DN, Jokes Collection-4, *Tatay Jobo Elizes, Aug2015* + + Book DO, Jokes Collection-5, *Tatay Jobo Elizes, Sep2015* + + Book DP, Beautiful Lie, *Joecel Jayme, Jan2016* + +

Permission had been granted by the author/authors to print their books under my free self-publishing service. They own copyrights to their works. Interested reader may request free reading of any of my booklist via online reading or ebook. Just email me.

Why I Publish Books By Tatay Jobo Elizes

Writings are timeless and they act as mirrors of history. I publish writings as they remain relevant anytime. You don't have to be a good writer to write something. The only requirement is to write in simple terms to be understood. I have seen a lot of good writings in the internet, in magazines and newspapers. But most writers have only one or two articles and therefore not enough material to be published as a book. And yet, many of them need to be published. So the idea of collecting all these various writings hit me. I myself cannot come up with enough material. I decided to offer my services to publish anybody's worthwhile writings in one fairly good sized book, in paperback or pocketbook form. Their ability to publish is solved in a nutshell.

I am offering these services free of charge because of the availability of print-books-on-demand (POD) system nowadays. I have acquired the knowledge the hard way. I am now in a position to help publish writings of anybody. I can produce the book, but it's not entirely free of cost on my part. I merely assume the cost.

Why put your writings in a book? And not just in the internet? I recommend that writings be retained in a hard copy or in book form or printed form for posterity. The book will always be there among your collections or libraries. Not all use the internet. The internet access has its technical problems. Writings in the internet may be erased erroneously. Free storage is hard to access. Paid storage may be returned or lost.

For those looking for a publisher, especially if you have a novel or many essays, I can produce the paperback book under your own authorship at no cost. I can produce art books, family tree books, family albums/pictorials, biographies, joke books, songhits books, travelogues, reunions, in color or black & white.

Notes about this picture book

This book can be displayed as coffee table book for family and guests. Each picture can be cut and framed. Just buy more books. This book is suitable for libraries and schools in Philippines and Pinoys abroad. It's a perfect reference material for study of history and heroes. It's suitable as gift for any occasion. It's a collector's item. Heirs of those persons and pictures shown may want to own this book for their own families.